D0625400

The author Norman Butcher (right) and technical illustrator Peter Holland experiment with a buddy-box system.

RADIO CONTROL
GUIDE

by
NORMAN BUTCHER

Artwork
Peter Holland

Photographs
Dave Hughes

Additional contributions by
**PETER CHINN,
ROGER BOWYER-LOWE,
JOE COETZER.**

© R.M. Books Ltd, 1982

First Published 1976
Second Edition 1978
Revised Edition 1982
Fourth Edition 1987
Reprinted 1989

*All of the models shown in photographs
throughout this book are from the
Radio Modeller Plans Range*

Published by:
The R M Books division
Chart Hobby Distributors Limited
Littlehampton · West Sussex · UK

ISBN 0 903676 12 5

Printed in England by Biddles Ltd., Guildford, Surrey
Filmset by New Rush Filmsetters Ltd., London E.1

CONTENTS

INTRODUCTION

WELCOME to Radio Control.

I don't know how you were introduced to this hobby—whether you saw a model aircraft being flown, or a boat sailed at the local site, whether you saw a copy of a monthly publication dealing with radio controlled models on a bookstall and idly picked it up only to become immersed, or whether you are a friend of a friend who builds models. The important thing is that you are nibbling at the bait and, by the time you have read this book, you will be hooked!

Now, what I intend to give you is a complete run-down of all the information you will need, initially, to enable you to choose the type of radio equipment most suited to your needs and pocket, to select a make which will give you satisfactory service, and to ally this to a model which will initiate you, successfully, into the pleasures of remote control.

That is what I am going to do, so, before I start, let me tell you what I am *not* going to do! I will not burden you with the theory of radio control because this has no place here, as it is likely to hinder rather than help in the choice of equipment. However, you *will* need to know the basic facts of which component serves which purpose, so that we all start on the same wavelength.

In its simplest form then, the transmitter you hold in your hand sends a signal to the receiver in the model which, in turn decodes this signal into an instruction to the servo(s) to operate rudder, elevator, motor, or whatever, to ensure the successful operation of your craft. This is all you need to know about that aspect.

I will not tell you how a model is made because, if you are a beginner to modelling, you will be building from a kit or plan, and these carry instructions to help the tyro through the building process, while, if you are an experienced modeller, who is only a beginner to radio control, then you will already know the answers. I will tell you, however, and in great detail, how to install your equipment in the model you have chosen because this, next to the ability to pilot the model (in the case of an aircraft), is the most important factor in determining its successful operation.

While it is possible to control any model by radio, this book will deal specifically with the most popular types – aircraft, boats and cars – but modellers whose interests lie outside these spheres will still find the contents of great value. After all, the selection and maintenance of equipment is a common factor, while the installation information, it will be found, may readily be adapted to special purposes too limited in appeal to warrant inclusion here.

This is an appropriate moment to explain that much of the installation information was originally published in "The Propo Book". When this first appeared, proportional control of a model was relatively new, but already destined to supersede all other types of control – as, indeed, was said in the introduction to the first edition. Today, to all practical intents and purposes, this has come about.

When "The Propo Book" was published, hundreds of established modellers were changing over to proportional and needed the installation advice which it offered. Now, 40,000 copies later, it is apparent that newcomers require much more information on selecting the most suitable radio for their own application, on buying a make which will give them long and satisfactory service, as well as on how to install it in a model, and then maintain it in good working order. Also, in the case of aircraft, they need advice on "how to fly", so as not to place at unnecessary risk their investment in model and radio.

All these services this book will provide!

CHAPTER 1

HOW A MODEL IS CONTROLLED

THE newcomer, seeing a model being operated for the first time, is impressed by the apparent ease, smoothness and seemingly effortless manoeuvring by the operator, followed by the safe return to earth (or harbour) with fine precision, yet this skill must be learnt. Before any attempt is made to do this, however, it will be necessary to understand how it is possible to control a model by the movement of

Fig. I

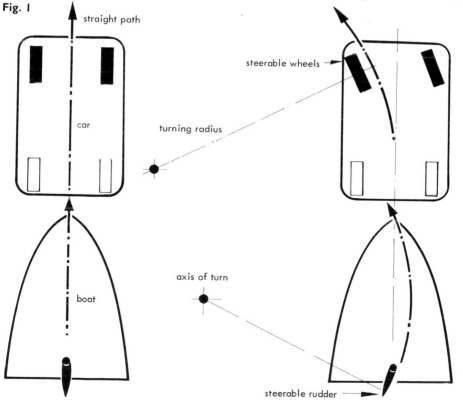

straight path

steerable wheels

car

turning radius

axis of turn

boat

steerable rudder

RADIO CONTROL GUIDE

various control surfaces. From this it becomes easy to appreciate that the control requirements of different model types demand radio control equipment of varying degrees of complexity. And, once it is understood what can be achieved with each type of equipment, from the simplest to the most complex (information which appears later on), it is a straightforward matter to decide the type of radio needed for each individual's requirement.

Everyone can grasp, probably from experience with the real thing, that the rudder on a boat, or the wheels on a car, when turned, cause the model to "follow" – Fig. 1. The control of an aircraft is, however, much more complex. Thus it must be understood that, without exception, forces other than the *mere turning of a rudder*, are necessary to "steer" an aeroplane.

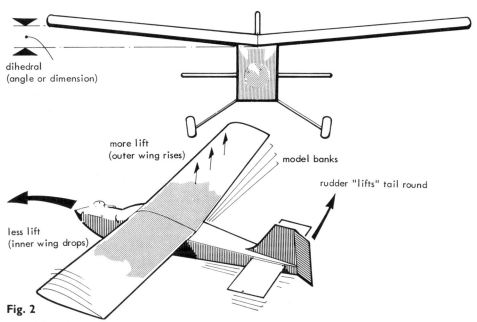

dihedral
(angle or dimension)

more lift
(outer wing rises)

model banks

rudder "lifts" tail round

less lift
(inner wing drops)

Fig. 2

The simplest models *are* steered by the rudder but, in order for this to be possible, the wings of the model must be tilted up to give what is known as the dihedral angle. Fig. 2 shows what this is and also how, when the rudder is operated, the model banks in a turn.

If the model has little or no dihedral, however, instead of the operation of the rudder making it turn, it will merely yaw, drop a wing and dive to the ground – Fig. 3. Therefore, in order to steer a model of *this* type, a different type of control is needed – aileron*.

*To be pedantic, aileron is not a "steering" control, it only *banks* the model so that the elevator can initiate the turn, which is why (apart from the Radio Modeller plan – *Banker* – the exception which proves the rule) to control an aircraft with aileron, it is essential to have a second control – elevator – as well. Refer to Fig. 5.

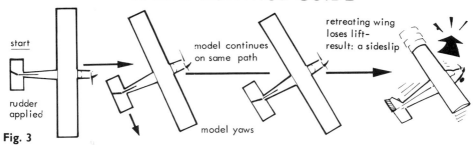

Fig. 3

A glance at Fig. 4 will show how operation of the ailerons will cause the model to start to roll or *bank*. This, though, will not make it *turn* and a further control – elevator – is necessary to complete the manoeuvre – Fig. 5. However, although a model cannot be steered by aileron without also using elevator control, the converse is not true, because elevator can be used to control pitch (up and down movement) on a model that is steered by rudder.

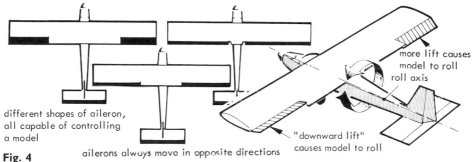

Fig. 4

Although a suitable design of aircraft may be flown, with a great deal of satisfaction, using solely rudder control, there is no doubt that having additional controls will add to the pleasure, by giving more precise control over the model itself. Moreover, as more advanced designs are chosen, more control is needed and it is common, nowadays, for models to be controlled by rudder, ailerons, elevator, and throttle control on the motor – this being known as "full house". There are yet further controls, but these are more in the nature of refinements and will be returned to,

Fig. 5

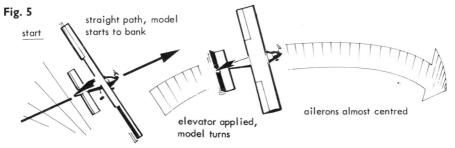

together with greater detail about the various progressions of control, from the simplest to the most advanced, in later chapters.

Having mentioned motor (throttle) control, now is a good moment to dispel a widely held misconception. It really is amazing how many people, on seeing a radio control model being operated for the first time, ask "how does it work when the engine stops?", assuming that the radio function is dependent upon the motor. Nothing is further from the truth, of course: otherwise how would it be possible to control a glider or a yacht? Anyway, everyone disproves this when the batteries are run down several times "bench testing"!

Now to get acquainted with the first technical term likely to be encountered at the model shop, or when other modellers are heard talking about various sets. The expression is "function", which is in no way mystical when it is understood that one function on a radio outfit will operate one control of a model. To take the simplest example . . . to control just one surface – say rudder – then all that will be needed is a single function outfit. Ah, but the rudder moves in two directions – left and right! True, but the servo always neutralises to its centre, so that the one unit gives two control commands – in this case left and right. (This is explained more fully in Chapter 4 – Fig. 19.) Exactly the same applies to all the other control surfaces (except that not all servos self-centre, but this will be explained later) so that each extra control to be operated will require an extra function*.

It is now possible to appreciate that, for a model such as a boat or car, the control requirements are simple and thus the equipment will be relatively inexpensive. The same applies to the simpler aircraft, but the greater the number of controls to be operated, the greater the number of functions required and hence the greater will be the complexity and cost of the equipment.

In anyone's entire modelling career, the purchase of a set of radio gear is likely to be the greatest single expense and, therefore, it is essential, in order to obtain the best value, to acquire a full understanding of exactly the equipment required.

---

*Although it is a "hangover" from a previous decade of equipment, it is still quite common to hear a "function" referred to as a "channel". To make this simple substitution confusing, however, some imported equipment names a single function as 2-channel! This is because two radio channels are required to command left and right rudder on the one servo and so on. This book, however, will stick strictly to the term *function* meaning, to be perfectly clear: *one function equals one servo, operating one control surface.*

CHAPTER 2

WHAT RADIO CONTROL EQUIPMENT LOOKS LIKE

SO far the discussion has been in general terms about radio control as such and the operation of models, which have doubtless so mesmerised as they were operated, that only the vaguest idea has been obtained of what the equipment itself looks like! Indeed, as all the "working" parts of the equipment are buried deep inside the model, it is probable that a receiver or servo would not even be recognised! It is a simple matter to rectify this . . .

Most radio equipment today is attractively packaged, so that all the parts can be clearly displayed by the shopkeeper, without removing them from the box. Just gaze into the window or showcase of any specialist dealer, and a bewildering variety of makes of equipment may be seen, but all with the same components in common – transmitter (often abbreviated, in print, to Tx.), receiver (often abbreviated to Rx.), servos, batteries, wiring harness, switch and various accessories.

First there is the transmitter, immediately identifiable as the biggest item in the box! Many and varied are the shapes, styles and colouring of transmitter cases, because this is the part of the outfit most susceptible to cosmetic sales appeal. Basically, however, it is a metal and/or plastic box, designed and balanced to be held comfortably in the hand, or suspended from a neckstrap — more of the reasons for this choice anon. Projecting from the top will be the aerial, which telescopes within itself for ease of carrying. Conveniently positioned on the front of the case, will be the control stick(s), (occasionally, in a unit intended specifically for use with boats or cars, a wheel will replace the stick), an on/off switch, protected so that it will not be moved unintentionally, and a meter to indicate radio output and/or battery state.

Transmitters not only vary in styling but also in size. Commonly, those for the cheaper outfits are smaller than those with a greater number of functions, but really it is convenience in use which dictates the size, as there is more than enough room in even the smallest units to accommodate the various electronic and mechanical parts. It must be borne in mind that the transmitter is the direct link with the model. Through it the operator "senses" how the model is responding, therefore it must feel right. Too small a unit could make hand movements seem clumsy, too large a one could mean too great a reach to the various controls, as well as being tiring to hold. Therefore, the transmitters of the best equipment have had much time and practical experience expended on determining the ergonomically correct layout and balance.

Next the receiver which, typically, will measure $2\frac{1}{4} \times 1\frac{1}{2} \times 1$ in. The case may be

RADIO CONTROL GUIDE

of either metal, plastic or a combination of both and, if it has a removable lid, (unsealed and designed to be removed, that is!) it is possible to marvel at the compactness and complexity of the components packed therein. Each receiver contains, basically, two separate (electrically, not physically separate) sections – the portion that actually receives the signal from the transmitter, and the decoder which transforms this signal into commands to the servos. Therefore, there is seldom any significant difference in the physical size between the receivers of the simplest one or two function outfits and the most complex 8-function units.

The connections from the receiver to the servos and batteries are made in either of two ways. The traditional method is for wires from each component to be connected with a plug and socket. An equally popular method nowadays, however, is for the receiver to contain a bank of sockets to receive plugs on the leads from the servos. In either case these are always polarised to ensure correct electrical connection. The lead from the battery is rather different, in that it is fitted with a socket and not a plug at the receiver end. This is because the battery lead is "live" and, therefore, a plug could short-circuit. The only other wire from the receiver is the aerial.

Fig. 6

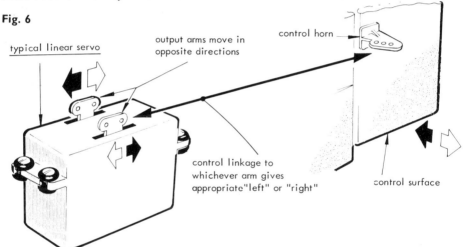

typical linear servo

output arms move in opposite directions

control horn

control linkage to whichever arm gives appropriate "left" or "right"

control surface

Servos

Normally a single function outfit will have exactly the same type of servo as a 4-function set of the same manufacture. It is common, however, for there to be a choice of servo output – linear or rotary. A linear servo has one or two arms on the top of the case, which slide in the required fore and aft direction to move the control surface(s) – Fig. 6. A rotary servo has a disc, or arm, which moves with a rotary action to a pre-determined limit, that is, it only "rotates" to and fro, not through 360° – Fig. 7. Occasionally a unit is found incorporating both types of output. The drawings do not show any specific make of servo, but a stylised unit which enables coupling to linear or rotary output units to be shown clearly.

Both linear and rotary outputs have their pros and cons, the advantages of one

12

RADIO CONTROL GUIDE

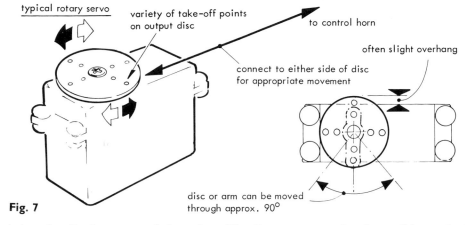

typical rotary servo

variety of take-off points
on output disc

to control horn

often slight overhang

connect to either side of disc
for appropriate movement

disc or arm can be moved
through approx. 90°

Fig. 7

being the disadvantages of the other. The linear servo makes it possible to obtain virtually a "straight run" from the servo to control surface, but the total amount of movement or "throw" obtainable from such a servo, is restricted to the equivalent of the movement of the arm, and may only be increased or decreased by adjusting the

Fig. 8

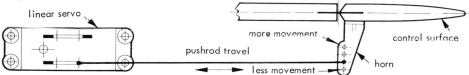

linear servo

more movement

control surface

pushrod travel

less movement

horn

position of the control rod on the horn — Fig. 8. If a greater (or lesser) degree of movement than is permitted by this adjustment is required then it will be necessary to use some form of mechanical leverage — Fig. 9.

On the other hand it is a simple matter to increase or decrease the throw from a rotary output servo, by varying the distance from the centre of the take-off point for the linkage, close to the centre for a short throw — Fig. 10a; further from the centre

Fig. 9

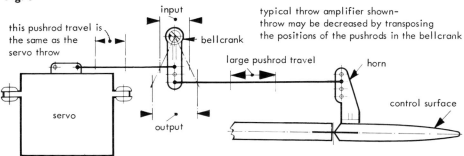

input

typical throw amplifier shown—
throw may be decreased by transposing
the positions of the pushrods in the bellcrank

this pushrod travel is
the same as the
servo throw

bellcrank

large pushrod travel

horn

servo

control surface

output

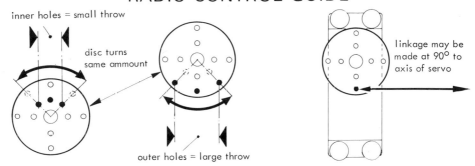

Fig. 10 a   **Fig. 10 b**   **Fig. 10 c**

for a large throw – Fig. 10b. Indeed, most servo output arms or discs are supplied pre-drilled to allow this*. Further, a rotary output servo may be mounted transversely in a model yet still permit direct coupling to a push rod – Fig. 10c. The disadvantage of a rotary output output, however, is that it is necessary to allow for the arc of movement – Fig. 11. What might well be called a swings and roundabouts choice!

The boat enthusiast has to contend with water penetration and condensation and, to meet this hazard, some manufacturers offer a special waterproof marine servo. Also, for specialist aircraft requirements, such as undercarriage retraction, a unit of greater than normal power, and possibly with extra throw, is required, and such are often available as "extras". Specialist servos of these types are nearly always rotary output, and normally of greater physical dimensions than standard units.

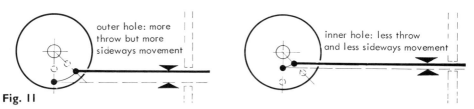

Fig. 11

Batteries

Here there are several options to look out for. With the cheaper sets it is normal for both the transmitter and receiver current to be supplied by dry batteries. In the case of the former, these may vary from a relatively large capacity 6 or 9 volt battery, to 4, 6 or even 8-pen cells, the transmitter case being designed around whatever type the designer prefers. If pen-cells are used, then a special battery box will be supplied, and this will be properly marked to ensure that the batteries are inserted in their correct polarity. Because of their low weight and compact size, allied to good electrical performance, the use of pen-cells in transmitters is quite popular.

To power a receiver, pen-cells are the only type of dry battery employed nowadays

*A rotary output disc with "offset" holes also makes it simple to incorporate differential movement into the control surface, but this complicated matter has a chapter to itself later on.

RADIO CONTROL GUIDE

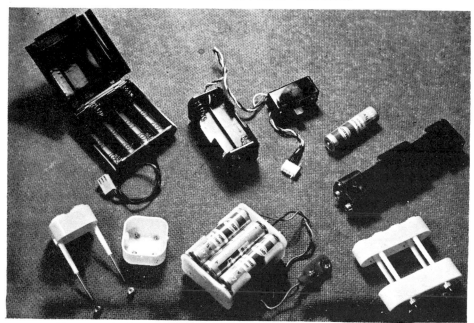

Above: a selection of different types of battery box, all for use with pencells.
Below: different shapes and sizes of nicad pack.

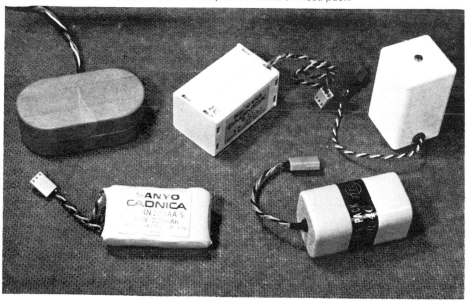

and, here again, a special battery box is normally supplied with the outfit. The lead from this box will often have, wired-in, an on/off switch that is designed to be conveniently mounted in the model.

The alternative to dry batteries, and normally standard equipment for all but the cheaper one or two function outfits, are rechargeable nickel cadmium batteries, generally referred to as nicads, although the term DEAC which is the name of the company which popularised this type of product, is still commonly used both specifically and generically. The advantage of the nicad type of battery is that it can be permanently installed in the model and wired to the various components, there being no need to remove it for replacement. Initially the cost is higher – quite appreciably higher – especially as a special charging unit is required (this is often supplied with an outfit, sometimes being built into the transmitter as an integral unit), but the convenience and long term saving, in not having to purchase replacement dry cells, is considerable.

A nicad unit is also more compact, because it does not need a battery box, although the weight is roughly equivalent to that of pen-cells complete with box. Unless an outfit is only available complete with nicads, an initial saving may be made by starting off with pen-cells, and adding a nicad pack at a later date. Also, it is possible to obtain nicads of the same shape and size as pen-cells and these may, of course, be placed in a normal battery box, to which some form of charging lead has been added.

It will be found that the actual shape of both battery boxes and nicads can vary considerably. The accompanying photographs show a selection of the shapes most commonly met. Also, there are normally two different nicad capacity "sizes" available, which are generally designated 225 or 500 (or a very similar number – i.e. 220 or 440 and so on). In effect, this means that the smaller unit is about half the physical size and weight of the larger but, therefore, will only have about half the operating life before needing recharging. Fuller details of this are given in the chapter on "Care and Maintenance".

Finally, there are the various accessories, which obviously differ from outfit to outfit but, commonly, include frequency pennant(s), servo mounting trays, neck strap and so on, and all of these will be dealt with in detail later on.

CHAPTER 3

THE PRINCIPLES OF CONTROL

HAVING now described what a radio control outfit comprises, it is time to explain a few basic principles of control, and this will make it easy to understand why the wide number of options, which various manufacturers make available in their equipment, are necessary.

First, though, it is necessary to understand exactly what is meant by proportional control. Now it is not the time to dwell on the problems and shortcomings of the past – the appended brief history will give a good idea of these – but newcomers should appreciate just how lucky they are to be entering the sport at a time when the sophistication of modern electronics has reduced the controlling of models to the simplest undertaking yet experienced by modellers. And all this is because proportional equipment does exactly what it promises – it gives proportional movement of the control surfaces of the model.

This is simple to understand if the parallel of driving a car is taken. At a curve in the road the wheel is not turned full lock, it is moved in proportion to the angle

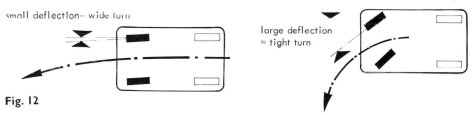

small deflection– wide turn

large deflection = tight turn

Fig. 12

to be negotiated – Fig. 12. Similarly with a model, except that, as the control stick on the transmitter is moved, so the servo in the model "follows" in similar increments and transfers the movement to the control surface – Fig. 13.

The uninitiated however, when handling a transmitter for the first time, are often puzzled why the steering stick(s) are spring-loaded to self centre. "Surely", they say, "you just position the stick to initiate a turn, and then make the necessary corrective movement when the model has responded, as required, to the first command?" In practice, in fact, this is exactly what does happen, except that the stick is not just positioned and then left alone until a corrective control is needed – it is held in the position required against the spring centring tension. (In fact, the stick is

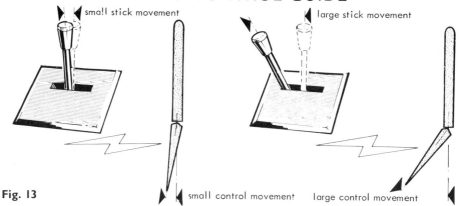

small stick movement

large stick movement

Fig. 13

small control movement   large control movement

never held completely still at all. Continually, slight corrective movements are being fed in, exactly as to the steering wheel when driving a car.)

The reason for having this centring action, is to provide an immediately identifiable and accurate control position reference. Shortly it will be explained how a model is trimmed to go straight, "hands-off", (i.e. with the control stick at neutral central position) and this is necessary because there is always a time lag between sending a command and seeing the response, especially with an aircraft. Therefore, unless it is possible to "find" this accurate neutral reference point of control, at which it is known the model will be flying in a straight line, the tendency is always to overcorrect and then overcorrect the correction, (the more so the further away the model), with the result that the steering course resembles the homeward path of a drunken cyclist – Fig. 14.

Non-centring controls

There are some controls, however, which are not required to return to centre, throttle being the most common example. Normally, in an aircraft, this is set at the required

Fig. 14

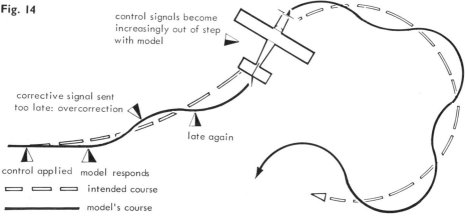

control signals become
increasingly out of step
with model

corrective signal sent
too late: overcorrection

late again

control applied   model responds

◻ ◻ ◻ intended course

▬▬▬ model's course

position and left undisturbed for long periods*. This does not mean that a different type of servo is necessary, as might at first be thought, but merely that, this time, the control stick on the transmitter does not self centre, being adjusted to stay in whatever position the operator requires. All that is necessary to achieve this is for the centring spring to be rendered inoperative, and the movement of the stick tightened up slightly, so that it does not slop about, then, as the stick is positioned in the required position, the servo stays in the same relative position. It is normally a very simple do-it-yourself job to render any stick either positionable or centring, so that the transmitter can be set up to suit the preferred "mode" of control – and this is a subject which will be discussed in detail in Chapter 5.

Just to be clear with a re-cap then, it is not the servo which is self centring or positionable, but the control stick on the transmitter. The servo merely obeys the command it is sent.

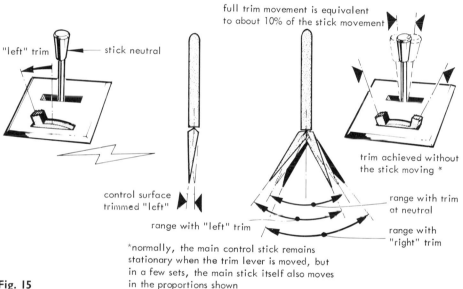

full trim movement is equivalent
to about 10% of the stick movement

"left" trim — stick neutral

control surface
trimmed "left"

range with "left" trim

trim achieved without
the stick moving *

range with trim
at neutral

range with
"right" trim

*normally, the main control stick remains
stationary when the trim lever is moved, but
in a few sets, the main stick itself also moves
in the proportions shown

Fig. 15

The trim facility

Before going on to discuss the various outfits, one final point to be cleared up is the trim control. Although, technically, it can readily be made available on every function of the outfit, in practice it will only be found on those operated by the main control stick(s). Either to the side of, or underneath the control stick, a smaller lever will be found, and this operates the trim control. By moving it left or right (or up or

*Racing cars, and, to a lesser extent boats, often use the throttle to assist the
steering as in full size practice and, in such cases, being in continual use, the
control is spring loaded, not to centre, but to the "slow" end of the speed range.

down) it will be noticed that the servo centring shifts towards the direction the trim lever is moved, typically to a maximum of 10% of the total servo movement in either direction – Fig. 15.

This is an extremely useful facility in that, during operation, a model can be trimmed, by shifting the servo centring, to move in a completely straight and level path. However   and this is very important advice to follow – although this control will be used to compensate, for example, for changes in balance as the fuel tank empties, it is never used as a permanent adjustment of trim. This is to say that, having trimmed a model using the trim lever, this adjustment is, as soon as possible, transferred permanently to the control surface, via the various adjustments in the linkages, and the trim lever itself is returned to centre. This is to ensure that there is an immediate visual check at the transmitter that all the controls of the model are in their correct relative positions before operation is commenced.

CHAPTER 4

THE BASIC EQUIPMENT CHOICE

NOW to consider the basic choice and layout of the various outfits starting with the simplest – a single function unit. As these are at the lowest end of the price scale, and are normally built down to a price, a certain spartan air to the appearance and fittings may be expected, (for instance there may be no output meter on the transmitter), but no compromise of performance should be expected or tolerated.

The single function transmitter may well be appreciably smaller than other units, and this is no disadvantage in that there is only one control stick to operate. This will be a simple single-axis unit, which may be moved left or right to give the appropriate control, and there will certainly be a trim lever, which is normally in the escutcheon of the main stick – Fig. 16. The receiver is unlikely to be much different in size or appearance from its bigger brothers except, of course, that there will be fewer wires leading from it – there's only one servo to connect to! And, talking of the servo, it will almost certainly be the same as those used with the more sophisticated outfits.

A choice of layout

With the 2-function outfit there is the first of the choices of layout – whether to have a transmitter with one stick or two – the explanation for this being in Chapter 5. The two stick transmitter will contain units similar to those on the single function outfit, except that one will be positioned to move horizontally and the other to move vertically. If, on the other hand, there is only one stick unit, then this will be of the dual axis type which may be moved left, right, up, down and all permutations in between – Fig. 17. Such a unit will also contain two trim levers – one for each axis of movement. In addition to the receiver and two servos, a rather more comprehensive selection of accessories is normally supplied with a 2-function system.

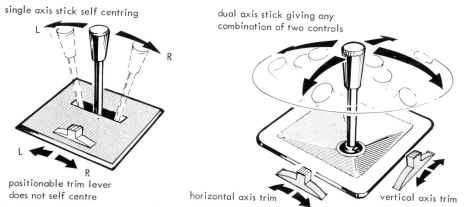

single axis stick self centring

dual axis stick giving any combination of two controls

positionable trim lever does not self centre

horizontal axis trim

vertical axis trim

Fig. 16

Fig. 17

Appropriately, there are three possible stick configurations with 3-function outfits! Probably there will be a dual axis stick on the right and a single axis stick on the left of the case. The alternatives are a dual axis stick and a positionable lever, or two single axis sticks and a positionable lever, see Fig. 22 and also illustrations in Chapter 5. The positionable levers would not offer a trim facility.

With equipment of three or more functions it must not be assumed that a full complement of servos, to suit the number of functions, is included in the quoted price. It is quite common for the quoted price of a three function outfit to include only two servos. In any case, it is normally possible to buy even the most advanced units with just one or two servos, and the advantages of this will be dealt with shortly.

The 4-function outfit is the most popular of all units for aircraft use. The vast majority of 4-function transmitters feature two dual axis sticks. There is a limited following, however, for the single stick outfit which, as might be expected, has a specially designed dual-axis stick, the top of which rotates to give rudder control, hence all three main controls of aileron/elevator/rudder are on the single stick unit – Fig. 18. On these outfits, motor control is via a separate positionable lever. Commonly, the quoted price for a 4-function outfit is inclusive of four servos.

Finally there are the 5-, 6-, 7- and even 8-function outfits. Basically, these are similar in layout to a two stick, 4-function unit, with the extra functions operated by switches and/or levers. As four functions will provide total control for all of the main control surfaces of an aircraft, as well as throttle control, the additional functions are intended for such operations as retracting undercarriage, operating flaps and so on. The former control is a strictly up/down operation, so the normal method of activation is a switch, which gives "up" in one direction of movement and "down" in the other. The flaps, however, require proper proportional control, so these are operated by a lever. Before buying a 5-function outfit it is wise to check that the operation method for this fifth function is suited to the proposed requirement, but any outfit with more than five functions could be expected to incorporate both types of operation. (A more detailed explanation appears in Chapter 5 – Fig. 30.) Normally the quoted price for these advanced outfits is inclusive of *four* servos.

Fig. 18

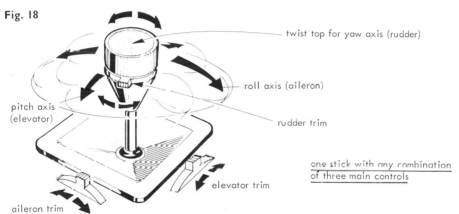

twist top for yaw axis (rudder)

roll axis (aileron)

pitch axis (elevator)

rudder trim

one stick with any combination of three main controls

elevator trim

aileron trim

Practical applications

That, then, sums up the basic choice and layout and, although both aspects will occur again, it will be easier to appreciate these finer points if the practical applications of the various outfits are first considered, and let the emphasis be placed on the word *practical!*

This is the point that must not be lost sight of – radio equipment, in the context of this book, is a means to an end and not an end in itself. Sooner or later, everyone meets an armchair expert who will bedazzle with his knowledge and pooh-pooh many of the limitations that have been (or will be) listed for various types of equipment. Such a person can be very plausible, but if asked to demonstrate his models, it will probably be found that he hasn't any! It is a tendency of such experts to look on the radio, and not on the model, as the end and, consequently, they are happy with a bench rig containing numerous bent pins and paper clips, which will perform the most complex command. Here, however, the concern is with controlling a model with equipment which can be bought over the counter and, if models are successfully and consistently to be operated, the limitations of the equipment chosen must be accepted.

Single function

With the single function outfit it is possible, successfully, and with considerable satisfaction, to operate many types of model. After all it must be remembered that, until relatively recently, a single control such as this, was all that radio control had to offer! Therefore, the sheer fun that can be obtained from today's reliability and proportional response must not be overlooked.

Obviously the single function will be employed to steer the model and, in fact, as was explained in Chapter 1, there are two commands available – left and right – Fig. 19. In a car these will give complete directional control, but there will be no means of stopping it (except physically) until the fuel is exhausted. The same applies to a powered boat, and here it is also necessary to judge to a nicety when the motor will stop, if there is not to be a long wait while the model drifts to shore. Marinewise, in fact, a yacht is a much better choice for single function, in that it can be steered to the bank to make adjustments to the sail trim.

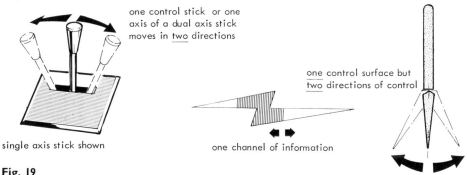

one control stick or one axis of a dual axis stick moves in two directions

one control surface but two directions of control

single axis stick shown

one channel of information

Fig. 19

With aircraft there is an enormous choice of so-called "single channel" designs (full details of the Radio Modeller range appears in the Radio Modeller Planbook) which will perform perfectly with just rudder control, although, here again, it is necessary to judge to a nicety when the motor will stop, if the model is to land in the correct area. Again, with gliders, both thermal and slope types, there are many designs available and, indeed, Dave Hughes devotes a complete chapter to rudder-only models in his book "Radio Control Soaring", a book which cannot be too highly recommended to those whose interest lies in non-powered flight.

Incidentally, it might be as well, in the context of aircraft, just to emphasise again the importance of having two controls available – left and right – even with the most basic equipment. This positive ability to send a command, which will give positive, proportional control for either direction of steering, has simplified the flying of models very, very much indeed, from the somewhat hit-and-miss business it once was. Also, as

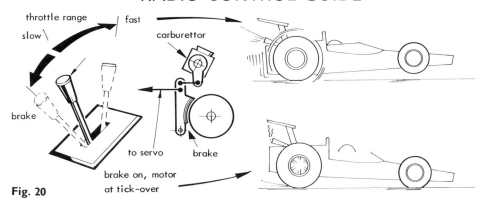

throttle range
slow
fast
carburettor
brake
to servo
brake
brake on, motor
at tick-over
Fig. 20

modern proportional equipment is very similar in size and weight to the single channel radio it has replaced, this means that hundreds of plans and kits, designed originally for this earlier equipment, will perform ever better with today's units.

A new world

It is with the 2 function units, however, that a whole new world begins to open up. For a car, 2-function provides all the control necessary, as not only does it give complete steering control, but the second function enables the model to be stopped, started or its speed varied at will. Here, also, is one of the exceptions which proves the rule, in that it is common with a car, to couple the throttle control to the brake, so that as the motor is throttled back beyond a certain point, the brake is progressively applied, hence the one function operates two controls – Fig. 20.

A similar situation applies to electric powered boats, where the throttle control gives forward in one direction from centre and reverse in the other – Fig. 21.

It will be noticed, though, that neither of these exceptions applies to a primary control – steering in a car, rudder in a boat – but only to a secondary control, in this case throttle, so that, if anything goes wrong, it will not be disastrous, in that steering control of the model is still available. With boats powered by an internal combustion

Fig. 21

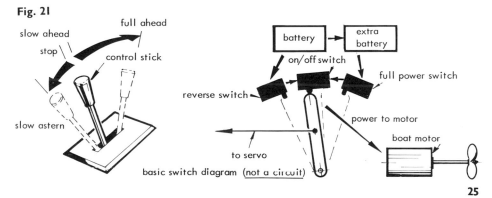

full ahead
slow ahead
stop
control stick
slow astern
reverse switch
battery
extra battery
on/off switch
full power switch
power to motor
boat motor
to servo
basic switch diagram (not a circuit)

engine, the second function would be devoted solely to throttle. In a yacht the main and foresails can be coupled together to a winch to give a degree of control equal to that of a power boat.

With aircraft, however, there are two types to consider. In a glider, the second function will be used to give elevator control, and this will then, as described in Chapter 1, enable the model to be "steered" using either ailerons or rudder. The former will certainly give much greater manoeuvrability, and enable most of the standard aerobatic figures to be flown, but rudder is much easier to install, especially for the beginner – it will be possible to make a more objective choice after reading Chapter 7 on suitable models.

A fundamental decision

With a powered aircraft, however, a rather more fundamental decision must be made. As with the glider, the second function could be used to provide elevator control, with the attendant advantages of manoeuvrability just described, and relying on experience to position the aircraft for landing when the motor stops. Indeed, many experienced fliers will say that it is a "waste" to use a function on a simple outfit "just for throttle".

Surely, though, this reflects a total lack of appreciation of the importance of this control? Certainly it is not essential but, once a model has been operated, both with and without this refinement, it becomes considered so. With throttle control, not only is it possible to gain, maintain, or lose height, at will, make touch-and-go landings and so on, but it also adds considerably to the safety of operation. Beginners often find the model becoming remote, even in danger of flying away, or their concentration flagging; throttle control enables them to end the session. During a flight interference might be suspected; again an immediate landing is possible. And, as the time to land approaches, the model can progressively be brought into the correct position for a neat arrival, instead of having to guess when the motor will stop, and then scramble to earth somehow, or else keep the model extra high for the last few minutes, waiting for the motor to cut out.

To sum up, it would be fair to say that, for a beginner, the choice should be rudder and throttle control. The more experienced flier can make his own choice because, with experience, comes the ability to bring the model safely in "dead stick" (as is said of a power model on the glide), while enjoying the advantages of greater aerobatic potential and manoeuvrability for the rest of the flight.

Virtually all, except for the very smallest, single channel designs will be able to accommodate the additional servo, whether it is used for elevator or motor control and, if the latter is chosen, it will be found that all but the smallest motors suitable for r/c models, are available in throttle equipped versions.

Three-function enters into the realms of "extra" controls for boats and cars – trim tabs on power boats, separate control of fore and mainsail for yachts, swivelling gun turrets on scale models, a separate braking system and so on. Aircraft, however, are beginning to come into their own. A power model, for instance, could be steered (aileron *or* rudder) and have elevator and throttle control, while a glider could go "full-house" with aileron *and* rudder and elevator.

The prospective purchaser of a 3-function outfit, however, must ensure that the

RADIO CONTROL GUIDE

disposition of the controls is suitable. Although almost any of the control dispositions available will be suited to boat or car use, this may not be so with an aircraft. For instance, if the intended use is in gliders, then, on an outfit with a dual and a single axis stick unit, the latter must move horizontally, whereas, for power flying, where the single stick would be throttle or elevator, it must move vertically. Again a transmitter with a dual-axis stick (or two single-axis sticks) and positionable lever is fine for power flying, but unsuited to full house gliding – Fig. 22.

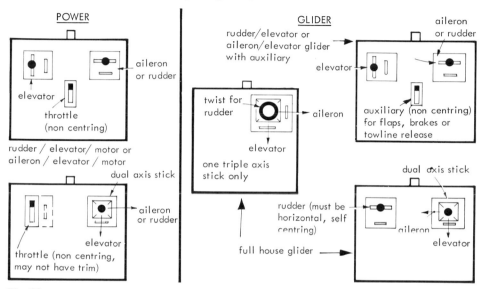

Fig. 22

And so to 4-function and the most popular (or desired) of all the outfits for the aircraft enthusiast. Apart from having the ability to operate yet more extras on boats or cars, the additional function has nothing to offer earth- or waterbound enthusiasts. Not so for aircraft though. Now it is possible to achieve what is popularly known as full house control – aileron, elevator, rudder, motor. (As has just been seen, gliders, having no motor, are "full house" with just the three aerodynamic controls, of course.) For the serious aircraft enthusiast there is no doubt at all that a 4-function outfit is the natural choice.

There are, however, more comprehensive requirements. The scale modeller, or competition aerobatic flier, for instance, often requires flap or retracting under-carriage facilities so, for them, there are 5-, 6-, 7- and 8-function units available.

CHAPTER 5
MODES

VERY few people are totally ambidextrous so, although most can manipulate with both hands, one is always much more under control than the other. With most activities this is of no great significance. Many fishermen will remember changing from right-hand winding to left-hand winding with a new type of fishing reel, with very little difficulty, and certainly no disastrous consequences to the fish – but, when it come to controlling a fast-moving model, there is a very different fish to play altogether! Here there is no "thinking" time at all – responses must be instantaneous and accurate. Therefore, it is imperative that the disposition of the controls of the transmitter is correct, so that responses are automatic – no thinking time is possible! To achieve this there is a choice of control known as "Mode" and, as there are only two modes available, they will be designated "Mode A" and "Mode B"[1].

Now this difference basically relates to the disposition of the primary[2] controls, so it is necessary to start by understanding what these are. The important point to appreciate is that no matter how complex the model, there will never be more than two primary controls and these are –

(a) directional control,

(b) elevation or control of height.

From this it is apparent that a boat or car will only ever have the one primary

1. Originally, and naturally, these were named Mode 1 and Mode 2 and referred to in the Propo Book as such. However, confusion has arisen as to which is which, some people speaking of what had been named Mode 1 as Mode 2, so, from hereon, reference will be to Mode A (named in the Propo Book as Mode 1) and Mode B (named in the Propo Book as Mode 2), so that here, at least, there will be consistency! In point of fact, it is unlikely that a modeller will talk of Mode 1 or Mode 2; Mode A or Mode B. Really these are only a convenient and precise method of defining, in a book such as this. In practice, modellers, shopkeepers and manufacturers, will talk of "throttle left" (Mode A) or "throttle right" (Mode B). But this is confusing to a "southpaw"; also it is incongruous for glider fliers to talk of "throttle" (even if in practice they do), so perhaps here, and especially with older fliers, both glider and power, the expression "single stick" (Mode A) will be used, and "two stick" (Mode B). This indeed, is a popular preference and, if it were not for the confusion with genuine single stick, (is there really any confusion because, after all, the mode is the same?), this latter is as good a definition as any, meaning that the primary controls are on one or two sticks. But all of these are far from being universal descriptions and, until one that really "clicks" is discovered, for clarity, in print at least, Mode A and Mode B it remains!

2. The secondary controls also enter into this, especially with cars and boats, but the explanation of the basic principle will be easier to follow if they are ignored for the moment.

RADIO CONTROL GUIDE

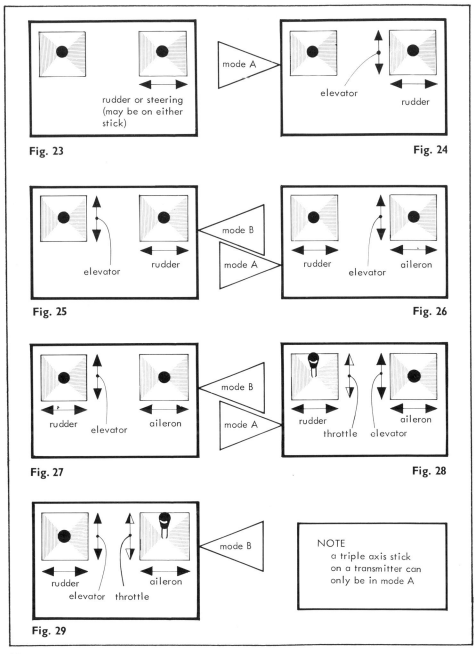

Fig. 23

Fig. 24

Fig. 25

Fig. 26

Fig. 27

Fig. 28

Fig. 29

NOTE
   a triple axis stick
   on a transmitter can
   only be in mode A

control, which is steering, via the wheels or rudder. An aircraft, however, may, depending upon its design, have elevator as well as steering, and, if this is so, the difference between Mode A and Mode B will boil down to whether the primary controls are to be operated by one hand or two.

Taking a 4-function outfit with two dual-axis sticks as an example, if this were used to control a boat or car, then the steering control would be from the horizontal axis of one of these sticks – Fig. 23*, and the same would apply to a rudder-only aircraft. It is when the second primary control of elevator is added that there arises a choice of mode. If, using the same 4-function example, elevator is added to the same stick that operates rudder, then operation will be in Mode A – Fig. 24. But, if the elevator is placed on the other stick, then the operation is in Mode B – Fig. 25.

Although, with an aircraft, there is a choice of steering control – aileron or rudder – when both are present only one will be the primary control and this will be aileron. (There are extremely rare exceptions to this rule but these are of no concern here.) Therefore, in Mode A operation, the primary controls of aileron and elevator are on one stick – Fig. 26, but in Mode B they are separated, one to each stick – Fig. 27.

To complete the arrangement for a 4-function outfit, the other secondary control, which is throttle, fills the remaining vacant stick axis, being placed with rudder in Mode A – Fig. 28 – and with aileron in Mode B – Fig. 29.

There is no point in reiterating all this by running through all the permutations of the various outfits, because the principle is the same throughout. However, so that there are no misunderstandings, Fig. 30 sets out the options diagrammatically and also "fills-in" the placement of the various secondary controls. A word of warning though; if the purchase of an outfit with less than four functions is contemplated – a watch must be kept on the limitations . . .

The majority of 2-function outfits available are two-stick and, therefore, operation is in Mode B. In a moment the importance of being in the same mode as other fliers in the area will be dealt with, so this must be watched. If a 3-function outfit for full house operation of a glider with aileron/rudder/elevator control is being considered, it must be checked that the stick configuration permits this. A unit with two single-axis sticks and a positionable lever is not suitable, refer to Fig. 30. If a true single stick 4-function outfit, with all the steering controls together – Fig. 18 – seems attractive, it must be remembered that operation is only possible in Mode A.

A primary can't be "saved"

Just to reiterate an obvious point, but one which many modellers never seem to grasp – it is the primary steering control which determines the mode. For example, modellers have been seen flying (or rather trying to fly) a rudder/elevator model with the rudder on the left-hand stick, and elevator on the right, as they were "saving" the horizontal axis of the right-hand stick for when they added aileron, to go full-house in Mode A:

---

* It should be noted that, although the explanations and drawings have assumed right-hand operation, there is no reason at all why a left-handed person should not transpose the controls. The importance of having an outfit which is not a "one-off" should be borne in mind, however, just in case it is necessary for someone else to "take over" when the model is airborne.

RADIO CONTROL GUIDE

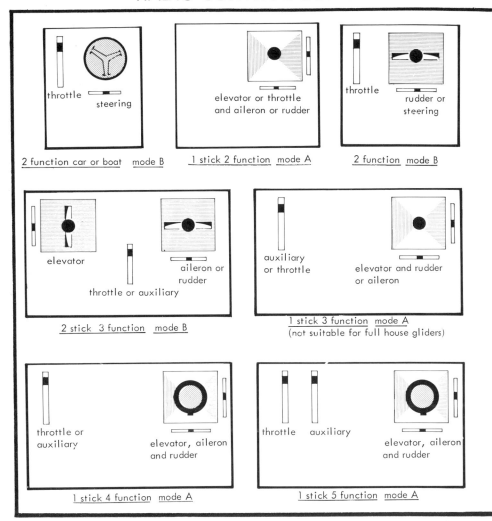

Fig. 30

(vice versa is equally common!). They had entirely failed to appreciate that a stick axis is not "saved" for anything of the sort, because when aileron *replaces* rudder as the primary control, it also replaces its location on the control stick.

To recap then . . . once this disposition of primary and secondary controls has been grasped, the reasons for a choice of control mode become obvious – the primaries can either be on one dual-axis stick – Mode A – or on separate sticks – Mode B. It is the reason for having this choice, and why it is so important to make the correct one, however, which needs further explanation – so back to the beginning of this chapter!

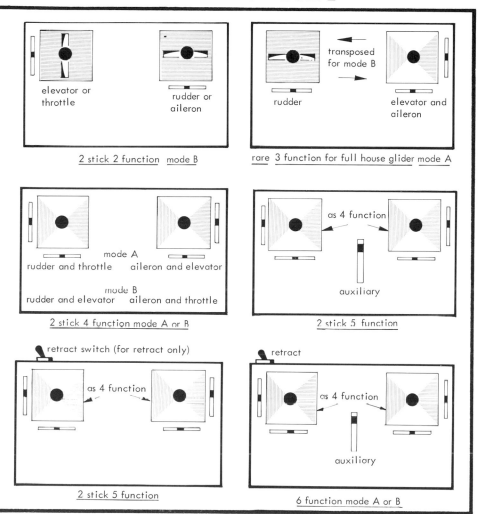

2 stick 2 function mode B

rare 3 function for full house glider mode A

2 stick 4 function mode A or B

2 stick 5 function

2 stick 5 function

6 function mode A or B

How the choice evolved

It is common to find modellers who have been flying for some years using Mode B because, when they learnt to fly in the pre-proportional era, technical reasons dictated the disposition of the controls in this manner. So, by sticking with it, they could convert to proportional without having to re-learn their flying technique. To many, however, it is more natural to fly a model like a "real" aeroplane, with the primary controls of steering and elevation on the one "joy stick". Therefore many modellers with no pre-proportional flying experience opted for Mode A. Or, perhaps, they did not realise a choice was possible and carried on with an outfit as supplied, and this could well have been in either mode!

Indeed, in those earlier days, it was seldom a simple matter to change the mode, so manufacturers tended to discourage the option. Perhaps it is for this reason that the choice of mode today tends to go in geographical regions, together with a preponderance of one or two makes of equipment. Therefore, it is easy to fall into the trap of saying "oh nearly everyone flies in Mode A (or B)". Even manufacturers do this because of this grouping effect, which makes it natural that modellers flying together should, without conscious choice, end up flying in the same mode. When writing this chapter the same error was very nearly made. Fortunately, 'phone calls round the country to model shops, manufacturers and so on, revealed the balance to be as near as anything 50/50!

Which mode to choose

Now it *is* possible to be able to fly both modes. Many competent fliers, for instance, prefer Mode B, but *can* fly Mode A (or vice versa), although this is usually confined to actual flying, it being preferred that an experienced "A" (or "B") flier should take-off and land. This is because their reflexes and instantaneous responses are tuned to their usual mode, whereas it is necessary to *think* what to do next when flying in the other mode. However, it is certainly not recommended continually to chop and change in this manner because one day, in a crisis, for just one fatal second, it will be forgotten just which mode is being flown!

It is important, therefore, to start off with the right mode, but the question is how to determine this? On the assumption that someone will be acting as tutor, it is sensible to be in the same mode, so that the model may be test flown by an experienced instructor. As has already been said, the choice of mode tends to go in areas, so there will be no difficulty in determining the most popular choice – the local model shop, which supplies all the equipment, will know! Therefore, the obvious choice is for this local mode but, even so, it would be unwise to choose an outfit where the mode cannot be changed. This point will be returned to in a moment because it must not automatically be assumed that the most popular local mode will, ultimately, prove the best for everyone.

Initially this should be the choice but, if difficulty in co-ordinating the control movements is experienced, then, assuming it to be an outfit where this is possible, the alternative mode should be tried. A word of warning though. Flying a model is like riding a bicycle; the technique has to be learnt. Therefore, it is not advisable to set off in (say) Mode A for a few minutes, decide this is no good and have a go at Mode B, progress no better, so swop back again and so on, ad infinitum. This will achieve nothing at all except broken models.

No, the initial chosen mode must be given a fair go, for at least an hour's flying. If at the end of this time, co-ordination does not come naturally, and the person teaching should spot such a basic fault probably before the pupil, then the alternative mode should be tried. This might well prove to be more "natural" in which case, with the experience now gathered, it will be realised at once that *the* correct mode has been found. If, on the other hand it seems no better, then it must be concluded the difficulty is because of a natural slowness in learning, so a change must be made back to the first mode, in which, by now, a fair bit of experience will have been acquired, and persevere.

This may sound a bit of a rigmarole, but is well worth the experiment, because there are so many cases where someone who thought they would never get the hang of co-ordinated movement, found a change of mode effected an almost miraculous improvement. And, certainly, there is no "best" mode – a succession of World Champions will testify to this!

The two basic methods of holding a transmitter and operating the control sticks. With Mode A (left) the primary controls are being operated with the fingers of the right hand, while with Mode B (right) the thumbs are used. If a neckstrap is used with Mode A, then it may be found easier for the left hand to operate the secondary controls, as it is not then necessary for the case to be held so firmly.

From all this it will be seen that, if it is proposed to buy a fixed function outfit (normally this will only be a 2- or 3 function, or a single stick 4-function unit, as the mode on two-stick 4's can normally be changed in a few minutes) it is strongly recommended that careful stock be taken of what modellers operating similar projects are using. Talk to them; all genuine modellers are willing to help a newcomer. Talk also to the local shopkeeper, (after all he is the man who will bear the brunt of any wrong advice) and then rely on what is said. Failing such help, the best advice would be to select an outfit giving Mode A operation for aircraft, as it seems that newcomers, in general, find it easier to co-ordinate the movement of only one hand. For boats and cars, however, opinion seems to be in favour of Mode B, and certainly the majority of 2-function outfits sold are in this mode.

Paradoxically, and in seeming contradiction to what has just been said, the same is applicable to 2-function units sold for aircraft use. Perhaps it is that where there are only the two primary functions to consider, two hands *are* better than one but, when it is necessary to co-ordinate both primary and secondary functions, then it is easier if the former are combined on one stick.

To sum up then, it is impossible to be categorical about which mode to choose, except to advise having the same as other local fliers. Failing this, a "dry-run" with each at the local model shop will make it possible to decide which feels more natural but, preferably, an outfit which enables a change to be made should be selected so that, if necessary, both may be tried in practice.

Finally, there is the question of how the choice of mode will influence the method of operating the control sticks. In Chapter 2 a neckstrap was mentioned. Now, watching fliers in action, it will be noticed that some suspend the transmitter from such a strap and operate the controls with their fingers, while others will hold it in their hands and operate the sticks with their thumbs. In general it is Mode B fliers who prefer the latter system, and Mode A fliers the former, although this is by no means a universal rule, so it is wise to experiment to find out which method will give the most precise "feel" of the model.

CHAPTER 6

WHICH OUTFIT TO BUY

HAVING noted the capabilities (and limitations) of each type of outfit, now to decide which is the most suitable. The easiest trap to fall into, when the first set of equipment is being purchased, is to buy one with too few functions. If everyone had unlimited funds, then this chapter would consist of the advice . . . "Buy a 6-function outfit and it will be possible to meet every conceivable requirement". This is not an ideal world, however, and most have to cut their garments with greater care.

Really, then, it is necessary to look at the problem in two ways. If money is the greatest consideration, then the best possible advice is for the most comprehensive equipment within the budget available to be bought and the model complexity adjusted to suit. A word of warning, however. It is vitally important to have an outfit which will give long and reliable service. Therefore, it is better for an outfit to have fewer functions and reliability, than every possible extra and not work! Which is not to say that an expensive outfit with limited functions, will be better than a cheaper one with more facilities!

Therefore no one should be discouraged from embarking into radio control, because it is possible to afford "only" a single function outfit. Endless hours of pleasure can be obtained from this, provided care is taken in selecting models suited to the limitations of the equipment, and there is further advice about this aspect in the next chapter.

It is when that bit extra can be afforded but there is reluctance to do so, on an unknown venture, that disappointment is most likely. It is important to remember that, becoming dissatisfied with a limited function set of "gear" and wanting to change it for something more comprehensive, is ultimately going to cost far more than buying the more comprehensive set in the first place.

Two things must be borne in mind. First, it is normally possible to buy, for example, a 4-function outfit with only one servo (adding the others as required at a later date). This will considerably reduce the initial cost, without restricting expansion, as progress is made to more adventurous models. Secondly, in these days of instant Access, Barclaycard and so on, it is possible to effect a long term saving with relatively modest initial expense.

There is no point whatever in buying equipment with more facilities than are needed, however. Intentions must, therefore, be examined carefully, and at length and then, if it is certain (repeat, *certain*) that the requirements will be met by a limited function unit, there is no point at all in paying the extra for a more comprehensive outfit.

Therefore, if ambitions are great but the pocket strictly limited, the best that can be afforded should be bought and modelling sights adjusted to suit the equipment. If simple yachts, power boats, or the simplest aircraft, are the main interest, a single function outfit will suffice. A 2-function unit will provide what is needed for all but the more sophisticated cars and boats, it will make the flying of powered aircraft even more practical, and is all that is needed for many forms of gliding. Three functions will satisfy the demands of all but the most advanced glider flier, will fill every requirement for the car or boat enthusiast, and will enable powered aircraft flying to be performed to all but the highest requirement. If the intention is to fly both glider and power models, however, it is virtually certain that only a 4-function (or more) outfit will meet the needs, because of the limitation of mode choice of a 3-function unit, as was explained in Chapters 4 and 5.

Long and hard thought is necessary before buying – the best way to save money is for the correct outfit to be purchased first time and this leads to what, for most newcomers, will be the milk in the coconut – which of the many makes on the market to buy? The answer is simple – the best that can be afforded! This need not necessarily mean striving to afford the most expensive outfit in its category, however, as will now be discovered!

Which make to buy?

Having just emphasized the importance of selecting an outfit with the necessary complement of functions, it must now be assumed that a decision has been made on this. Therefore, and assuming it meets this requirement, the logical choice is the make, or makes, of equipment most popularly used by the local fliers – after all, if it were unreliable and crashing models, they would not be using it! Enquiries should be made as to why such a local preponderance exists, however. If it is because the local stockists are able to provide spares and service then, obviously, no better choice can be made; if not, then some pointed questions must be asked. Very few modellers are unwilling to discuss such matters with a totally uninhibited freedom!

At this stage though, it is necessary to beware of the local know-all! Of the many individual makes on the market, it is impossible to single out one (except for a manufacturer of course!) and say "that is the best", so anyone who unreservedly claims this is not to be believed. Someone may, in all good faith, think Brand X which, inevitably, happens to be the brand he is flying at the moment, is the best and, for him, it is. He may add "I tried Brand Y but it was useless".

In this case a second opinion must be taken. In all probability this person will say that Brand Y is the only set worth buying, and Brand X is useless. Now this might lead to the supposition that both are suspect – not a bit of it. It is the human failing towards "brand loyalty" which is suspect, plus the fact that no one likes to admit

*An attractive sport biplane for .61 motors, **Acrobits** is compact – 48½ in. wingspan – yet has plenty of wing area, makes it easy for the less experienced to handle.*

Designer's photo

that what he currently owns is not the best choice, because this reflects upon his own judgement.

Unlike an engine — which may be seen (or heard) to be running well or badly — to all but the really experienced, generally, a radio outfit is a go/no-go unit — it either works or it doesn't! If this happens on the ground, the answer is obvious but, if it happens in the air, the model will crash and this leads many people to think that equipment failure' causes all the crashes and, therefore, the equipment in use at the time must be a type to avoid. This is not true. Based on years of experience, it can be stated that, very seldom indeed, when related to the numbers involved, is equipment failure the cause of a crash.

Close personal investigation of many crashes convinces that, in nine cases out of ten, the cause of a crash is pilot error (either in flying, construction, assembly or inadequate pre-flight preparation), or — rather less likely — outside interference. Unlikely? Not a bit of it. To go no further than personal experience of writing-off many models, in only one case was equipment failure diagnosed after a thorough and impartial analysis. The other causes ranged from cold fingers, incorrect depth perception, flying the "wrong" model, thinking the model was going away when, in fact, it was not, "stalling" it by using too much elevator on both landing and take-off (the most common cause of "locking on aileron and rolling into the ground"!) to over indulgence in liquid optimism.

Now it is very tempting each time to blame the wreckage on "them" — the manufacturers — because, just as few people have ever spoken to a bad driver (when they are wrapped in their tin boxes audible communication is difficult), so an incompetent pilot is an even rarer bird! Nevertheless, after a crash, the pilot will know, and so will all experienced modellers watching, where the fault lay.

Now is a good moment to consider "interference" briefly, because it has a close, almost an indistinguishable, affinity with the radio failures just discussed. In other words, nine times out of ten it is an excuse for incompetence. There are, however, the tenth occasions and these will be discussed in a later chapter.

Returning to the question of radio trouble — and certainly this can be experienced with a particular outfit — it is to be hoped that it shows up on the ground, and the manufacturer sorts it out before a model is lost. This is generally the case and all is well, but sometimes confidence is lost, and the set is traded in for another of a different make. This is normal in all things, from cameras to motor cars.

Occasionally, though, someone who has bought and had trouble with practically every set on the market will be met. The wise man will run a mile before being cornered and bored to tears with the tales of woe! Most experienced modellers know someone like this and they also know people who own Mr. A's ex-sets, bought at bargain prices, and with which there has never been a subsequent moment's bother. Moral: if there is someone for whom nothing works — the wise man will wonder why.

Now the thought might have occurred that all equipment is faultless, and only the customer is wrong, but this also in untrue! If modellers using the local field are flying successfully with a particular brand (or brands, but seldom will more than two or three be in general use) of equipment, then it may safely be assumed that it is reliable, and that any tales of disaster may be ascribed to more personal reasons!

RADIO CONTROL GUIDE

It is unwise, however, to just rush off and buy one of these sets, because there are factors, other than reliability, to consider.

Type of servo output

Although, nowadays, very little difference will be found in the physical size and weight of servos, hence it is unlikely that any make could be excluded from consideration on these grounds, in Chapter 2 an aspect was mentioned which could influence choice – whether there is a linear or rotary output. To all practical intents and purposes, for general applications, the choice is immaterial.

For certain specialist uses, however, there may well be a requirement for one or the other. If a choice had to be made, then rotary output is certainly the more versatile, in allowing easy throw adjustment and, marginally, therefore, is to be preferred to the linear type, even though the direct push-pull coupling of this makes many installations simpler than with rotary. Fortunately, however, many manufacturers offer a choice and, of course, there is no reason whatever, why both linear and rotary output servos of the same make should not be intermixed in an installation.

In subsequent chapters, many installation requirements will be found where the ideal take-off from the servo dictates that it moves in a specific direction in answer to a given command. This is known as the "sense" and Fig. 31 shows how

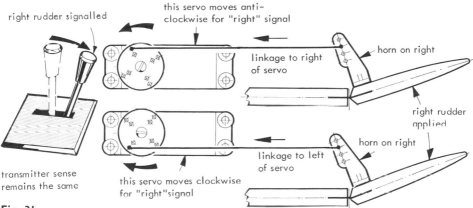

Fig. 31

this may vary by 180°. Take right rudder, where it will be seen, in one sense, the take-off is from the right-hand side of the servo, whereas in the other sense, the take-off point is at 180°. Aileron control is, perhaps, the most common installation where a servo with the correct sense is vital for proper working, so it is common for manufacturers to have available servos in either sense. Very often, in fact, with all outfits (other than single function, obviously!) servos in either sense are supplied with the unit, and identified with a colour or letter coding. In any case, a manufacturer can always reverse the sense of a servo if necessary, but it is better for the choice to be ready to hand when an installation is being made.

Also, as was stated in Chapter 4, it is normal for a manufacturer to use the same

RADIO CONTROL GUIDE

basic servo for his entire range; further it is quite common to find a servo manufacturer supplying almost identical units to different radio manufacturers; so, obviously, there is quite a degree of overlapping in this field.

Finally, the question of batteries. In Chapter 2 the alternative shapes and capacities were described, so it is necessary to make sure that the pack in the outfit chosen is suitable both physically (see Chapter 8) and for capacity. As a general guide it will be found that only the smallest, or very specialised model, cannot accommodate all standard pack shapes but, if there is a problem, an outfit must not arbitrarily be rejected. It is usual for alternative shape packs to be available to special order.

Similarly with capacity. A manufacturer may have standardised on, say, a 500 cell but have the 225 size available to order. Alternatively a 225 might be "standard" – the requirement might be for a 500 – perhaps a weekend's flying without access to charging facilities – so, here again, if there is doubt it is wise to enquire, because this is the simplest part of an outfit to "customise".

AM or FM; 27, 35 or 459 MHz?

Model control equipment may be operated in the UK on three frequency bands — 26.970 to 27.270; 35.010 to 35.200 and 458.5 to 459.5MHz. For many years 27 and 459MHz were the only available frequencies, and technical limitations restricted the use in practice to the 27MHz band only. Ever increasing use of this band, not only by modellers but CB ('Citizens' Band'), medical and other operators, eventually led to the introduction of 35MHz *exclusively for aircraft,* while increasing technical advances made 459MHz equipment available for all model use. These three frequency bands are, themselves, sub-divided into varying numbers of "spot frequencies" which are controlled by a pair of crystals — one each for the transmitter and receiver — and it is this facility which permits many models to be operated simultaneously within the specified band width. Originally all 27MHz equipment was AM (Amplitude Modulation) and could only be operated at a spacing of 50kHz, thus allowing six models to be operated simultaneously. Increasing development plus the introduction of FM (Frequency Modulation) reduced the spacing to 25 kHz and the number of models able to be operated to 13. Equipment on the other frequencies has, however, been designed from the outset for FM operation at 10kHz spacing, thus allowing much greater individual useage within the bands.

Costwise, the lowest priced equipment is 27MHz AM, followed by FM on the same frequency, then 35MHz with 459MHz tending to be the most costly. In appearance all are generally identical except that 459MHz equipment has a short, stubby, transmitter aerial (about 3in. long) making visual identification simple.

When it comes to buying, if cost is the prime consideration, the 27MHz AM set must be the first choice. Be warned, however, that its use may be restricted by interference from other (CB, medical etc.,) users of the band and, hence, aircraft modellers are recommended to pay the extra for 35 or 459MHz equipment. Operators of models which do not have the operational range, and hence proneness to interference of an aircraft high in the sky, may well find that 27MHz AM equipment is totally satisfactory but, even so, the extra cost of FM might prove a better longterm investment. Of course, those who wish to use their equipment to operate both aircraft *and* other types of model are excluded from the 35MHz band and must choose either 27 or 459MHz equipment.

RADIO CONTROL GUIDE

Although, technically, by using all the various spots available on all of the frequencies it is possible to fly many, many models simultaneously from the same site, in practical terms, for everyday club use a limit of about 6 to 8 is generally enforced. The reason for this is that, even when concentrating at ten tenths, a pilot has only to glance away from his model for a fraction of a second and, when he looks back, his angle of vision will have widened to encompass all the other models in the sky! In the ensuing panic he concentrates on the one which seems to be responding to the signals he is sending, only to find, too late, that his was the model which peeled off and crashed!

All modern outfits use plug-in crystals which enable the operator to select which spot on the band he will use. They do not, however, permit "instant conversion" from 27 to 35MHz or vice versa merely by plugging-in the appropriate crystals, even should they physically fit. In practice it will be found that two or three pairs of crystals will be adequate to allow ample useage time on even the most crowded sites, provided proper control is exercised and observed as described in Chapter 19.

The schedule of agreed spot frequencies for the 27MHz and 35MHz bands appears on page 240, together with the standard recognition colour or number code for displaying on the transmitter aerial — in the form of a flag or pennant. Spots on the 459MHz band are also precisely defined, but possible re-allocation of certain of these means that details of those currently in use must be obtained from a dealer.

The price of an outfit normally includes the cost of one pair of crystals, and the purchaser can often specify which spot he would like these to be on. Before doing so (or buying additional pairs), the advice of the shop and, if possible, the local club, should be sought so as to select crystals which will spread the use of the band most evenly among local users.

Tutelage suitability

Having discoursed at length on the choice of modes, it will have been gathered that the choice should always tend towards an outfit where the stick operation may readily be changed. Allied to this is the question of learning to fly and tutelage. Without doubt the best method of pilot instruction is via a "buddy-box". This is a facility which enables the tutor to plug (via a multi wire cable) his own transmitter (or, occasionally a specially made "dummy" transmitter) into that of the pupil. A "dead man's button" enables the instructor to over-ride the pupil's transmitter and take control of the model should difficulties arise. Normally the two transmitters must be in the same mode (again emphasizing the importance of starting out with the popular local mode), but a few makes do permit dual instruction with either transmitter in either mode.

Almost as good a method of instruction is for the tutor to "stand-by" the pupil, ready to take the transmitter from him, or hand it to him, as the situation demands. Obviously, for this method of instruction, buddy-box facilities are not necessary, so a saving in the initial cost of the outfit may be expected. Further, it is wise to consider the advisability of paying for something with a "once only" use — unless, of course, a change of role to become a tutor in due course is envisaged!

To sum up thus far . . .

(1) A choice should be made from the most popular locally used equipment, provided

proper local sales and service facilities exist. If they don't, an enquiry as to why this equipment is preferred to a make with local service is advisable, before a decision is reached.

(2) The equipment selected must meet the requirement for initial training, inter-changeable frequencies, and so on.

(3) Do the servos offered with the outfit meet all requirements? (A complete newcomer, having only read thus far, will be forgiven for saying "how on earth do I know?" Therefore, he should read on. Later, most conceivable variations of installation, in all types of model, are discussed and a much clearer idea of what each particular mod-elling requirement will demand will become clearer.

(4) A "loner" must make a careful study of all adverts and pay particular attention to servicing convenience, because this really is the nub of the matter – easily available servicing, preferably (although this is far from being commonly possible) where the set can be delivered, rather than having to rely on the post.

Suppose, however, the equipment decided upon doesn't meet these requirements. Just suppose that, Brand X, of excellent reputation and with a local service agent, is as aesthetically appealing as water in a pub? Then the individualist will buy the brand he fancies and, if it is one of the esoteric foreign models, with no British servicing facilities, will just have to put up with the inconvenience when it needs servicing – because it will, eventually!

"You gets what you pay for!"

Where does price enter into all this? It will certainly govern the number of functions and the quality of the finish and "feel" of the outfit, although there should be no compromise on reliable operation at any price.

Function for function, however, there is little to choose between sets of similar quality. Indeed in this, as in any other field, the saying "you get what you pay for" is as good a truism as any. No one expects to buy a Rolls-Royce for the price of a Mini; neither can they expect a set costing £100 to offer everything that one costing £200 can, especially, perhaps, in the way of after sales service. Neither must it be assumed, however, that because an outfit is more expensive, it will be more reliable, or give better service, than one costing a lot less. It may well have more features and facilities, plus a much better "feel" and quality of finish, but no radio can do more than "work" reliably and accurately. With the exception of degree of accuracy of response, it can almost be said that a radio either works or it doesn't.

Which comes right back to the beginning – it is impossible to do better than follow the example of successful local fliers . . .

CHAPTER 7

CHOOSING
THE RIGHT
MODEL

NOW that it is known what radio control equipment does, its limitations as well as its potential, it will have been decided how many functions will be needed, and a choice made from the bewildering array of equipment at the shop. So, now to find a suitable model to use it in, and here there are two categories of reader to consider — the complete newcomer and the experienced modeller, who is only a newcomer to radio control. Therefore, two words of advice — one for each category!

To the total beginner: Being over-ambitious can prove self-defeating. Many models, which are quite suitable for training purposes, may offer too much of a constructional challenge — make sure that the model chosen is both easy to complete, as well as to operate.

To the experienced modeller: The ability to construct an advanced model may lead to the supposition that the suitable trainer may be by-passed — pride comes before a crash, and the highest failure rate is among those who think they know enough to miss out the initial stages.

To be fair though, if the choice is for non-flying models, then the whole situation is far less fraught. Although not recommended, provided throttle control is available, it is possible to start off with a racing car or a high-speed boat. But throttle *is* essential — as even a relatively experienced operator will confirm that controlling either of these devices flat out, while waiting for the motor to stop, is guaranteed to sweat off a few pounds in weight!

An aircraft, however, is a totally different kettle of fish, because it has to be controlled in three dimensions. After all, a boat or car, remains earth or water bound, and the biggest disaster which can befall is to run into some obstruction. With an

---

Heading photo shows a most popular sports/aerobatic model, **Sky Chief**, *for .29 to .40 motors and four-function radio. It has a span of 52 in.*

*Not for the beginner, but ideal as a first fully aerobatic glider, **Pedro** features quick construction, has a 49½ in. wingspan and requires three-function radio.*

aircraft there is the *third* dimension of height, and this is the problem to be overcome by learning to fly.

A relatively complex scale boat or car can be built as a first radio controlled project, in the reasonable expectation of obtaining a degree of success. Note – degree – because all things are relative, and the more models built, the more success in operation is achieved.

With an aircraft, however, the only guarantee, following the building of a scale type design as a first project, is failure! If ever the thrill of flying a model with effortless ease is to be achieved, then it is essential to start with the correct design.

The allure of a scale *Spitfire* or *Hurricane* or even a four-engined *Flying Fortress* may seem irresistible, for all such models can be flown, and flown with seeming ease, by radio control. It is the pilot, however, who is making it look easy by his skill – skill built up through many hours of practice. He started at the humblest level, so must everyone.

What has to be learnt is a skill in control and, if what has been said makes this seem difficult, this is not so. There is no more skill required in learning to fly a model, than there is in learning to drive a car. Each requires the four basic principles –

(a) the right vehicle;
(b) application;
(c) concentration;
(d) some initial perseverance.

Obviously no-one who does not possess (b) and (c), and (d) would have read this far, but what about (a)?

RADIO CONTROL GUIDE

Well, the sad truth is that anyone who possesses the last three virtues tends, by his very nature, to think that he can get off the ground with a project which every expert will say is too ambitious. He *will* get off the ground, but the return will be quicker, and very spectacular. And, this is a basic truth, not in any way related to the equipment.

A trainer is essential

It is very tempting to believe that, because equipment which will give control over all the surfaces used to fly a full sized aircraft has been bought, that it is possible to skip the simple training model stage, and go straight on to that *Spitfire* with flaps and retractable undercarriage. This is not true. It is still not true even for the pilot of a full-sized aircraft, and the reason — pause to think about it — is obvious.

In a full size machine the pilot is sitting in the cockpit, and every required correction of course or attitude communicates itself to him immediately. This is not so with a model — here the flier is detached from what is being controlled, the only contact being visual and, to a very much lesser degree, audible. This being so, the need for any correction only becomes evident when the deflection from the flight path is obvious. So obvious, in fact, that too much correction is applied and often the model veers in the other direction, the result being a wild zig-zagging, undulating flight path. (Refer back to Fig. 14.) The answer, of course, is *anticipation* and, when a flier has learnt to anticipate the correct control responses then, effectively, he has learnt to fly — with one other reservation . . .

When a model is coming towards the pilot the steering controls are reversed in that *his* right is the model's left and so on. Of course, if he always faces in the same direction that the model is travelling, this never happens, but only a contortionist, straining to look over his shoulder, or even between his legs for inverted flying can do this! Seriously, the answer is simple, but must be practised from the very first operational attempts, and this is never to think of the transmitter control stick's right or left, but only of the *model's right or left* and thus controlling will always be in the correct "sense". Obviously the same also applies to a land or water vehicle but, as has been said, to a much lesser extent, because their operation is only two dimensional.

Which model to choose

For those with an interest in boats then, for single function, a yacht or relatively slow power model is ideal. For something more spectacular, such as a racing or scale boat, then a 2-function outfit, to enable throttle control to be achieved, is almost essential. In yachts the extra function, when used to give sail control, will add enormously to the fun. Similarly, with cars; for other than very slow moving vehicles, a second function will be almost essential.

With aircraft, however, as was said earlier, there are probably hundreds of designs, ranging from the simplest, to quite sophisticated scale types, which were designed to be flown with rudder-only control. The Radio Modeller Planbook contains numerous designs of all types, and there are also many commercial kits. The fact that the majority of these were designed for "single channel" control is no handicap. It may be necessary to use a little ingenuity in re-arranging the equipment installation, but the actual flying is going to be much easier and more precise than ever it was with the older equipment. Further, with the larger size of models in this category, there is normally more than enough space and weight carrying ability for an additional servo to give either throttle or elevator control, so the owners of 2-, or even 3-function equipment should not pass over this rich hunting ground.

Obviously, to learn to fly* one of the more sophisticated designs should not be selected, always it must be remembered that the terms "single channel" and "easy to fly" are not synonymous. Therefore, what is needed is a model which is relatively slow flying to allow thinking time, which will fly "hands-off" while the thinking goes on, and will not respond suddenly or viciously to some ham-fisted control signals.

Among gliders, the simple thermal soaring type generally meets these requirements while, for anyone living near a suitable slope soaring site, then a similar type, but adapted to the more specialist requirements of slope soaring, will again prove quite suitable. In similar vein, power enthusiasts will find that the so-called "powered glider" types are among the simplest from which to learn the basic principles of control.

Now this has rather supposed "going it alone" and hence what is needed, effectively, is a free-flight model whose natural sedate flight pattern can be interrupted by radio! It is surprising just how quickly it is possible to pick up the rudiments of control by interrupting the natural flight path of a model of this type and then, in no time at all, be ready for more ambitious projects. Indeed, with rudder-only control of a properly trimmed and adjusted model, flown in suitable weather conditions, there is very little which needs to be "taught".

With an instructor available, however, it is possible to start straight away with the so-called "intermediate" trainer, which normally requires at least two functions, on rudder and elevator, with often a third for motor. Ideally, the latter should be chosen because from this it is an easy step to greater things. Even for the owner of a 4-function outfit, the intermediate rudder/elevator model is as good a jumping off point as any, although, if progress is quick, then the urge to try aileron control is great, and there are available a selection of designs to start training, using rudder, then adding aileron later on.

Given a really suitable model, there is, of course, a lot to be said for the owner of a 4-function outfit starting off full-house and, in the Radio Modeller Plans range, there is a trainer designed with this specific purpose in mind. It is RM 50 *Big-Wig* and it also incorporates flap control for those with a suitable r/c unit.

The greatest temptation, especially if the instructor is a really competent flier, is to start off with too ambitious a project. All too often this leads to frustration — the instructor being more often in control than the pupil — and disappointment. The real secret of success is to be content, initially, with learning the secret of control with a "forgiving" trainer. Once it is possible safely to solo such a model, weekend after weekend, without continual repair sessions, it is time to think of something a

---

*This aspect is dealt with in detail later, here the prime concern is with model choice.

RADIO CONTROL GUIDE

Big Wig is a large, slow-flying model, especially designed as a trainer for those who wish to start full-house. It also incorporates optional flaps for slow landings but, if these are to be used, a five-function outfit will be required. Designed for .61 motors it has a wingspan of 80 in.

Designer's photo

little more advanced and then, when this is mastered, the 6-ft. span scale *Spitfire* with working flaps and retracting undercarriage. Ah dreams . . . . .

Helicopters

For those whose interest is helicopters, the problems are somewhat different. There is no equivalent to the fixed wing "free-flight with radio guidance" type of model, so an instructor, while not absolutely necessary, would be a distinct advantage.

The difficulty in flying a helicopter is not that things happen quickly, but that too much happens at one time. Most fixed wing models can be (and usually are) flown for much of the time using only two of the available four functions. Flying a helicopter, however, requires the simultaneous use of all four functions, with the added complication that the operation of each will affect and require a correction from the remainder.

Flying any type of model is a balancing exercise. A fixed wing model may be compared to balancing a broom handle on the index finger, a helicopter to balancing a broom stick on each index finger!

While many people have learnt to fly helicopters without previous fixed wing experience, such must be an advantage. Firstly, from a construction point of view, helicopters require accurate building and a sound radio installation, so any previous experience must be helpful. Secondly, fixed wing flying experience will help in judging the position of the helicopter in the air. The absence of a large wing makes it difficult to judge the attitude of the model. Also, the experienced flier will start off straight-

49

RADIO CONTROL GUIDE

*One of the most popular scale designs is the **Piper Cub**, because its simple construction and slow flying characteristics make it an ideal choice for those who expect even a trainer model to look like the real thing! Of 71 in. wingspan it is designed for .29 to .35 motors and four-function radio but will, in fact fly without the use of ailerons.*

away by flying the model and not the "box"; both skills which are more easily learnt from a simple fixed wing trainer.

There is, however, one disadvantage faced by a fixed wing pilot taking up 'copter flying and that is that, in case of difficulty, he will instinctively close the throttle, which will turn a difficult situation into a disaster. With a helicopter, in case of emergency, the thing to do is to *open* the throttle to gain height and thus thinking time.

Finally, what of the many other model types which can be controlled by radio? There are radio controlled model trains, tanks, puppets, motor cycles, theatres and so on, but, in relation to the three main divisions – aircraft, boats, cars – these are very much specialist, one-off, projects. Nevertheless, although their own peculiar problems do not, therefore, merit detailed discussion, it will be found that the general principles of control requirement, operation and installation described for other models, can readily be adapted.

And now to those general principles. It must be assumed that equipment is chosen and a suitable model built, and all that remains is to get one installed in the other and become operational. The chapters which follow will first deal with aircraft installations, because they give the most comprehensive coverage of the subject and are, by the very nature of the model, the most demanding. Following this will be a relatively brief section detailing those aspects of boat and car useage which are not covered by general aircraft installations, but, it must be borne in mind, that it really is these basic aircraft requirements which are the nub of *any* successful installation, so this section must not be skipped over, or the most vital information of all will be missed.

CHAPTER 8

INSTALLING THE SERVOS, RECEIVER AND BATTERIES

Ask any manufacturer or shopkeeper, and he will say that the most consistent cause of equipment failure is incorrect installation, and this is why so much space is devoted to a detailed description of the many aspects of this, together with the various methods of solving the problems involved. Because of the wide diversity of servo choice, most of the illustrations show a stylised unit, representing either dual-linear or disc output. Therefore, the various couplings shown are adaptable to all types of servo.

Before getting down to specific cases, some emphasis on general points:

1. A servo must never be allowed to stall or overload. Stiff linkages, mechanical stops, or linkages fouling, are the common causes and the result is always excessive battery drain, and usually a ruined servo and crashed model. *Linkages must always be completely free – a servo may have 4 lb. pull, but it operates most efficiently and accurately under no-load conditions.* Therefore, ideally, all linkages to control surfaces should be so free that the surface will "fall" under its own weight, when the pushrod is disconnected from the servo. Care must be taken to avoid having a linkage "jam" so that the servo does not reach its full commanded travel. This is most common with throttle, and can put sufficient drain on batteries to result in control of the model being lost.

2. The servo must always be mounted in accordance with the manufacturer's instructions with regard to insulation from vibration. Those mounting grommets are not there for fun; they ensure the equipment works, despite the pounding of the engine.

3. If a "block" installation, for easy transfer of the servos from one model to another – as detailed later – is being made, each individual servo must still be mounted in the "tray" so as to be vibration-insulated, and not rubbing against other units.

4. The popular servo-mounting tape is, like most things, satisfactory if used properly. If used without consideration of the transmission of vibration or torsional strains to parts of the servo case not designed to absorb them (for example, if the linkage is the least bit stiff), the case may be distorted, causing uneven gear wear and even disengagement of the gears in extreme cases. Many servos are expressly designed and stressed to be mounted via grommets, or grommet mounted spring clips, and installing them in a

51

model in any other way could invalidate a guarantee. The correct way to mount servos with tape is detailed later.

Planning the installation

With the foregoing points in mind, the layout of the various components is now planned so that the "runs" to the various controls are as straight as possible. At this stage it is assumed that a model with the disposition of the control runs and the control horns, which determine the connection of the servo in relation to its direction of travel,

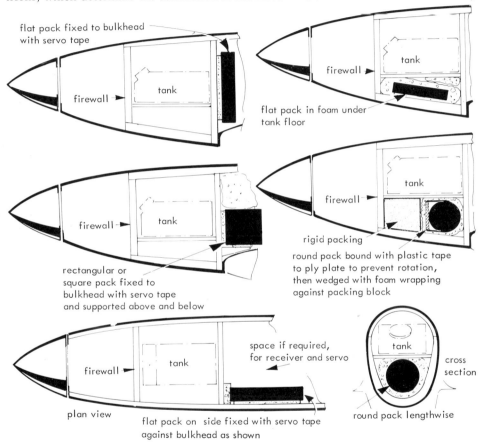

flat pack fixed to bulkhead with servo tape

tank

firewall

firewall ▶

tank

flat pack in foam under tank floor

firewall ▶

tank

firewall ▶

tank

rectangular or square pack fixed to bulkhead with servo tape and supported above and below

rigid packing

round pack bound with plastic tape to ply plate to prevent rotation, then wedged with foam wrapping against packing block

firewall ▶

tank

space if required, for receiver and servo

tank

cross section

plan view

flat pack on side fixed with servo tape against bulkhead as shown

round pack lengthwise

Fig. 32

is on the bench, as is usually the case when a model is built from a kit or when an ARTF has been bought. If scratch building, the disposition of the controls may be worked out during the construction of the model to suit the sense and method of mounting the servos, although, even here, problems not foreseen early enough may arise. The recollection of a model careering all over the place, through overlooking the fact that left rudder/nosewheel on a model upside-down on the bench, becomes right rudder when the model is taking-off, still causes a blush to rise to the face in many quarters!

In most cases, access to the equipment is via the wing opening and, apart from allowing for the obvious differences (and potential reversals just mentioned), installations are identical in both high and low wing models. Even with a non-aerobatic model, however, gravity must never be relied on to keep any part in place. A receiver nestling comfortably in its foam bed in the bottom of the fuselage will be all right on the bench, but it must be secured before the model is turned all ends up to get it in the car. This is an inviolate rule: everything must be secured. Batteries, receiver, servos, switch, plugs, sockets, harness and individual wires – in short, nothing must be left unsecured or unsupported.

In addition to considering the control runs when planning an installation, the balancing of the model must also be borne in mind, so that the c.g. is correct without ballast (if possible). With modern miniature servos it is normally easy, having determined the disposition, merely to move them fore or aft until the balance is correct, and this will be dealt with more fully in a moment. Modern equipment, being small and light, the effect of such movement is not great, but the heaviest part of the airborne unit – the power pack – must never be placed anywhere other than at the front. This, then, is the first parameter and although, depending on the model, some tolerance of fore and aft placement is possible, this must not be at the expense of absolutely secure fixing.

Fig. 32 shows typical methods of locating a flat, round or square pack. The flat type may be fixed to the bulkhead or fuselage side with servo tape, which will also

Fig. 33

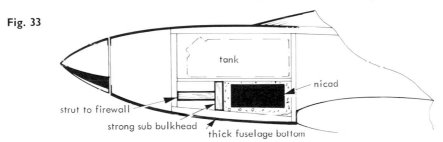

strut to firewall

strong sub bulkhead

thick fuselage bottom

tank

nicad

provide vibration insulation. Round or square types should be wrapped in foam before being slid in place. Normally, once installed, the battery is so well tucked away that inspection is difficult, so it is important that the wires are adequately supported. Especial care must be taken to ensure the pack cannot rotate, this being the most common cause of a lead fracturing.

Often, with a battery placed at the nose of an aircraft, it is effectively in a tapered "box". Without proper support as shown in Fig. 33, in a heavy landing, to say nothing of a crash, it will try and burst out – Fig. 34 – which will not only damage the model, but shear the battery leads as well.

A similar situation to this can arise with gliders. Here, of course, there is no

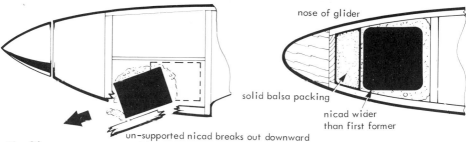

nose of glider

solid balsa packing

nicad wider
than first former

un-supported nicad breaks out downward
and forward in a heavy landing

Fig. 34

Fig. 35

motor or tank to consider, so the power pack is normally placed in the extreme nose. This point will, of course, have been considered when selecting the equipment, and an outfit with a suitably shaped nicad bought! In case not, however, the battery must not just be placed in anyhow, but supported properly – Fig. 35.

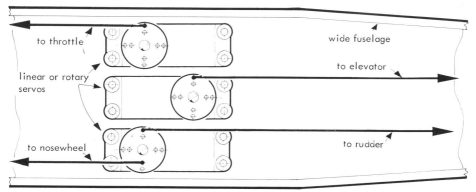

to throttle

linear or rotary
servos

to nosewheel

wide fuselage

to elevator

to rudder

Fig. 36

Now to planning the servo layout in the fuselage, and it is most important always to bear in mind the necessity for having the straightest possible runs for the pushrods, to avoid binding and backlash. Therefore, the servos must be disposed and juxtaposed until this occurs. Figs. 36, 37 and 38 show the three most common dispositions, which are arrived at by logical process. The tank is behind the engine with the steerable

Fig. 37

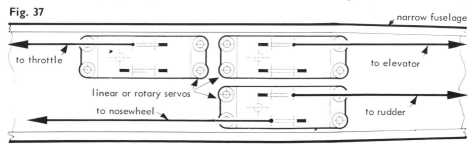

narrow fuselage

to throttle

linear or rotary servos

to nosewheel

to elevator

to rudder

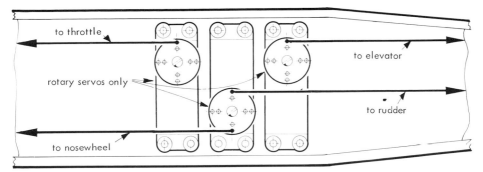

Fig. 38

nosewheel between the two, ergo, the throttle and rudder servos are positioned as near as possible to the fuselage sides, and the nosewheel horn positioned on the opposite side to the throttle arm.

It will be noted that, where the servos are placed lengthwise in the fuselage – Figs. 36 and 37 – either a rotary or a linear output may be used. Only rotary output units, however, may be used for transverse mounting as in Fig. 38.

In the drawings, the nosewheel take-off from the servo is shown as being on the opposite side from the rudder pushrod. While the nosewheel take-off should always be from the output nearest the side, the rudder pushrod may be taken from either side, to

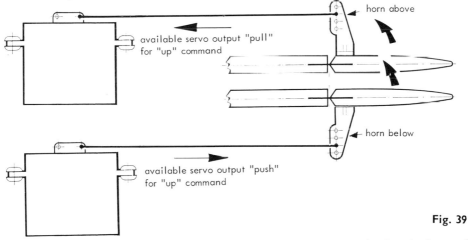

Fig. 39

suit the direction determined by the horn, even if this does mean altering the internal disposition of the elevator pushrod. If, however, the control horn is moved from the bottom to the top of the elevator, or from the left- to the right-hand side of the rudder or nosewheel, this will reverse the sense of the control action – Fig. 39.

Obviously it is not feasible to illustrate every possible arrangement, and only the most popular layouts are shown here, but even if, for example, certain models' layouts necessitate having two servos side by side, and the third (throttle) well forward, or perhaps three servos in a straight line, (which may call for a little initiative), nonetheless the basic principles of the installation remain constant. And, the most important constant of all is for there never to be any compromise on ensuring the proper geometry for the control runs. While, as will be shown in a moment, it is advantageous to have all the servos mounted as a unit on a tray, this must always remain a secondary consideration to the importance of having the correct control runs, as described in succeeding chapters.

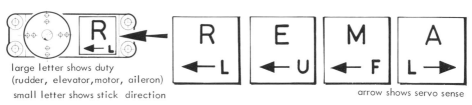

large letter shows duty
(rudder, elevator, motor, aileron)

small letter shows stick direction

arrow shows servo sense

Fig. 40

This leads to an alternative consideration of the problem, which is to determine the servo position first, and then lay out the control runs to suit. Certainly, when scratch building, this is often feasible, in which case it offers the best possible solution. But, in practice, it is amazing how often "Murphy's Axiom" is applicable! Therefore, although the temptation will exist to make a simple "block" installation and bodge about with endless contortionist bends in bits of wire to get the runs correct – temptation exists to be resisted! The end result of a bodge-up is always so much backlash and lost movement, that the model itself could well be placed in jeopardy.

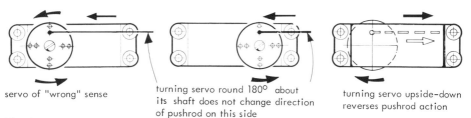

servo of "wrong" sense

turning servo round 180° about its shaft does not change direction of pushrod on this side

turning servo upside-down reverses pushrod action

Fig. 41

Therefore, unless it is possible to have both a block servo installation *and* the correct control runs, the former must be sacrificed. It may, initially, take longer, and require more ingenuity, to mount the servos piecemeal in the correct position, but the end product will be a trouble free installation – better than which cannot be achieved!

It is a good idea for each servo to be marked with its function, and rotation or direction of drive, as in Fig. 40. The plugs and sockets or connectors are marked R – Rudder, E – Elevator, A – Aileron, M – Motor, and so on. With this form of notation throughout everyone will understand – it is much better than "auxiliary, 1, 2, 3", etc, as it is all too easy for the plugs or linkages to be mixed up when fitting out a

RADIO CONTROL GUIDE

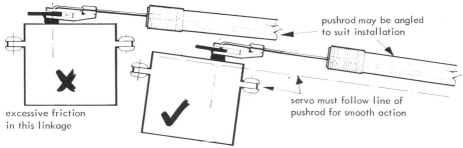

excessive friction
in this linkage

pushrod may be angled
to suit installation

servo must follow line of
pushrod for smooth action

Fig. 42

new model, when transferring gear to a different model, or even after inspecting the
gear whilst carrying out a service!

This method of identification should also serve as a reminder, by means of an
arrow, that the direction of a servo cannot be reversed by turning it round, but that
this can be achieved by turning it upside-down, if feasible — see Fig. 41.

Another aspect of planning is to make sure that, having got the servos correctly
arranged, operation does not lead to binding. Fig. 42 shows a common mistake which

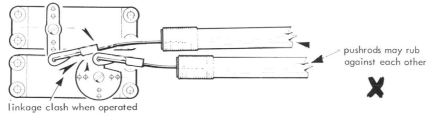

pushrods may rub
against each other

linkage clash when operated

Fig. 43

leads to excessive friction in the linkage, and Fig. 43 shows an even more common
installation error.

Having decided on the disposition, all the controls are operated to their maximum
travel (including trim) and in every possible combination, to make certain that neither
the pushrods nor the servo outputs themselves will foul. Fig. 44 gives a good example of

Fig. 44

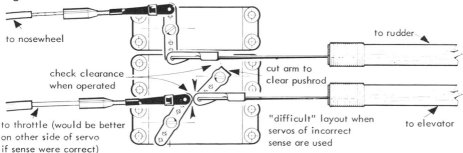

to nosewheel

check clearance
when operated

to throttle (would be better
on other side of servo
if sense were correct)

cut arm to
clear pushrod

"difficult" layout when
servos of incorrect
sense are used

to rudder

to elevator

what, on the face of it, seems a perfectly practical linkage – which, indeed it is, provided there is clearance at the point indicated by the arrow, when both motor and elevator are not only at their extremes of travel, but also with the full appropriate trim selected.

Having determined the position of the servos, their actual position in the fuselage must be decided. The model is assembled with the engine, batteries and so on installed, and the receiver and servos placed (wedged in place with a piece of foam if necessary) in the relative determined fore and aft position. The c.g. is then checked and the position of the receiver and servos adjusted until the correct balance is achieved. Provided, physically, there is enough room in the model, it doesn't matter if the receiver is in front of, or behind, the servos, which, being the heaviest single unit, may have to be placed well fore or aft to achieve balance. Having marked where the servos must be, the model is dissembled for them to be fixed in place.

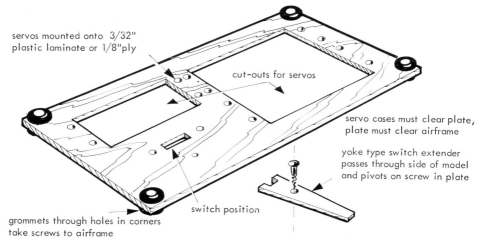

servos mounted onto 3/32"
plastic laminate or 1/8"ply

cut-outs for servos

servo cases must clear plate,
plate must clear airframe

yoke type switch extender
passes through side of model
and pivots on screw in plate

switch position

grommets through holes in corners
take screws to airframe

Fig. 45

The majority of servos have lugs which are fitted with grommets and there is no better way of installing these than by mounting them in a servo tray, as this makes for both neatness and easy interchangeability between models. A selection of commercial trays is shown in the accompanying photograph (often one of these trays is supplied with an outfit), but if there is not one such which suits the servos or model, then it is a simple matter to make one from good quality $\frac{1}{8}$in. plywood or a similar material as shown in Fig. 45.

Many commercial trays have moulded-in spigots, designed to prevent the mounting grommets being compressed so much that they fail in their purpose of insulating the servos against vibration. This is very important, and Fig. 46 demonstrates the right and wrong way of screwing a servo down! Should it be necessary to use nuts and bolts (self-tapping screws are not suitable in thin servo trays, or with metal brackets, where the tip of the screw will protrude through the material) then a spacer

RADIO CONTROL GUIDE

Plugs and sockets should always be identified—see text and Fig. 40.

A selection of commercial servo trays for mounting two and three units. Note switch sliders and aileron mount.

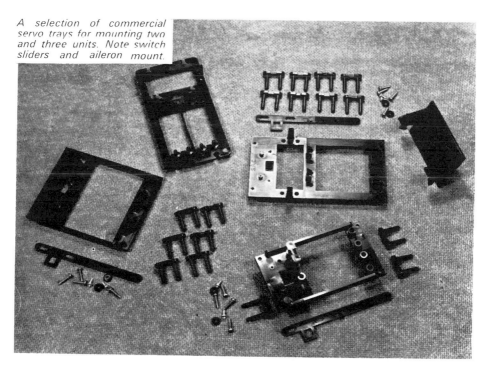

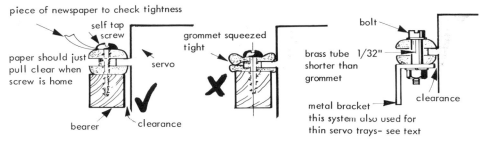

piece of newspaper to check tightness
self tap screw
paper should just pull clear when screw is home
servo
grommet squeezed tight
bolt
brass tube 1/32" shorter than grommet
metal bracket
this system also used for thin servo trays– see text
clearance
bearer
clearance

Fig. 46

tube should be fitted in the grommets. This should be about $\frac{1}{32}$in. shorter than the thickness of the grommet, and will prevent overcompression, whilst allowing the bolts to be really tight – Fig. 46 again.

It is equally important that there is adequate clearance between the bearer (or any part of the structure) and the case of the servo, so that there is no risk of trans-mitted vibration. Also some servos have the cable exiting in such a position, that the rails or trays will have to be notched to permit free clearance when installing or removing the servos. Not only will this prevent damage to the cables, but also remove another potential source of transmitted vibration – a cable squeezed against a bearer.

It is quite common for a servo tray itself to carry mounting grommets and, therefore, the servos may be mounted more rigidly in such a tray, relying on the normally larger tray grommets to insulate the entire "block". Again, though, it is important that, once installed, there is sufficient clearance all round to ensure that no part of the unit (and this includes the tray itself, of course) will come into direct contact with the structure. Normally, about $\frac{3}{32}$in. is adequate and this should always be checked out by placing a finger on each servo in turn (or the entire tray, as appropriate) and then applying a firm pressure in all directions. In a correctly mounted unit, there will be a feeling of firmness but not rigidity and, without forcing anything, but just applying a firm pressure, there should be about $\frac{1}{16}-\frac{3}{32}$in. "float" in all directions – Fig. 47.

Of course, not all servos are lug mounted, some being designed especially to be mounted on spring clips, the accompanying photo showing a typical example. It will be noted that the clips are fitted with grommets, and the foregoing advice on mounting is,

Fig. 47

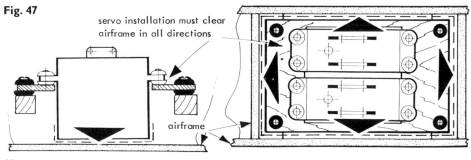

servo installation must clear airframe in all directions

airframe

RADIO CONTROL GUIDE

Above: *servos designed to be mounted in metal spring clips. Note the mounting grommets in the clips, which are available for both upright or sideways mounting of the servo.*

Below: *a selection of commercial mouldings for mounting lug type servos. None of these clips has grommet insulation, this being provided by the servo grommets.*

therefore, equally applicable. Also, there is no reason at all why the clips should not be fitted to a plywood tray to allow easy interchangeability between models, although it is such a simple matter to clip a servo in or out, that many modellers prefer to have a set of clips fitted in each model.

There are also available spring clips for use with lug mounted servos – see the accompanying photograph. These clips are not normally fitted with mounting grommets, the design being such that spigots engage in the actual servo grommets, enabling them to fulfil their proper function.

Now to mount the clips, tray, or individual servos, as the case may be, into the model and, for the latter two, the normal method is to screw them to wooden bearers. Woodscrews are far from being the best for fixing – better are the "PK" or self-tapping type. The rails are pre-drilled slightly smaller than the screw, to avoid the wood splitting as the screw is wound down. Any straight-grained hardwood is suitable for the rails but, in some applications, it is preferable to use hard balsa – more about this later.

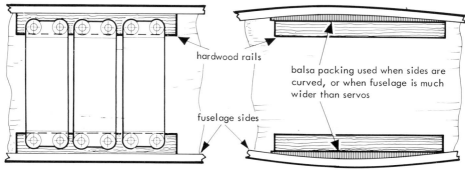

hardwood rails

balsa packing used when sides are curved, or when fuselage is much wider than servos

fuselage sides

Fig. 48

By far the best location for the rails is along the fuselage side – Fig. 48 – as this spreads the load most evenly. Often it is not possible to do this, however, and alternatives must be sought. A selection of ideas is shown in Fig. 49, one of which should suit all but the most stubborn case!

It must, though, always be borne in mind that this servo "block" is relatively heavy and, if it tears free in a crash, or even just a heavy landing, the damage to both the airframe and any other equipment in front (the receiver perhaps?) to say nothing of the servos themselves, will be considerable. All conscientious modellers will take especial care here, because they are probably the type who always wear a seat belt for the same (well almost the same) reason.

Ah, but what if the model doesn't permit a block installation? Well, on no account must there be a bodge-up of the control runs, so this leaves only the alternative of mounting the servos individually. Servos using a clip mounting should present few problems here – the correct relative place is determined and they are screwed to the fuselage side, floor and so on or, if necessary, a special platform or bulkhead is fitted.

With servos of the lug mounting type (when a clip mounting attachment is not

RADIO CONTROL GUIDE

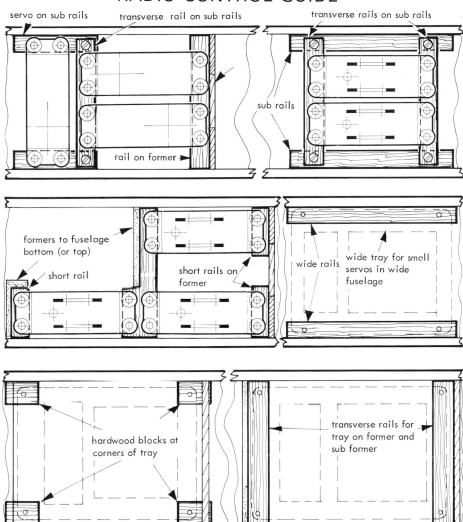

Fig. 49

being used), the best solution, undoubtedly, is for them to be screwed to individual runners. It is often difficult, however, to mount such runners (or, indeed screw-mount servo clips) in the required position. Therefore, it will often prove more convenient to use servo tape, but careful note must first be taken of the limitations of this material.

Servo tape, which is obtainable at model shops, is a sponge plastic strip with contact adhesive on both sides. The sponge plastic serves two purposes; it provides vibration insulation, and it allows for any slight unevenness in the surface to which the tape is fixed. This ensures that all the adhesive is in contact with the surface. The tape sticks best to smooth non-absorbent surfaces. The smooth surface of a servo case, or the plastic or metal base of a servo clip, is perfect for a good adhesion but, if the servo is not to become detached from the airframe, any wooden surface must be "skinned" with a coating of balsa cement which is allowed to dry, before any attempt is made to tape-fit the servos.

As mentioned earlier, however, care must be taken to fix the tape to the servo so as not to impose torsional, or vibration, loads to parts of the servo case not designed to carry them. The former is unlikely to occur unless the linkages are in the slightest degree stiff, and the latter is ensured by selecting a tape which has at least the same degree of resilience as the normal mounting grommets. If there are any doubts about the case twisting, it is wise to use tape over the whole area not just a strip of tape at each end as is usual.

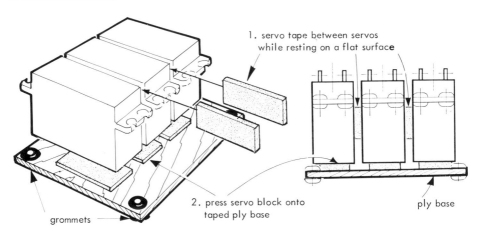

1. servo tape between servos while resting on a flat surface

2. press servo block onto taped ply base

ply base

grommets

Fig. 50

Servos fixed with tape are removed by slipping a sharp modelling knife between the servo and the structure, and cutting through the foam plastic. The remains of the tape are then removed by "peeling" with the fingers. Fresh tape has to be used for the next installation. Old tape must never be re-used by coating it with contact adhesive. It will have been cut unevenly when removing it from the model and this means it will no longer afford any vibration damping at all, as it will be filled up with adhesive, thus destroying the flexibility of the tape material.

It is possible to make a unit installation using tape as shown in Fig. 50, where the servos are taped to a removable ply plate, which is then mounted in the model. The additional tape between each servo is to ensure they do not touch each other, and also to make the whole unit firm.

Servo tape must not be exposed to fuel spray or exhaust fumes as this can, in time, soften the backing adhesive and cause the servo to move, or even become

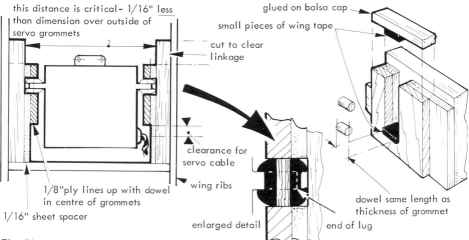

this distance is critical – 1/16" less than dimension over outside of servo grommets

cut to clear linkage

glued on balsa cap

small pieces of wing tape

clearance for servo cable

wing ribs

1/8"ply lines up with dowel in centre of grommets

1/16" sheet spacer

enlarged detail

end of lug

dowel same length as thickness of grommet

Fig. 51

completely detached. Tape fixings should be checked periodically as, if exposed to the sun's rays – or central-heating – the tape can "dry out", and become easily detached.

Fitting the aileron servo

The aileron servo is best positioned in the thickest part of the wing but, in doing this, the spar must not be cut into or weakened in any way. The actual position, and the question of whether the servo is to be placed on its side or upright, will depend entirely on the linkage employed. A favourite method, for a servo flat in the wing, is to make a tight-fitting housing to fit the servo lugs complete with rubber grommets. Such a housing may be made from hard balsa faced with ply – Fig. 51. Pieces of dowel are fitted into each grommet to prevent them compressing too much and hence allowing the servo to float endwise, Fig. 52 showing the right and wrong way. The servo may also be screwed to a removable ply plate as in Fig. 53.

Other methods of mounting must, of course, depend on the servo, but it may be

Fig. 52

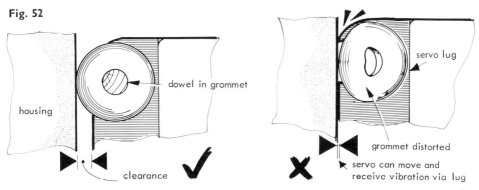

housing

dowel in grommet

clearance

servo lug

grommet distorted

servo can move and receive vibration via lug

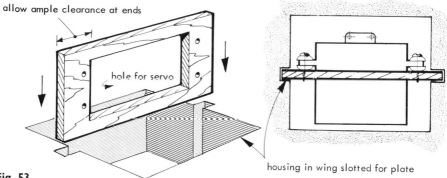

allow ample clearance at ends

hole for servo

Fig. 53

housing in wing slotted for plate

taped in place or screwed to rails, as in the fuselage installation. This latter is normally only used with upright servos and these generally project above (or below) the wing into the fuselage. This is where a hard balsa rail should be used. In a rough landing, a wing held on with rubber bands might slew to one side, in which case the screws will tear from the balsa without damaging the servo or the fuselage. It is simpler to plug a torn hole and re-screw the servo in place, than to have to repair a split fuselage side and pay for a servo overhaul!

Also – and this is of greater initial importance – allowance must be made for the overhang into the fuselage. This lesson is normally learnt the hard way, by not discovering that the aileron and fuselage servos and linkages foul each other, until the wing is fixed in place ready for flying. With the wing just resting on the fuselage there is clearance but, as it is pulled down securely by the rubber bands, the whole lot interlock!

Owners of spring-clip mounted servos will find that the manufacturers generally supply clips dimensioned for both upright and sideways mounting of the unit, the latter reducing the height appreciably. There is also on the market a selection of specialist mounting brackets for use with lug mounted servos, enabling them to be

Fig. 54

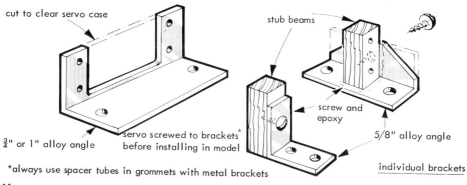

cut to clear servo case

stub beams

screw and epoxy

$\frac{3}{4}$" or 1" alloy angle

servo screwed to brackets* before installing in model

5/8" alloy angle

*always use spacer tubes in grommets with metal brackets

individual brackets

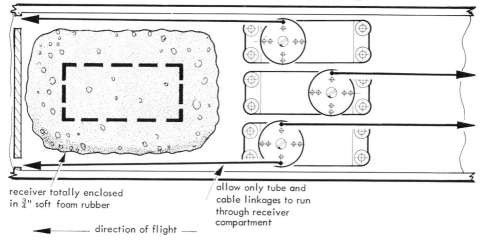

receiver totally enclosed
in $\frac{3}{4}$" soft foam rubber

allow only tube and
cable linkages to run
through receiver
compartment

◄——— direction of flight ———

Fig. 55

installed on their side. Of course, there are occasions where a commercial unit is unsuitable for a particular job, but it is a simple matter to devise home made alternatives and Fig. 54 suggests some ideas to work from.

Installing the receiver

Having positioned the servos, now to tackle the receiver mounting. The modern unit is so small and light that, generally speaking, no consideration need be given to the weight affecting the balance, except that the foam rubber packing may equal, or even exceed, the weight of the unit itself. Figs. 55, 56 and 57 show typical positions for the receiver and all are applicable to either high or low wing models.

The only points to watch are that the foam (not foam plastic but foam rubber) is adequate (about $\frac{3}{4}$in. thick) to protect the unit both from vibration and shock in heavy

Fig. 56

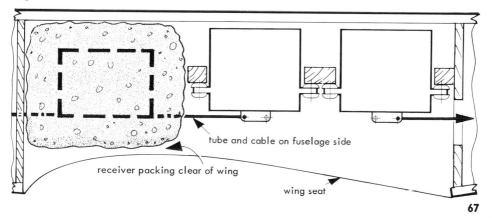

tube and cable on fuselage side

receiver packing clear of wing

wing seat

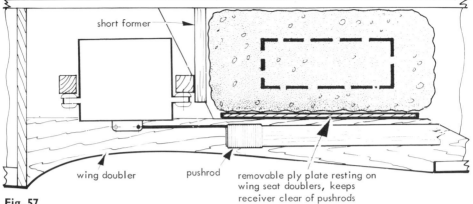

short former

wing doubler   pushrod   removable ply plate resting on wing seat doublers, keeps receiver clear of pushrods

Fig. 57

landings. Also, there must be sufficient slack in the harness and aerial, to allow for the "float" of the receiver inside the rubber. Finally, the aerial is exited from the fuselage by the shortest feasible route, and not run adjacent to the servos, so as to avoid the possibility of picking up interference from the servo motors.

A knot in the aerial "holds" against the inside of the exit hole, so that there is enough slack to allow the Rx to "float" even though, as is normally the case, the aerial is pulled tight externally by a rubber band. Indeed, it is important that no direct strain is placed on any of the leads as they exit from the units. Therefore, it is usual to support these by binding with thread or adhesive tape, as shown in Fig. 58. Some

Fig. 58

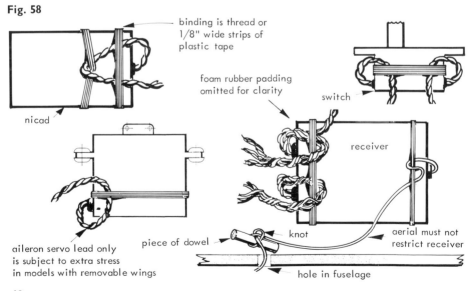

binding is thread or 1/8" wide strips of plastic tape

foam rubber padding omitted for clarity

switch

nicad

receiver

aileron servo lead only is subject to extra stress in models with removable wings

piece of dowel

knot

aerial must not restrict receiver

hole in fuselage

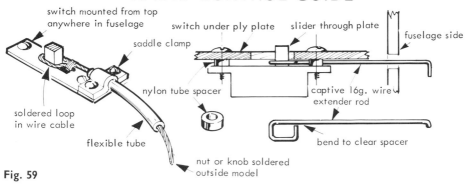

Fig. 59

outfits require access to the inside of the receiver to change crystals and, with these, it is undesirable to "seal" the case with binding as shown, so an alternative – adhesive tape to the side of the case perhaps? – should be found. Certainly, it is unwise to forego this precaution, because if the receiver is constantly being removed and replaced as the crystal is changed, its leads will be in even greater need of support than those of a unit which lies undisturbed.

Disposition of ancillaries

With all the main items now in place, it only remains to install the switch and dispose the harness, plugs and sockets, neatly and securely. If, for convenience sake, the switch is fixed to the fuselage side, it must always be on the side away from the engine exhaust and so positioned and identified that the on/off selection is obvious, but not liable to accidental switching. Many switches are provided with an extra long slider designed expressly to pass through the thickness of a fuselage side. With a slide switch, however, many prefer to mount it inside the fuselage and operate it via a pushrod as shown in Fig. 59. Many of the commercial servo trays incorporate a switch mounting, with either pushrod operation or a lever and yoke. The home made servo tray which is shown in Fig. 45 incorporates the latter system.

It is important that no wires, plugs, or sockets are left unsupported and free to

Fig. 60   **Fig. 61**

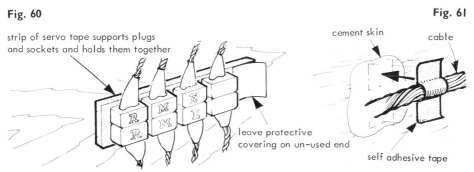

float about. The most common system is to dispose the wiring along the top or bottom of the fuselage, and cover it with foam rubber or plastic wedged, or held in place, by strips of self-adhesive tape. If this easy solution is impossible, the methods shown in Fig. 60 to support plugs and sockets, and strips of tape as in Fig. 61 to secure the harness to the fuselage side, will be found to be both effective and neat.

Electric powered aircraft models

The only problem that these pose, which is not common to normal powered models and gliders, is in the sheer weight of the batteries. At the beginning of this chapter the importance of securing the r/c battery, so that it could not break loose and damage the other components, was emphasised. The power source for an electric motor is, perhaps, ten times as heavy as the r/c receiver battery, so it can readily be seen that the havoc this can cause, should it break loose in a crash, could be devastating.

Obviously the layout of the model and the necessity to achieve the correct balance will be the determining factors but, if it is possible for the r/c equipment (including its batteries) to be positioned aft of the motor battery pack, this will provide the best possible insurance policy for the equipment!

*   *   *

It was very difficult to decide whether this chapter or the succeeding one would appear first, because both are so mutually interdependent. Indeed, in practice it is impossible to separate installation and equipment mounting, from linking the servos to the control surface but, for clarity, this false distinction was made. Therefore, before fixing the servos in place, read on . . .

CHAPTER 9

PUSHRODS

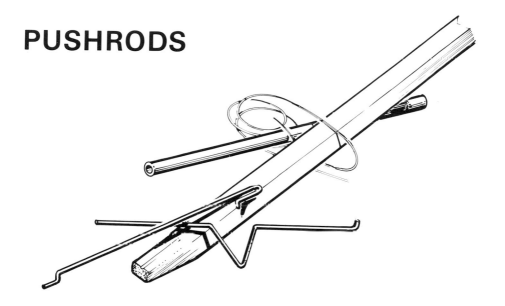

THERE are three methods of linking servos to the surfaces they are to operate — pushrods, tube and cable, and the closed-loop (or "pull-pull") system. The first two are by far the most popular, and are almost certainly the only type likely to be encountered at this stage, because the closed-loop system, although it has many, albeit somewhat specialised, attributes, is seldom found in an "every-day" model.

Undoubtedly, the "best" system, where there is a straight and uncluttered run (i.e. there is no danger of fouling the structure or other control rods) from the servo to the control surface or a bellcrank, is the pushrod, because this gives the lowest mechanical loss. Although, ideally, the rod should run in a completely straight line, this is seldom practical. Therefore, some adjustment of either, or both, wire ends is permissible. Such bends must never be excessive, however, or the pushrod will tend to bow under compression and straighten under tension, with consequent loss of control resolution — Fig. 62.

If it is difficult to achieve a straight run, then it is better to use a tube and cable linkage. Moreover, there are linkages — especially to throttle or steerable nosewheel —

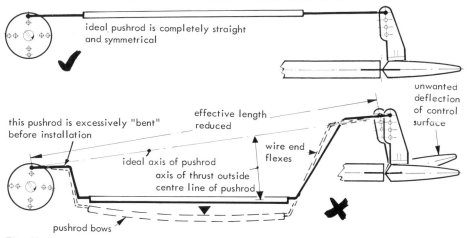

ideal pushrod is completely straight and symmetrical

unwanted deflection of control surface

this pushrod is excessively "bent" before installation

effective length reduced

wire end flexes

ideal axis of pushrod

axis of thrust outside centre line of pushrod

pushrod bows

Fig. 62

where not only is a straight run virtually impossible to obtain but where, anyway, some form of sealing is desirable to prevent the ingress of fuel. This is where the tube and cable linkage will be used almost exclusively. As has been said, the closed-loop system is more specialised, so will be dealt with after the more popular methods have been discussed.

First then, pushrods and, for such a simple item, the design requirements are – surprisingly – quite stringent. The pushrod must be light; too much weight increases the shock load to a servo and other parts of the linkage, when a model makes a rough landing. It also gives the servo extra work to do and, in extreme cases, can affect the servo resolution, because of excessive transmitted vibration from the engine – Fig. 63. The pushrod must be reasonably rigid. If it either twists or bends it will cause the control surface to change position, relative to the servo output arm, as the model executes manoeuvres. The pushrods themselves must be designed so that they cannot foul each other, or bind against the fuselage and jam the controls. They must connect readily to the servo and to the horn on the control surface and, finally, must break in a bad crash, so that the damage to the servos is minimised.

Wire-ended balsa pushrods

The only pushrod that combines all these requirements, yet is simple to make, is a balsa pushrod with wire ends. There are other materials which may be available

Fig. 63

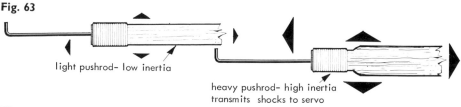

light pushrod– low inertia

heavy pushrod– high inertia transmits shocks to servo

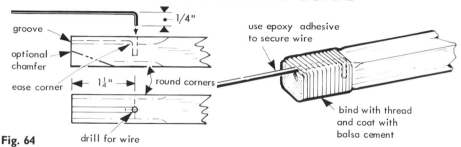

Fig. 64

groove

optional chamfer

ease corner

$1\frac{1}{4}$"

round corners

drill for wire

1/4"

use epoxy adhesive to secure wire

bind with thread and coat with balsa cement

(hardwood dowel is tempting because it looks so neat, but it does not meet the requirements for lack of whip or inertia) but, except for very special applications, it is best to stick to balsa. The choice of the grade of balsa used for pushrods, however, is important; it must be straight grained and soft – but not ultra-soft, or there will be difficulties in attaching the wire end.

The section should be $\frac{1}{4}$in., $\frac{3}{8}$in., or $\frac{1}{2}$in. square (or round, if preferred) depending on the size of model and the length of run. Soft balsa of large cross-section is much better than hard balsa of smaller section, as it has a greater resistance to bending than a smaller section of equal weight. It also has better self damping, which can resist the building-up of resonance which might, otherwise, cause the rod to vibrate and lead to loss of control.

A wire extension is fitted to each end of the rod for the purpose of connecting to the servo and horn. 16g. wire is generally used, because it is the minimum size for safety, and the holes in control horns and discs are normally of this size. It is not necessary to struggle with hard-to-bend piano wire, as there are at least three other materials which are more satisfactory for most applications; silver steel, mild steel – or bicycle spokes! Yes, seriously – some of the latter are available in 16g. and have a threaded end, which will be useful in other applications. All these materials bend more easily than piano wire, thus enabling an accurate shape to be formed. Aluminium, brass or copper wire, must not be used as these are far too soft.

Wire ends are fitted to the balsa by grooving the ends of the balsa rods lengthwise, bending the wire $\frac{1}{4}$in. at 90° and pushing it into the balsa about $1\frac{1}{2}$in. from the end. The joint is coated with balsa cement and bound with thread – Fig. 64. The corners of the rods are rounded off at each end so that the thread does not sink in and loosen with use. If the balsa is very soft, a pre-coating of balsa cement prevents the ends being crushed by the binding. An even more secure method is to double the wire

Fig. 65

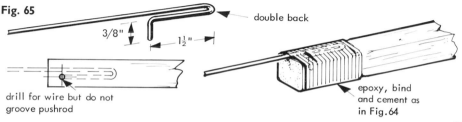

double back

3/8"

$1\frac{1}{2}$"

drill for wire but do not groove pushrod

epoxy, bind and cement as in Fig.64

73

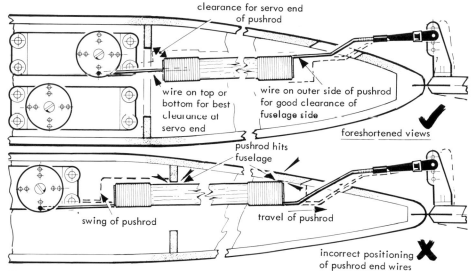

clearance for servo end
of pushrod

wire on top or
bottom for best
clearance at
servo end

wire on outer side of pushrod
for good clearance of
fuselage side

foreshortened views

pushrod hits
fuselage

swing of pushrod

travel of pushrod

incorrect positioning
of pushrod end wires

Fig. 66

back on itself after bending the end. This reduces the chances of its twisting and gives a larger area for cementing and binding – Fig. 65. Balsa cement is recommended for the joints because it shrinks as it dries, so holding the wire even more firmly.

The wires may be bound on to the top, bottom or side of the balsa rod, depending on the clearance available in the fuselage. Fig. 66 shows this, and also how allowance must be made for the "swing" of the pushrod, while in Fig. 67, is shown how similar allowance must be made in the exiting of the pushrod from the fuselage. In addition to rubbing against the fuselage sides, the pushrods can also bind together. Fig. 68 shows what happens if the wire ends are bound on to the rods without thought to this, and Fig. 69 how the pushrods should be arranged, while Fig. 70 shows how additional clearance is often possible by staggering the pushrods vertically as well as laterally.

The clearance between the pushrods themselves and the fuselage sides, top, and

Fig. 67

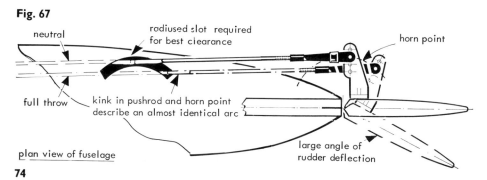

neutral

radiused slot required
for best clearance

horn point

full throw

kink in pushrod and horn point
describe an almost identical arc

plan view of fuselage

large angle of
rudder deflection

RADIO CONTROL GUIDE

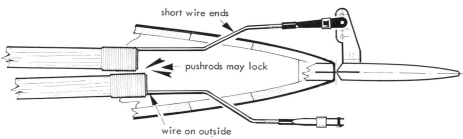

short wire ends

pushrods may lock

wire on outside

Fig. 68

bottom, must be checked with both elevator and rudder at every extreme of movement, not forgetting that, with full trim applied, the total travel is normally increased.

Although the wire at the control surface end has to be long enough to exit from the fuselage, the wire at the servo end is normally much shorter, but not so short as to

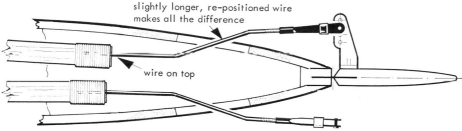

slightly longer, re-positioned wire makes all the difference

wire on top

Fig. 69

allow the balsa part to hit the servo when the pushrod moves fully forward – Fig. 71. This applies to all the servos, irrespective of whether the output is linear or rotary. It is important, also, to ensure that there is enough clearance at this point to allow a

Fig. 70

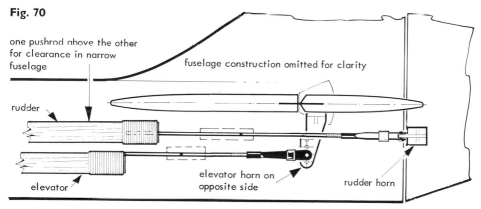

one pushrod above the other for clearance in narrow fuselage

fuselage construction omitted for clarity

rudder

elevator horn on opposite side

rudder horn

elevator

75

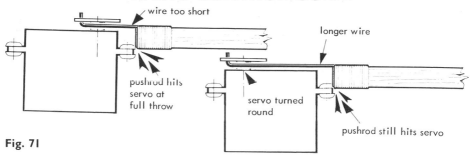

wire too short

longer wire

pushrod hits
servo at
full throw

servo turned
round

pushrod still hits servo

Fig. 71

servo to be turned round the other way, as might be necessary to avoid fouling output
levels of adjacent servos.

"Short" pushrods

In certain cases, relatively short linkages are possible, such as those from servo to strip
ailerons, or between bellcranks and horns. These pushrods may be of plain wire, there
being neither need nor space to interpose a balsa section. Aileron linkages are dealt
with in more detail later but here is a case where, in spite of a relatively long run, a

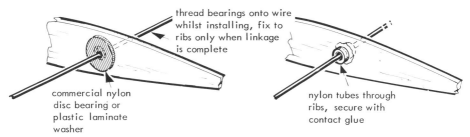

thread bearings onto wire
whilst installing, fix to
ribs only when linkage
is complete

commercial nylon
disc bearing or
plastic laminate
washer

nylon tubes through
ribs, secure with
contact glue

Fig. 72

wire pushrod is permissible. 16g. piano wire is often used, because it offers reasonable
resistance to bending. It is supported throughout its length by the wing ribs through
which it passes, and offers quite low friction. A commercial plastic guide, designed to
be glued to the ribs, is available, but a plastic washer or short length of nylon tube
make suitable alternatives – Fig. 72. If desired, softer wire ends may be added to the

Fig. 73

1/2"min.

tin both ends

place together whilst the
solder is molten, bind with
fuse wire, resolder in model
sliding to correct length

"V" notches to introduce solder

thick wall brass tube

split tube aids solder flow

Fig. 74

piano wire, using either a lapped and bound joint or a piece of brass tube. See Figs. 73 and 74 respectively.

In certain applications – rudder pushrods on boats, or the relatively short push-rods in helicopters for instance – a rod which is more rigid than unsupported wire and yet of smaller cross section than balsa is normally required. Here aluminium tube can provide an excellent solution. A wooden plug, drilled to take a wire kink or quicklink, is epoxied into either end as shown in Fig. 75. Such a rod is not really suitable for

1/2"long 3/16"beech dowel drilled for wire

wire pushrod end

3/16"bore alumimium tube

carefully de-grease tube and wire and epoxy all three together

Fig. 75

longer runs as the weight/whip/size ratio is inferior to balsa but, for up to about 12in., it can be extremely neat as well as practical – see photograph.

Tube and cable

In talking of "tube and cable" controls (sometimes known both commercially and

A typical nylon in nylon tube and cable, shown here with the type of saddle clamp recommended for intermediate support of the outer—see text.

generically as "Snakes") the reference includes any system of the Bowden cable type, whether it be wire cable in a nylon outer tube; wire cable in a PTFE outer; nylon tube in nylon tube; PTFE tube in nylon tube; or nylon in PTFE. Of all these, it has been found that the latter two types give the most friction-free and hence consistent results. The commercial tube-in-tube type of snake can be bought in two types – semi-rigid for straight, or almost straight rudder/elevator linkages, or more flexible for use when there is a marked curve in the system.

Deservedly the tube and cable system has proved extremely popular, because of its versatility in use. Inevitably, even in a dead straight run, the slight friction between the inner and outer tubes presents a drag which is not present with a push rod, and this drag will increase quite noticeably as bends or curves are introduced. And it is not only the friction which will increase, but also the end float. Fig. 76 illustrates how this can vary from zero to $\frac{1}{4}$in. or even $\frac{3}{8}$in. with the same piece of tube and cable!

Further, if this end float is too great, it will prevent centring of the control surfaces, and result in inconsistent flying. Also, the increase in friction in the tube/cable will, again, result in inaccurate centring, and will also cause increased battery drain and servo wear. Therefore, despite, or perhaps because of its versatility, it is apparent that the use of a tube and cable linkage must always be planned with its limitations in mind.

Obviously, there are many applications where, despite having a straight run from the servo to the control horn, a tube and cable is to be preferred to a balsa pushrod. Perhaps the concern is with internal appearance through an open cockpit, or that the disposition of interior detail will mean there is insufficient clearance for a balsa rod. In such cases a tube and cable (or closed loop which will be dealt with shortly) should be used, provided it may be supported. Sag, or whipping caused through vibration, in a long run, can lead to centring variations. Fig. 77 shows this, while Fig. 78 suggests some methods of providing support, and there are also available a selection of commercially made cable clamps as shown in Fig. 83.

The importance of arranging the servos so that a straight control run is possible has already been emphasized. There are installations, however, where a reasonably small deviation from the dead straight run may be accommodated by the use of a tube and cable. The emphasis must be on "reasonably" because, reverting to Fig. 76, it is so easy to introduce end float in a tube and cable system, that it should be pondered

Fig. 76

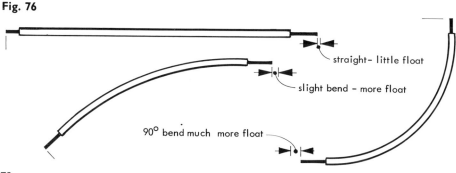

straight– little float

slight bend – more float

90° bend much more float

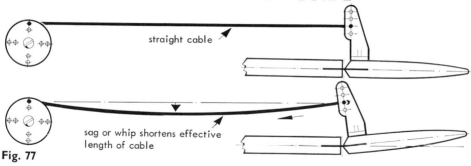

straight cable

sag or whip shortens effective
length of cable

Fig. 77

why a lot of money is spent on a radio outfit with 99% servo resolution, only to negate it with an inadequate linkage!

Unfortunately, the tube and cable system is so simple to install and hook up, that this rather basic point is sometimes overlooked, or conveniently forgotten. There are some installations, however, where it is the only practical system and, for throttle and nosewheel links, tube and cable should always be used because any slight drag or

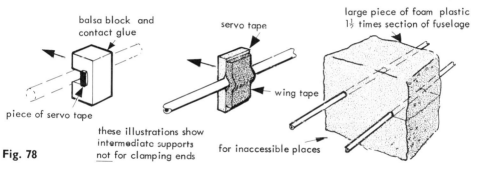

balsa block and
contact glue

servo tape

large piece of foam plastic
1½ times section of fuselage

wing tape

piece of servo tape

these illustrations show
intermediate supports
not for clamping ends

for inaccessible places

Fig. 78

end-play is relatively unimportant on these controls – and more than compensated by the ease of installation. Also, a slight bend in a linkage, especially the nosewheel, is beneficial in that it provides some degree of shock-damping friction – Fig. 79.

With tube and cable control linkages, particular attention should be paid to the clearances at each end. All the drawings showing linkages in this book have, for the sake of clarity, followed a standard diagrammatic pattern – they are not to scale. A

Fig. 79

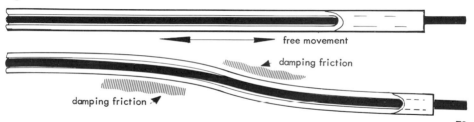

free movement

damping friction

damping friction

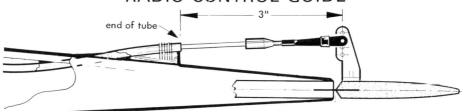

Fig. 80

particular model might require extra clearance, or slight variation from the standard theme, so, in every case, the following precautions must be observed:

1. Freedom of the inner cable to bend as it follows the arc of a lever, horn or bellcrank.

Fig. 81

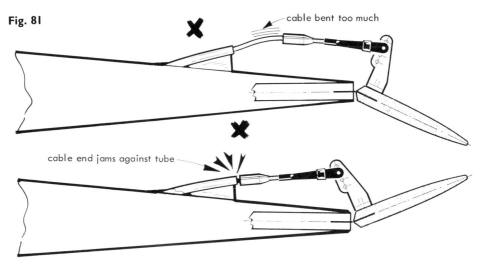

About 3in. minimum must be allowed for this — despite what may be seen on some models! Fig. 80 shows the correct control disposition and Fig. 81 how not to do it!

2. Later the junction of a wire end to a cable inner will be described. This inevitably expands the inner part, so the 3in. clearance at the cable end must be from the unexpanded point — Fig. 82.

Fig. 82

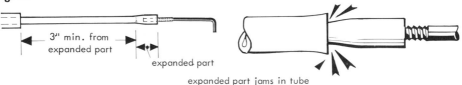

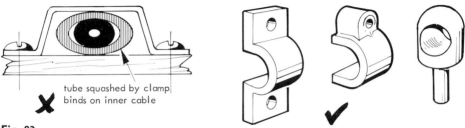

tube squashed by clamp
binds on inner cable

X

✓

Fig. 83

3. Correct matching of inner and outer components of the cable to provide float-free action, without lost movement or noticeable friction.

4. An outer tube must never be clamped with anything that can distort the tube and introduce friction – Fig. 83. The methods shown in Fig. 78, or the special clamps manufactured for the purpose and sold at model shops must be used, as these will hold the tube firmly without distorting it. A selection of clamps is shown in Fig. 83.

5. The outer cable must be bonded securely to the airframe at both ends; if it is free to move at all there will be lost movement between the servo and the control surface. Nylon or PTFE tube does not bond easily, so the outside should be carefully roughened to form a key. It can then be coated with glue, bound to a suitable piece of balsa, care being taken not to deform the tube, and then glued to the appropriate part of the airframe – Fig. 84. Contact glue works well inside the model, but it softens if exposed to fuel, so if this is likely an epoxy glue must be used.

Closed loop systems
The final method of connecting a servo to a control surface is not, in the strictest sense of the word, a *pushrod* at all, but a "pull-pull", or closed loop, system. Originally it was introduced by scale modellers, anxious to give added authenticity to their models by simulating the system in the original aircraft. The system has now found wider acceptance, however, where lightweight and absolutely precise operation are given

Fig. 84

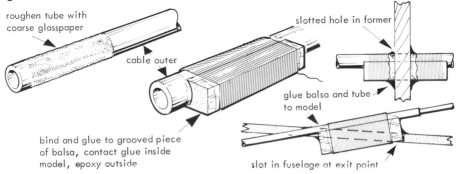

roughen tube with
coarse glasspaper

cable outer

slotted hole in former

glue balsa and tube
to model

bind and glue to grooved piece
of balsa, contact glue inside
model, epoxy outside

slot in fuselage at exit point

RADIO CONTROL GUIDE

right   rigid pushrod (push-pull)   pull for "right"

two horns

left

rotary or linear servos both suitable

pivot

bellcrank with same throw as horns

control line wire or fishing trace wire

pull for "left"

holes in horns in line with hinge

cables too tight when full control is applied

✗

horns too far ahead of hinge

sideways movement introduced

loss of resolution

✗

horns too far aft of hinge

Fig. 85

priority over a rather more demanding installation procedure and a more precise setting up requirement.

The principle of the system is shown in Fig. 85. From this, it is apparent that, for it to work at all, there must be a precise coincidence between the hinge line of the control surface and the attachment point to the horn, irrespective of whether a linear or rotary output servo is used. It is not essential, however, that the control wires should run in a completely straight line between the servo and the control horn, as is shown in Fig. 85. Fig. 86 shows how tubing may be used to direct the control run and so by-pass

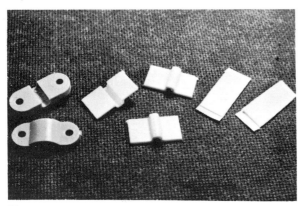

Commercial mounting saddles of various sizes are readily available. They may be screwed in place, or alternatively fixed with contact glue or double-sided tape.

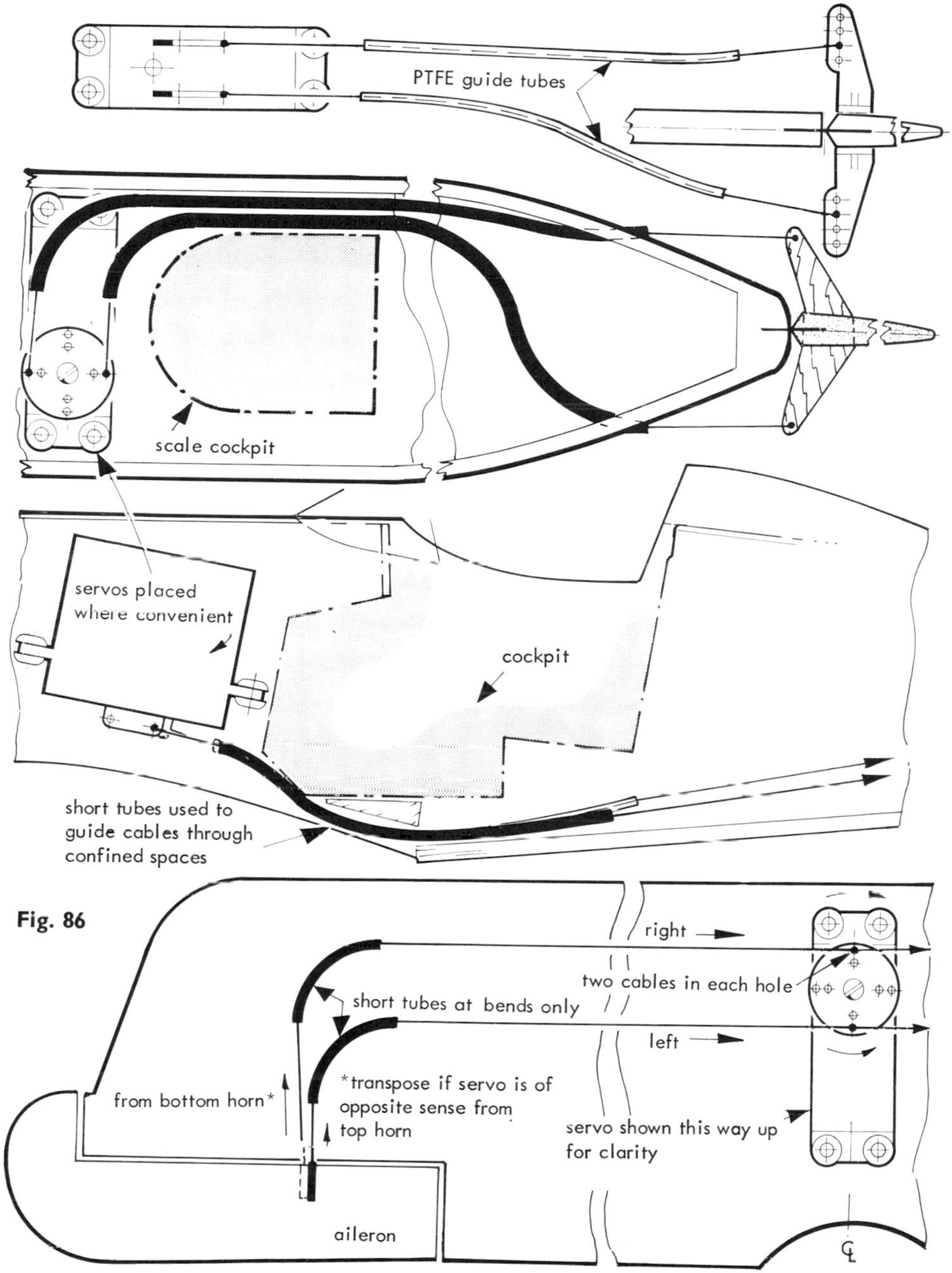

RADIO CONTROL GUIDE

PTFE guide tubes

scale cockpit

servos placed
where convenient

cockpit

short tubes used to
guide cables through
confined spaces

Fig. 86

right ——▶

two cables in each hole

short tubes at bends only

left ——▶

from bottom horn*

*transpose if servo is of
opposite sense from
top horn

servo shown this way up
for clarity

aileron

certain areas – a scale cockpit for example. Although, obviously, this will introduce some drag (as opposed to the zero drag of a straight-through coupling) this is negligible, even with bends as tight as 1in. radius, and can be discounted for all practical purposes. It is important, however, that the tube be securely fixed along its length by clamping, binding, gluing and so on to the structure, otherwise the tube itself will "move" with the cable and introduce back-lash and lost movement.

The choice of cable depends on the model. For all general purposes stranded control-line wire is ideal, but this is usually too thin for accurate scale models. Thicker wire may be obtained from fishing tackle shops, where it is sold as wire trace, and is available in a range of thicknesses. The wire is normally nylon covered and this covering need only be removed at the ends, where it is attached to the horn. PTFE is the ideal material for the tubing and, as there is no necessity for a snug fit, it is often convenient to use tube from a standard tube/cable set up, as this may be bought at model shops.

CHAPTER 10

PUSHROD END CONNECTIONS

NOW to consider the various types of pushrod ends – the means of attaching the pushrods to the servos, control horns or bellcranks – and the obvious progression is to start with the simplest and most "basic" methods, and progress to the more sophisticated ones, which include commercially available, or shop-bought, accessories.

Joggles

The simplest way to connect a pushrod to a servo or bellcrank is the "joggle" or "kink". This is made by bending the end of a piece of wire, which should be a working fit in the output hole of the servo disc, into a joggle shape as shown in Fig. 87. The bend radii must be as sharp as possible and are best formed by hammering the wire, whilst it is clamped in a small vice or, better still, in a hole in a piece of hardened steel. Bend "A" is made first, the wire removed and re-inserted to make bend "B" – both bends being 90°. (It is easier to have the wire longer after bend "B", so that it can be clamped securely, it being cut back to the required length after bending.)

Joggles are more easily formed from mild steel, but if piano wire is used it is annealed by heating to red heat and allowing to cool slowly. It must not be inserted into the nylon bellcrank or servo output until it is quite cool, or it will enlarge and

Fig. 87

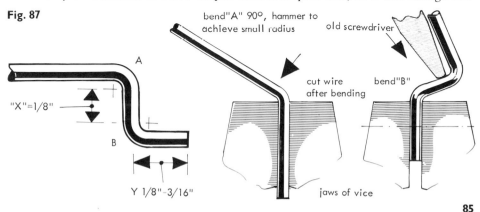

bend"A" 90°, hammer to achieve small radius

old screwdriver

cut wire after bending

bend"B"

"X"=1/8"

A

B

Y 1/8"-3/16"

jaws of vice

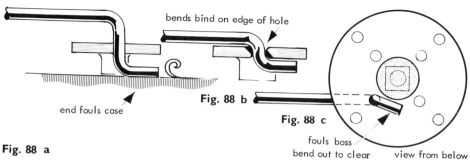

bends bind on edge of hole

end fouls case

Fig. 88 b

Fig. 88 c

fouls boss
bend out to clear

view from below

Fig. 88 a

distort the hole. It is much easier to use mild steel rod, however, as this has adequate strength in short lengths.

A common mistake, in forming joggles, is to make the distance "X" – Fig. 87 – too long, so that the wire end binds on the servo case, or may even drop into one of the slots present in some cases – Fig. 88a. If too tight, due to being too short or badly shaped, it will bind in the disc or lever – Fig. 88b. If dimension "Y" – Fig. 87 – is too great, the end will bind on the boss of the servo disc or lever, when the latter turns, particularly if one of the inner holes is used, as in Fig. 88c. It will then be necessary to bend the end outwards slightly. Some servos have quite a large boss, and it will almost certainly be necessary to make such a bend with this type. Commercially available joggles, known as "Kinks", are available. These have been designed to fit the optimum number of applications and are recommended to those who do not like making fiddly bends in pieces of wire. They may be joined to wire ends by means of a brass tube collar, as shown in Fig. 74.

Plain pin

The end of the wire of the pushrod is bent at 90° for about $\frac{1}{4}$ in. With a rotary output servo similar to that illustrated, the output arm is unscrewed and dropped over an

Fig. 89

Fig. 90

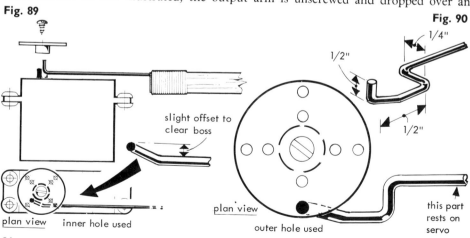

slight offset to clear boss

plan view   inner hole used

plan view

outer hole used

1/4"

1/2"

1/2"

this part rests on servo

RADIO CONTROL GUIDE

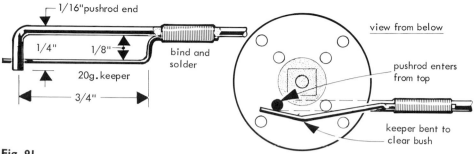

Fig. 91

Fig. 92

upwards-facing pin, before being screwed back onto the servo – Fig. 89. When in place, the pushrod cannot drop out. This method may be used with disc or lever outputs, but it is important that the pushrod cannot jam against the disc centre and, to ensure this, it may be necessary to bend it slightly.

If the disc or lever is wide enough to clear the case, the pushrod is prevented from dropping out by bending the wire, as shown in Fig. 90. This additional kinking prevents the wire dropping out, because it rests on the servo case under all conditions. It also has the advantage of ensuring that the rod cannot foul on the shaft, as mentioned earlier. The disc or lever is removed to enable the wire to be fitted, as before.

Pin and keeper

The disadvantage of both joggle type and plain pin attachments is that it is necessary either to unscrew the servo arm/disc, or remove the bellcrank or horn, when disconnecting the pushrod. A more satisfactory method is for a 20g. piano wire "keeper" to be fitted to the wire end, as shown in Fig. 91. The dimensions are typical for most applications, and the keeper is sprung tightly against the pin part. In use, the keeper is prised aside while the pin is inserted, then it is passed under the disc or linear output lever, or on the opposite side of the bellcrank or control horn, where it retains the pin on the device.

The same precautions apply to ensure that the wire or, in this case, the keeper, does not foul the boss of the servo lever or disc. The solution is the same; it is bent out a little to clear, as in Fig. 92. In both cases, if the pushrod is positioned on the top of the disc, lever or arm, with the pin pointing downwards, towards the servo case, the wire must be cut short enough to clear the case in all positions.

Clevises

A commercially available device, known as a clevis, provides an almost "instant" pushrod end connection. These are marketed under various brand names, such as Kwik-link, Q-Link, Adjusta-Rod, etc., and are now used by the vast majority of r/c modellers in preference to any home-made devices, generally providing neater and more satisfactory – not to mention quicker – connections. They comprise a metal or nylon fork, with a pin attached to one arm. The other arm is prised aside to allow the pin to be fitted into the horn, whereupon it springs back into place and retains it. A

87

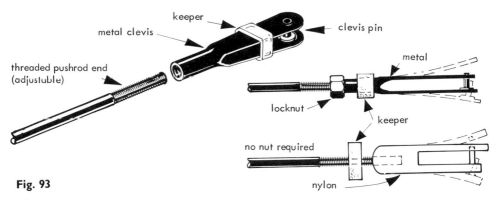

keeper

metal clevis

clevis pin

threaded pushrod end
(adjustable)

metal

locknut

keeper

no nut required

Fig. 93

nylon

safety sleeve (a $\frac{1}{4}$in. length of $\frac{1}{8}$in. bore fuel tubing is ideal) is then slid up over the fork as an extra precaution against its opening under flight loads or vibration. The fork terminates in a length of mild steel rod, which is fixed to the pushrod direct (if it is long enough), or soldered to the home-made pushrod end wire. Typical clevises are shown in Fig. 93.

An important point is that these clevises are threaded, and screw onto a threaded end of the rod, thus providing for fine adjustment of the control surface neutral, in relation to servo neutral. A locking nut is usually provided with the metal type, to set it in position once adjustment is finalised. This is useful in that it maintains the settings of the linkages, even should the surfaces be disconnected for any reason. For instance, it is usual to disconnect the clevises from the aileron horns when transporting a model in a car, so as to avoid possible distortion of the linkage, should the wing happen to be inadvertently rested on the corner of the aileron. The lock nuts will prevent the otherwise relatively loose-fitting metal clevis from vibrating around on its thread and taking up a "false" position.

Nylon clevises, on the other hand, are an inherently tight fit on their rods and will not move unless deliberately twisted round. Nylon clevises being more pliable, offer better protection to the servo in the event of a bad crash, as they will often wrench clear without damage. If a nylon clevis is used on a stamped metal horn (such as the central elevator joiner type – see Chapter 13) it is important that any rough burrs

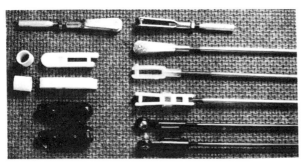

A selection of clevises in metal and nylon. Note that there are plastic keepers on some, but others have a special moulded pin which clips securely in place. The wise modeller will, however, still make a 'belt and braces' job with a home-made keeper— see text.

around the hole are smoothed off, as these could cut through the nylon pin and cause loss of control.

If possible a nylon clevis should be used on the engine end of the throttle linkage, as there is a great deal of vibration here and a throttle lever attached to a metal clevis induces electrical noise, which could interfere with sensitive receivers. For the same reason, a metal-to-metal joint, such as might be found when a metal horn or bellcrank is attached to a metal clevis, should not be used, neither should wire parts be allowed to rub against screws or other metal objects.

Some earlier proportional outfits were so sensitive to this metal-to-metal noise that even a nylon clevis which had a metal pin had been known to give interference when connected to a metal horn or throttle arm! The answer, in such cases, was to remove the pin and solder it into the horn, then hook the clevis back over it. Nylon bushes are commercially available for inserting into metal control horns when using a metal clevis or pin-and-keeper. (There are more details about this bushing system, and other means of suppressing metal-to-metal noise in Chapter 12.)

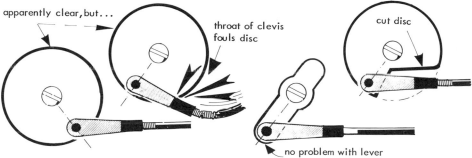

Fig. 94   **Fig. 95**

If a commercial clevis is used on a disc output of a servo, it will be found that it generally jams solid when the disc rotates away from the direction of the pushrod – Fig. 94. This stalls the servo, because it prevents full movement in one direction. The answer is for the disc to be cut to give clearance – or for a lever output to be used instead – Fig. 95. Nylon may be cut easily with a hot knife, but at least $\frac{1}{16}$in. of material must be left round holes or the clevis will tear out under load. Special clevises with an extra long yoke are sometimes available from specialist shops and, naturally, these are to be preferred for connections to discs.

It is essential that at least one adjustable clevis be used in each linkage – it doesn't matter at which end – because, if the neutral positions of the control surfaces (both, in the case of ailerons) are not readily adjustable, it will be impossible easily to trim the model to fly "hands off".

It is not usual to have an adjustable clevis at each end of the pushrod. In fact, it is only rarely that this is desirable, and it is more usual to have the adjustable end positioned where it is most easily accessible. For instance, if the elevator has the horn on one side, it will be external and this is where the adjustable clevis would best be fitted. If, however, a central elevator horn, with the connection inside the fuselage is

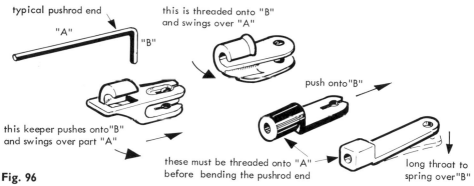

typical pushrod end

"A"

"B"

this is threaded onto "B"
and swings over "A"

push onto"B"

this keeper pushes onto"B"
and swings over part "A"

these must be threaded onto "A"
before bending the pushrod end

long throat to
spring over"B"

Fig. 96

being used, then the adjustment will best be made at the servo end (albeit usually requiring the wing to be removed for access), so that is the logical place for the adjustable clevis to be fitted.

For connections not requiring adjustment, there are various types of plastic "keeper" available in the shops – some of very ingenious design – for easy clip-on or swing-in fixing, removal of servos, for interchanging between models and so forth. Fig. 96 shows some examples of these.

Other systems

Many ingenious alternative methods of linking a push-rod to a servo disc have been thought up and some aileron attachments (which can, of course, be adapted to other uses) are shown in the next chapter. Most of these devices are "one-offs", but a commercial unit for attaching a plastic cable end to a servo is shown in Fig. 97.

Various junctions

There are obviously a large number of combinations in which the various types of clevises may be used, but the following cases are the most common, and show how the various types of linkages may be joined to either wire pushrod ends, or to the clevis itself.

Stranded wire cable to wire

The notched tube method may be used here – Fig. 98 – but it is important that the

A selection of clip-on and swing-in keepers— note the varying length of 'throat' on some to accommodate the swing of a servo disc.

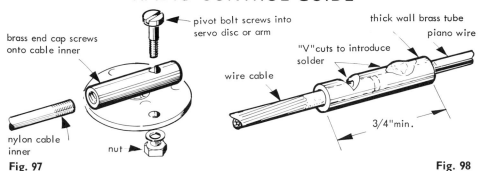

brass end cap screws
onto cable inner

pivot bolt screws into
servo disc or arm

thick wall brass tube

piano wire

"V"cuts to introduce
solder

wire cable

nylon cable
inner

nut

3/4"min.

Fig. 97

Fig. 98

solder does not make the stranded part rigid for too great a distance, as this would prevent it flexing, and possibly also increase its diameter enough to cause it to jam in the tube.

Stranded cable to clevis

Some clevises are made of nylon and it is possible for a stranded wire cable to be fixed direct to these. The method is to push the end of the cable into the hole occupied normally by the pushrod, then a steel modelling pin is inserted through the nylon at right-angles to the cable, so that it passes between the strands. This spreads the strands apart and locks them in the clevis – Fig. 99. This is a modification of a nylon clevis which has been supplied with a metal pushrod, but there are now on the market several types of nylon clevis specifically designed to be fitted to cable. One has a circular hole in its side, through which a blob of solder may be secured to the end of the cable – Fig. 100. Another has a hollow piece of brass studding, which serves as adjuster, into which the cable is sweated, but not while the clevis is attached! – Fig. 101.

In the same way, metal clevises are obtainable with turned metal threaded ends which are hollow, to receive a cable – Fig. 102. Some cables are sold with these clevises already soldered in place. It will be found neater and more satisfactory to use these specially made clevises, than to fit wire-ended ones to the cable, by binding and soldering the latter, though this may, of course, be done if nothing else is to hand.

Nylon or PTFE tube to wire

Nylon clevises intended for use with double tube ("Snakes") linkages have a short length of studding (threaded rod) of about $\frac{1}{16}$in. diameter, which serves both for

Fig. 99

do not tin

nylon clevis

Fig. 100

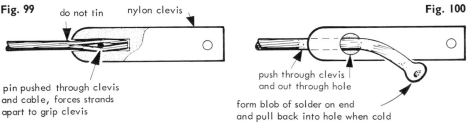

pin pushed through clevis
and cable, forces strands
apart to grip clevis

push through clevis
and out through hole

form blob of solder on end
and pull back into hole when cold

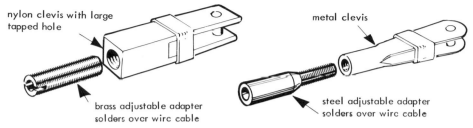

nylon clevis with large
tapped hole

metal clevis

brass adjustable adapter
solders over wire cable

steel adjustable adapter
solders over wire cable

Fig. 101   **Fig. 102**

adjustment (by twisting the clevis on it) and attachment, by screwing it into the inner tube where it cuts its own thread – Fig. 103. This makes a firm connection which can be tested by suspending a weight from it. An alternative type for use with tubing of too small a bore to accept a threaded rod, has a hollow-headed adaptor to screw onto the outside of the tube – Fig. 104.

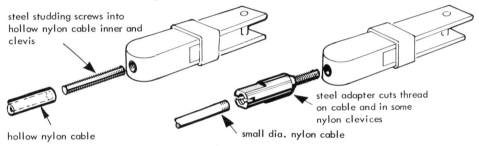

steel studding screws into
hollow nylon cable inner and
clevis

steel adapter cuts thread
on cable and in some
nylon clevices

hollow nylon cable

small dia. nylon cable

Fig. 103   **Fig. 104**

It may be, however, that it is required to fit, say, a wire-ended clevis – either metal or nylon – to the inner tube. In such cases, wires which are not already threaded (this is where the bicycle spokes come in!) could have a thread cut on them – for example, a 10BA thread for 16g. wire. Screw-cutting dies are quite cheap and are a worthwhile addition to the modeller's toolbox, but must not be used on piano wire or they will not last long!

If the wire is of so small a diameter that it slides straight into the tube, it must be built up in thickness by adding a piece of brass tube, or a coating of solder – Fig. 105. A neater way is for some thin copper wire to be wound over the end of the rod, soldered and wiped clean while the solder is still molten. This forms a primitive thread, but one which is adequate for locking into the cable – Fig. 106 – although it

Fig. 105   **Fig. 106**

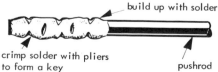

build up with solder

crimp solder with pliers
to form a key

pushrod

pushrod

thin copper wire soldered

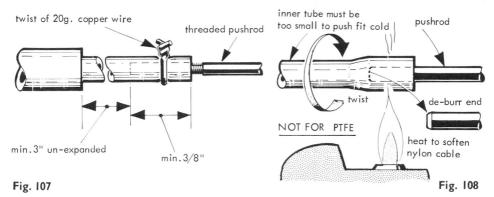

twist of 20g. copper wire

threaded pushrod

inner tube must be too small to push fit cold

pushrod

min.3" un-expanded

min.3/8"

twist

NOT FOR PTFE

de-burr end

heat to soften nylon cable

Fig. 107

Fig. 108

may be necessary to experiment with different thicknesses of wire binding to achieve a good tight fit. In all these cases, the joint is made doubly secure if the inner tube is crimped onto the wire with a single turn of copper wire, as shown in Fig. 107.

Nylon tubes may be expanded to allow a wire which is of too large a diameter to be inserted. They will soften if held for a few seconds over a flame, when the wire should be inserted, and will shrink back as they cool and grip the wire tightly – Fig. 108. Additional security may be ensured by first notching the wire to key it into the softened tubing and crimping it with a turn of wire as just described.

If a threaded rod, as mentioned earlier, is used, a locking nut, even though it may look workmanlike, is not required as tightening it will withdraw the rod from the tube!

Closed loop systems

Without doubt the easiest end of all is a loop bound with soft copper wire and soldered. Some form of adjustment and spring loading, to take up any slack which may develop is, however, obviously desirable, and Fig. 109 shows a very simple system which does both. The angle of the bend "X" can be increased or decreased with a pair of pliers, until the control surface centres with the servo at neutral, or the tension adjustment is correct. Normally, there is always a very slight "slack" in the cables as, if they are too tight, accurate centring is impossible, while, if there is too much slack, the same occurs but for the opposite reason! Therefore, a little trial and error adjustment is always

Fig. 109

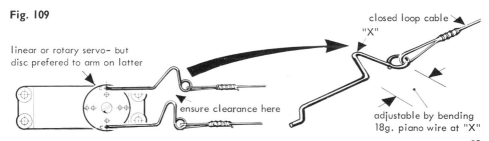

closed loop cable

"X"

linear or rotary servo– but disc prefered to arm on latter

ensure clearance here

adjustable by bending 18g. piano wire at "X"

necessary with each new installation. Of course, a kink or quick link may be soldered to the cable, using any of the methods described, and this will provide easy attachment and adjustment, just as with other "pushrods".

Soldering stainless steel

Earlier, wire fishing trace was mentioned as a suitable cable, but this is normally of stainless steel and hence rejects ordinary solder. However, a stainless steel flux can be purchased from specialist tool shops and this enables a satisfactory joint to be made in the usual way. This flux is also extremely handy for "difficult" soldered joints where the solder doesn't want to "take" but it is extremely corrosive and the joints must be thoroughly cleaned after soldering. Also, it tends to "splutter" as the iron is applied, so skin, and especially eyes, must be kept well clear or protected.

PTFE – a warning

When there is a need to do any soldering on metal which is in close proximity to PTFE material, it should first be disconnected. PTFE gives off a highly poisonous vapour when heated to a temperature high enough for soldering metal, so the soldering iron must be kept well away! For the same reason, it is not possible to expand PTFE tube by heating, as previously described for other types.

CHAPTER 11
AILERON LINKAGES

C HAPTER 8 described how to mount the servo in the wing and Chapter 9 the various types of pushrod, so now, as a separate consideration, the various forms of aileron linkage will be explained before going on to describe the geometry of the control horns and hinging of the control surfaces. As was said earlier, there is some jumping about and breaking off, seemingly in the middle of a subject, but this is to ensure that various aspects are explained in digestible detail! To get the full picture, it is necessary to read Chapters 8-17 in conjunction with each other.

Basically there are two types of aileron — strip and inset — and the linkages to the latter will be described first, because strip ailerons introduce a new form of "pushrod" not previously mentioned.

Pushrod/bellcranks

Having stated a preference for pushrod operation of controls, this is a good starting point and, for the first time, a bellcrank is introduced directly into a linkage to a control surface. It is important that this is correctly mounted to ensure trouble-free operation. Not so tight as to impose unnecessary strain on the servo, yet not so loose as to introduce unwanted backlash into the system. Fig. 110 shows the correct way of

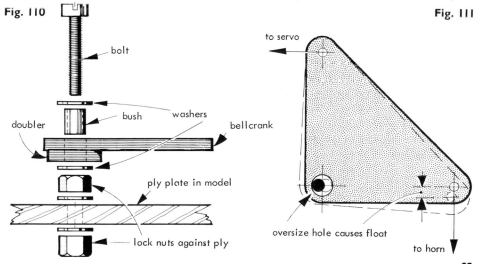

Fig. 110

bolt

bush

washers

doubler

bellcrank

ply plate in model

lock nuts against ply

Fig. 111

to servo

oversize hole causes float

to horn

95

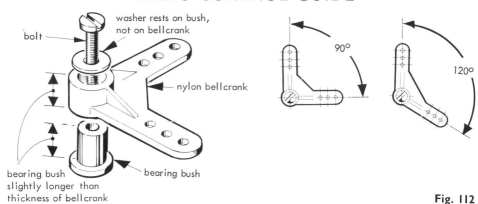

bolt

washer rests on bush,
not on bellcrank

nylon bellcrank

90°

120°

bearing bush
slightly longer than
thickness of bellcrank

bearing bush

Fig. 112

mounting a home-made bellcrank, with the thickness of the bush determining the degree to which the bolt is tightened, while Fig. 111 shows the importance of ensuring that the bearing holes are a good fit! Most commercial bellcranks, which are normally moulded from plastic, incorporate a bearing bush of this type – Fig. 112 shows two typical examples – and, in practice, these will be used for convenience sake, unless the correct size or angular disposition for a special job is not available.

Fig. 113 shows a typical installation – and Fig. 114 shows how, at the construction stage, it is a simple matter to reverse the sense of control by moving the bellcrank through 180°, which adds weight to earlier comments on planning the installation. Provided the main pushrod passes through wing ribs or supports such as in Fig. 72, 16swg. piano wire is quite adequate up to a distance of about 15in., from servo to bellcrank (which covers most applications), but beyond this, a built-up pushrod, as

Fig. 113

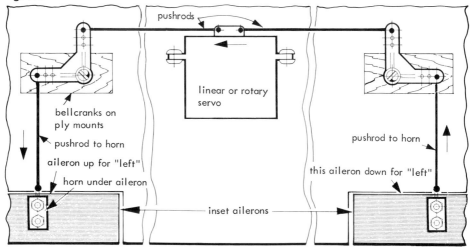

pushrods

linear or rotary
servo

bellcranks on
ply mounts

pushrod to horn

aileron up for "left"

horn under aileron

pushrod to horn

this aileron down for "left"

inset ailerons

RADIO CONTROL GUIDE

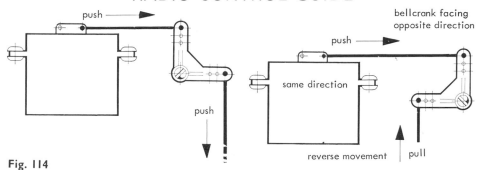

Fig. 114

described in Chapter 9 should be used. The rod from the bellcrank to the control horn is, of course, short enough to need no additional support. It is often helpful to incline the bellcrank to allow the correct geometry to the control horns – Fig. 115 –

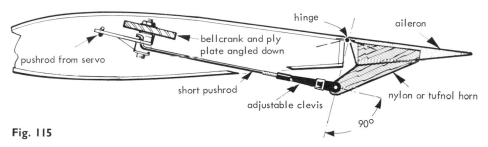

Fig. 115

also, it is sometimes constructionally convenient not to have joggles or clevises at the pushrod/bellcrank junction, and Fig. 116 shows how to do this safely. The pushrod must not press down on the rubbing piece so hard as to cause binding or friction, while if a servo with rotary output is being used, allowance must be made for any "rise" as it moves in determining such clearance, and also when cutting the slots through the wing ribs – Fig. 117.

With this type of linkage it is possible to make the main pushrod in one piece,

Fig. 116

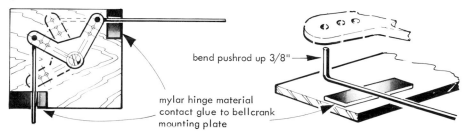

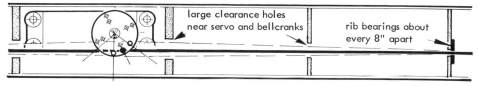

large clearance holes
near servo and bellcranks

rib bearings about
every 8" apart

Fig. 117

with the connection to the servo as in Fig. 118, which allows basic adjustment for centring of the system, final fine adjustments being made via the clevises to the control horns. With a linear output, the set-screw assembly (it is simple for owners of a lathe to turn one up, but ideal substitutes are to be found inside many domestic electrical fittings) may be locked tight to the servo output but, with a disc, it must be free to rotate, to allow for the rotary movement. The wheel collet connection is, of course, only suited to linear outputs.

Fig. 118

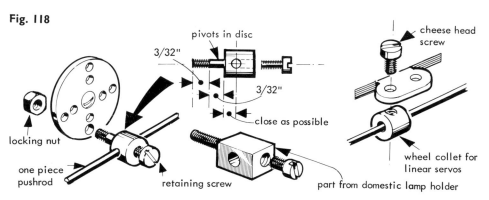

pivots in disc

3/32"

3/32"

close as possible

cheese head
screw

locking nut

one piece
pushrod

retaining screw

part from domestic lamp holder

wheel collet for
linear servos

An alternative is for a simple wire link to be made up – Fig. 119 – bound to the wire and soldered when in the correct position. The servo disc must be removed before soldering or the heat will soften it. Fig. 120 shows another method, where a piece of nylon or PTFE, fixed to the wing, prevents the connector falling out. This system is often the only one that allows easy removal of a servo. Yet another method

Fig. 119

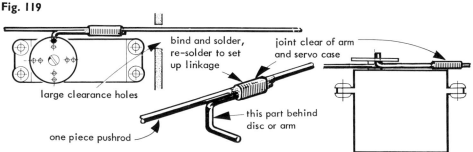

bind and solder,
re-solder to set
up linkage

joint clear of arm
and servo case

large clearance holes

this part behind
disc or arm

one piece pushrod

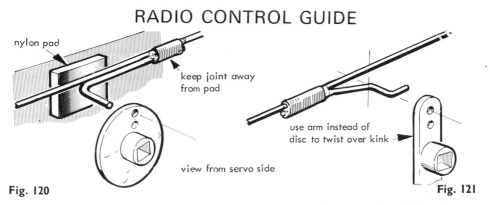

nylon pad

keep joint away
from pad

use arm instead of
disc to twist over kink

view from servo side

Fig. 120

Fig. 121

is to use a joggle end, twisting it on to the servo output, then screwing this back on to
the servo – Fig. 121. Linear servos may be connected via a pair of clevises as shown in
Fig. 122.

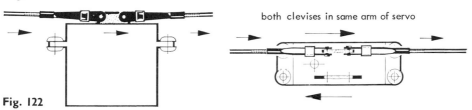

both clevises in same arm of servo

Fig. 122

Pushrod or tube and cable or . . .

A study of Fig. 123 will show that, for any aileron control system where the control
horn is a reasonable distance outboard of the fuselage, it is only a matter of choice, or

Fig. 123

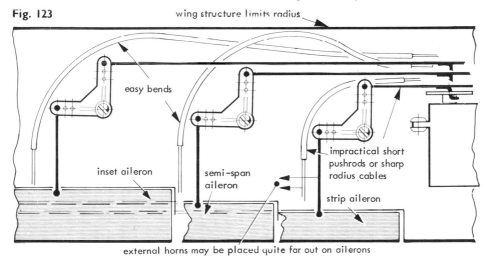

wing structure limits radius

easy bends

inset aileron

semi-span
aileron

impractical short
pushrods or sharp
radius cables

strip aileron

external horns may be placed quite far out on ailerons

preference, whether push-rod or tube/cable is used. However, in any system where the horn is adjacent to, or inside, the fuselage, neither is really suitable, as there is either an impractically short pushrod to allow for the "rise" of a disc output servo, or an undesirably tight radius for tube and cable. In these circumstances, therefore, a different system altogether will be used and this will be described shortly.

Tube and cable?

In Chapter 9 the necessity for having as straight a run as possible for the tube and cable was emphasised but, with a wing, a 90° bend is unavoidable unless the model design permits the use of the system shown in Fig. 124. In any case a tube/cable which gives the minimum backlash compatible with free movement, must be selected – refer back to Fig. 76 in Chapter 9.

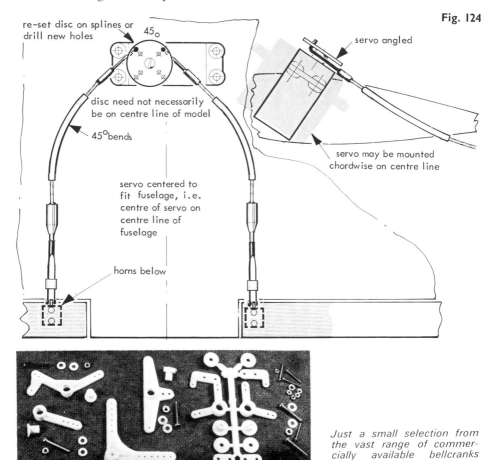

Fig. 124

re-set disc on splines or drill new holes

45o

servo angled

disc need not necessarily be on centre line of model

45° bends

servo may be mounted chordwise on centre line

servo centered to fit fuselage, i.e. centre of servo on centre line of fuselage

horns below

Just a small selection from the vast range of commercially available bellcranks and similar accessories.

RADIO CONTROL GUIDE

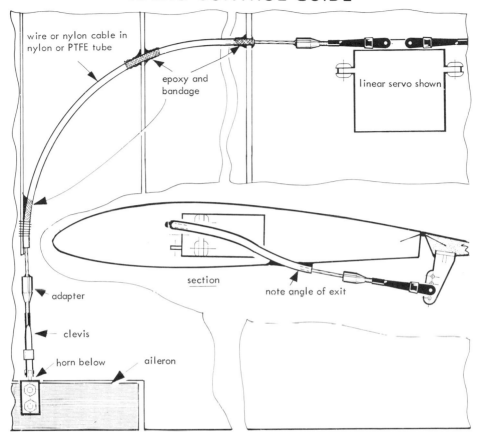

wire or nylon cable in
nylon or PTFE tube

epoxy and
bandage

linear servo shown

section

note angle of exit

adapter

clevis

horn below   aileron

Fig. 125

It is equally important that the outer cable is secured – care being taken that it is not squashed in any way – at close intervals, so that it does not "move" and increase the backlash. A good practice is to glue it as it passes through ribs, or at about 4in. intervals, with a contact or an epoxy adhesive and a strip of bandage. Roughening the cable outer with sand-paper gives an adequate key, even with PTFE.

At this stage also, attention must be paid to the angle and position at the exit of the outer, in relation to the aileron control horn. Fig. 125 illustrates all these points, and Chapter 13 will explain why the correct geometry at the cable exit point is so important.

Fig. 125 also shows the layout of a typical tube/cable installation, and Fig. 126 shows how the control sense may be reversed by turning the servo through 180° in cases where it is not practical to connect to the opposite side of the output lever or disc.

If, as is usual, there is a separate tube and cable to each aileron, the two ends

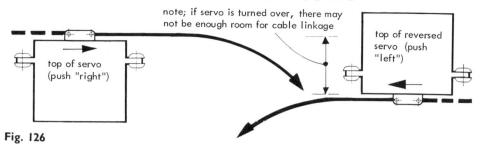

note; if servo is turned over, there may not be enough room for cable linkage

top of servo (push "right")

top of reversed servo (push "left")

Fig. 126

must be connected to the servo by any of the means already described. Both must be attached to the same side of the servo output of course and Fig. 122 showed a typical hook-up to a linear servo.

A rotary output can pose problems, in that two clevises or joggles cannot be forced into the same hole! In such case the inner cable halves should be joined with a length of wire and the coupling made as in Figs. 118, 119, 120, 121 and 127. In order to avoid the introduction of differential movement (Chapter 16) at all times the take-off hole of the disc and the "run" of the pushrod must be at 90° to the servo drive when the latter is at centre. Therefore, the method of re-arranging the position of the output holes as shown in Fig. 124 is only applicable to the linkage illustrated, and will not work if the run is parallel to the servo case.

If it is possible to install the inner cable in one length, then the link-up problem is simplified and connectors as illustrated in Fig. 127 make a simple and easily adjusted attachment to the servo. This system is obviously also applicable for use with wire pushrods, while the connectors shown in Fig. 118 are equally suited to tube and cable.

Strip ailerons

From Fig. 123 it will have been noted that a strip aileron is one which extends virtually the full length of the wing trailing edge. At one time almost every model had ailerons of this type, but fashion then decreed a reversion to the inset type. Now, however, the growing realisation that, whatever the theoreticians say, in practice

Fig. 127

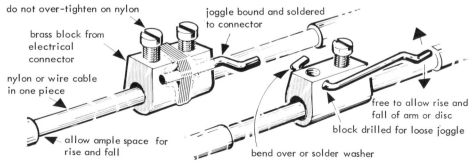

do not over-tighten on nylon

joggle bound and soldered to connector

brass block from electrical connector

nylon or wire cable in one piece

free to allow rise and fall of arm or disc

block drilled for loose joggle

allow ample space for rise and fall

bend over or solder washer

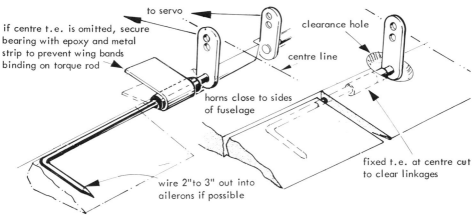

if centre t.e. is omitted, secure bearing with epoxy and metal strip to prevent wing bands binding on torque rod

to servo

clearance hole

centre line

horns close to sides of fuselage

wire 2"to 3" out into ailerons if possible

fixed t.e. at centre cut to clear linkages

Fig. 128

there is no discernible difference in the performance between the two types, has enabled modellers to again use them with a clear conscience!

There are many structural and practical reasons why the strip aileron is popular, not the least being that the entire wing can be built, covered and painted before they are attached, and this represents a great saving in building time and effort. Their only practical disadvantage, compared with the inset type, is that often it is not easily possible to make an immediate visual check to determine whether they are properly aligned, or have not been knocked out of alignment in a bad landing.

As it is usual for the control horns to extend into the fuselage, precautions must be taken to ensure that the wing is aligned accurately, so that the horns cannot foul other control rods, etc. Also, in the event of a rough landing with the wings slewing, it

Fig. 129

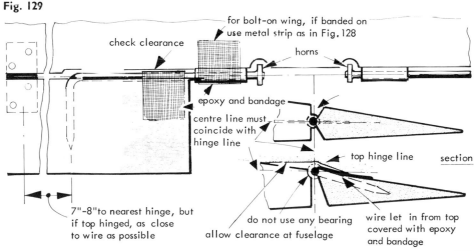

check clearance

for bolt-on wing, if banded on use metal strip as in Fig. 128

horns

epoxy and bandage

centre line must coincide with hinge line

top hinge line

section

7"-8"to nearest hinge, but if top hinged, as close to wire as possible

do not use any bearing

allow clearance at fuselage

wire let in from top covered with epoxy and bandage

103

RADIO CONTROL GUIDE

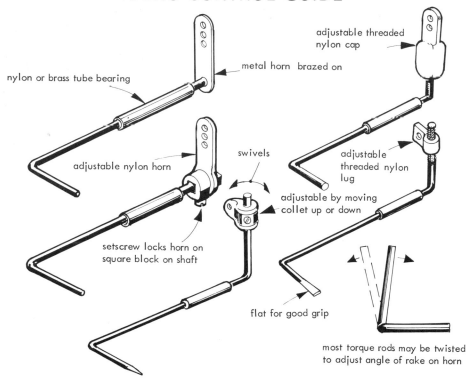

nylon or brass tube bearing

metal horn brazed on

adjustable threaded
nylon cap

adjustable nylon horn

swivels

adjustable
threaded nylon
lug

adjustable by moving
collet up or down

setscrew locks horn on
square block on shaft

flat for good grip

most torque rods may be twisted
to adjust angle of rake on horn

Fig. 130

Fig. 131

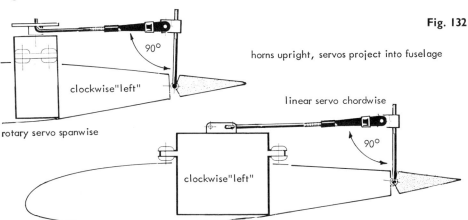

Fig. 132

90°

clockwise"left"

horns upright, servos project into fuselage

rotary servo spanwise

linear servo chordwise

clockwise"left"

90°

Two types of torque rod for operating strip ailerons, showing different means for adjusting the throw. Note the bearing tubes.

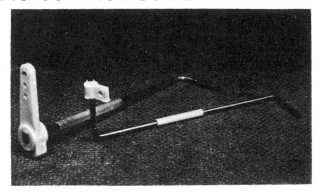

is possible to damage the horn and the fuselage side. Therefore, it is advisable that the wing be keyed in position and that regular checks of the alignment be made.

It is usual for the strip ailerons to be operated by a different type of "pushrod" from any previously described, in fact, it is not a pushrod in the proper sense at all, but a torque-rod, and Figs. 128 and 129 make its construction and method of operation clear, while Fig. 130 shows a typical selection of commercial types.

In use, the only points to watch are that the aileron hinge line is coincident with the centre of the torque rod, that on a wing held in place by rubber bands, there is

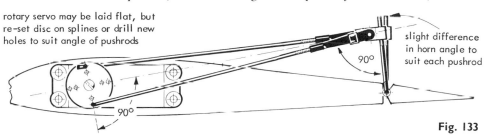

rotary servo may be laid flat, but re-set disc on splines or drill new holes to suit angle of pushrods

slight difference in horn angle to suit each pushrod

90°

90°

Fig. 133

adequate clearance between the fuselage side and the aileron to clear these, and that the bands do not hinder the operation of the rod. Inside the fuselage there must, of course, be adequate clearance for the horns and pushrods.

Figs. 131 and 132 show linkages from the servo to the horn, using disc and linear outputs with an upright mounted unit, and Figs. 133 and 134 show slightly

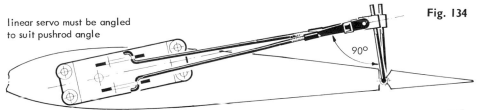

linear servo must be angled to suit pushrod angle

Fig. 134

90°

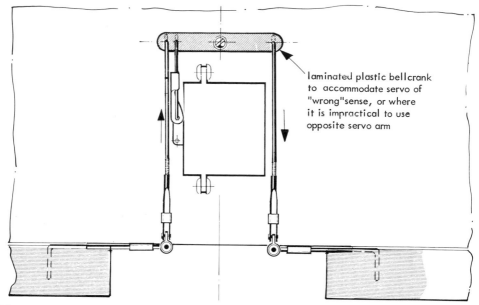

laminated plastic bellcrank
to accommodate servo of
"wrong"sense, or where
it is impractical to use
opposite servo arm

Fig. 135

more complex systems with a side mounted servo. For this system to work properly, the aileron horns must be very close together and in line with the disc or levers. Fig. 135 shows how to use a bellcrank with a single linear output servo. This type of linkage was very popular at one time and commercial bellcranks may be adapted. The method of mounting the servo itself was, of course, described in Chapter 8.

CHAPTER 12
THROTTLES AND STEERABLE NOSEWHEELS

THE special problems of throttle and steerable nosewheel linkages can be very frustrating. Indeed, it is not untrue to say that often more time is spent in getting these two functions absolutely right than on all the other linkages put together!

To deal with throttle first, the following requirements must be met:

(a) the throw must be sufficient to operate the throttle fully, but not so great that the servo is stalled;

(b) care must be taken to make sure no electrical noise is generated, as throttle linkages are the main source of this;

(c) as with all other linkages, there must be a minimum of lost movement or backlash.

(This latter point is often glossed over because the throttle is "unimportant" – it is to those who are sloppy in their modelling – but in that case, the whole model will be so indifferent that the pleasure of flying with a really "tight" throttle link will not be appreciated anyway!)

As was said in Chapter 8, a tube/cable linkage is normally to be preferred, and Fig. 136 shows the correct way to connect a throttle pushrod to a linear output servo for either "sense". With a rotary output, to prevent binding, allowance must be made for the "swing" of the cable. Initially the tube should be fitted as close as possible to the servo, afterwards cutting off about $\frac{1}{8}$in. at a time until the movement is free. It is helpful if the tube is left about $\frac{1}{4}$in. longer than the ideal, so that its mouth can be

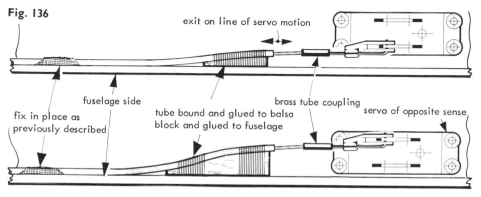

Fig. 136

exit on line of servo motion

fix in place as previously described

fuselage side

tube bound and glued to balsa block and glued to fuselage

brass tube coupling

servo of opposite sense

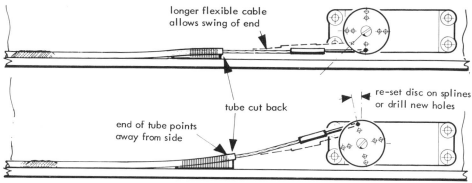

longer flexible cable
allows swing of end

re-set disc on splines
or drill new holes

tube cut back

end of tube points
away from side

Fig. 137

"belled" with the tip of an old ball point pen or metal knitting needle, warmed over a match. Fig. 137 shows the correct method of connecting to a rotary output servo (again for either "sense"), and Fig. 138 how not to do it!

Now to consider the degree of travel required . . . A popular system is to arrange the travel so that the total movement of the servo, including trim, operates the motor from full throttle to cut-off. In practice, this means setting up with the servo at full throttle position, and the trim at its extreme of travel in the same direction. Then, leaving the trim where it is, the throw is adjusted so that, with the throttle lever at "slow", the throttle itself is at a safe, semi-fast, tick-over speed for in-flight manoeuvres, etc., but a bit on the fast side for landing. By moving the trim to about mid-position, the motor is slowed to landing speed, then when the model has been taxied back to the start line, moving the trim to fully slow cuts the motor. With a good slop-free linkage, this system is obviously as precise as the resolution of the servo, and that means absolutely consistent results every flight.

This system is preferred because of the additional control it gives, and it is easy enough to set up so that there is slight excess of movement at either extreme of practical throttle response travel (but not reaching the stops), so that the servo is never stalled. However, it does mean unscrewing the throttle stop on the motor and, for some reason or another, many modellers seem reluctant to believe that a servo is as accurate as the throttle stop for precise slow running!

If such be the case, then it is essential to have some form of slipping device, or over-ride, in the linkage, to be certain that the throttle is fully "home" on its stop

Fig. 138

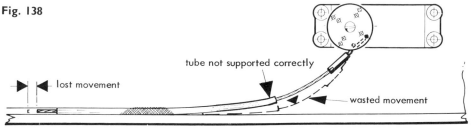

tube not supported correctly

lost movement

wasted movement

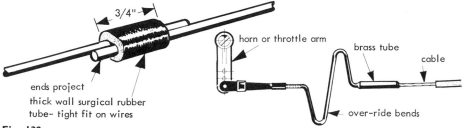

3/4"

ends project
thick wall surgical rubber
tube- tight fit on wires

Fig. 139

horn or throttle arm

brass tube

cable

over-ride bends

Fig. 140

without stalling the servo. Throttle response is markedly non-linear and while, at the slow running position, even the tiny amount of lost movement in, for example, a servo gear train, can be sufficient to change the tickover from slow to just too fast for a comfortable landing speed, at full throttle the same amount of lost movement would have no effect at all.

Fig. 139 shows the simplest possible slipping link which is incorporated in the straight run of cable alongside the engine, where it provides insulation against electrical

Fig. 141

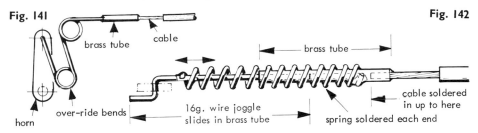

brass tube

cable

horn

over-ride bends

16g. wire joggle
slides in brass tube

brass tube

cable soldered
in up to here

spring soldered each end

Fig. 142

noise, caused by the cable touching against the motor, and is also well lubricated, which is essential to maintain smooth, consistent action. This system also provides the simplest possible adjustment of length. Other popular and easy to make systems are shown in Figs. 140 and 141, with a more sophisticated version in Fig. 142.

More sophisticated still is the over-ride incorporated on the servo disc itself, and shown in Fig. 143. With this, it is possible to actuate the throttle manually, so that

Fig. 143

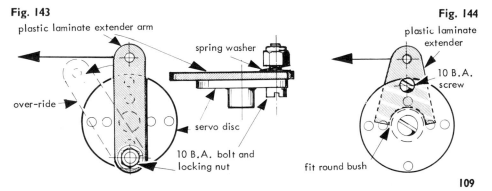

plastic laminate extender arm

spring washer

over-ride

servo disc

10 B.A. bolt and
locking nut

Fig. 144

plastic laminate
extender

10 B.A.
screw

fit round bush

109

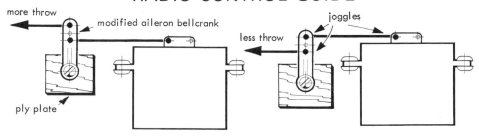

Fig. 145   **Fig. 146**

engine checks can be made without using the radio, which can be a very real advantage as is explained later. It will be noted that this type can be designed to increase the throw of the servo, which is essential for satisfactory operation of some motors. Obviously, it is a simple matter to vary the throw of a rotary output servo, by merely varying the distance of the take-off hole from the hub as in Fig. 144. To adjust the throw of a linear output servo is, however, only slightly more difficult, as is obvious from Fig. 145 which gives increased movement, or from Fig. 146 which shows how to decrease the movement. Varying the relative hole/pushrod positions also gives fine adjustment of the amount of throw possible. An equally simple system may, of course, also be used to reverse the sense of the servo if required – Figs. 147 and 148 – which also show how the same system can be used to bring the pushrod alongside a fuselage side. There are available a selection of commercial units which permit easy adjustment of throw and also manual over-ride operation.

Electrical noise, which has been mentioned several times, is the "noise" generated by a metal-to-metal joint, such as that between a metal clevis, and a metal throttle arm, vibrating. Although it is always bad practice to have metal-to-metal joints in a model, in general, the only two likely to affect the receiver and cause glitches are those on nosewheel and throttle. This is because the control rod itself runs immediately adjacent to the receiver and servos, and hence radiates the interference. Therefore, it is usual (and always recommended) to use a nylon clevis at the pushrod/throttle arm junction. However, this may not be practical in some installations, in which case the joint must either be electrically bonded, or the arm drilled out and a plastic bush (commercial ones are available) inserted as in Fig. 149. Some manufacturers get over this problem

Fig. 147   **Fig. 148**

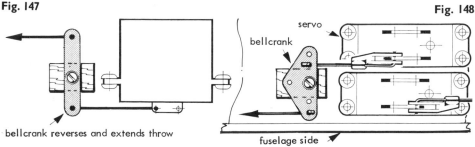

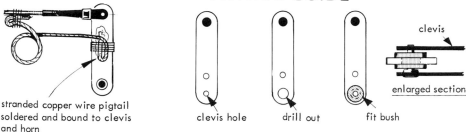

stranded copper wire pigtail
soldered and bound to clevis
and horn

clevis hole   drill out   fit bush

clevis

enlarged section

Fig. 149

by using a nylon throttle arm so that a metal clevis, which is more compact than a nylon one, can be used.

Electric powered models

Although there is no "throttle" as such on an electric powered model, it is advisable to have the facility to switch the motor on or off. Any typical servo has more than enough power to throw a switch of the type recommended for this purpose, so it is only a matter of devising a simple linkage to operate it. The one important point to watch is that the servo can move over its full commanded travel without stalling or, if there is any possibility of this, to install one of the slipping linkages which have just been described.

Steerable nosewheel

Many of the comments on the throttle linkage are applicable to the nosewheel, especially the importance of getting the correct "run" from the servo, although this is, of course, also governed by the "run" to the rudder, as discussed in Chapter 8. As the

Fig. 150

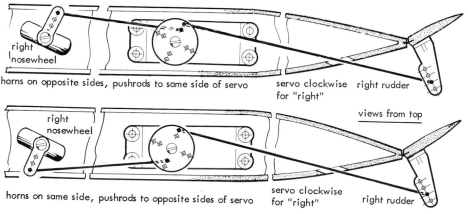

right
nosewheel

horns on opposite sides, pushrods to same side of servo

servo clockwise
for "right"   right rudder

right
nosewheel

views from top

horns on same side, pushrods to opposite sides of servo

servo clockwise
for "right"   right rudder

nosewheel often takes the brunt of the landing load, obviously this must not be transmitted to the servo, so some form of shock absorbing link is incorporated. The systems shown in Figs. 139, 140, 141 and 142 have all been used successfully, but the latter three are to be preferred as the nosewheel usually returns to its correct tracking after the shock is absorbed. It may also be helpful to use the systems shown in Figs. 145, 146, 147 and 148 to adjust the throw, as it is normal for the nosewheel throw to be about half that of the rudder, or reverse the sense, so that the servo take-off nearest the fuselage side can be used.

It is easy for the relative sense of movement of the rudder and nosewheel to be confused, and Fig. 150 shows how various permutations of servo output and horn position can achieve the same end.

With all nosewheel linkages it is advisable to take the same noise precautions as for throttle.

CHAPTER 13
CONTROL HORN GEOMETRY

M OST modellers use commercial control horns, and these are normally moulded in nylon, some typical examples being shown in Fig. 151. The amount of "throw" is usually determined by the provision of several connecting-holes for the clevis, at varying distances along the horn – the nearer the connection to the surface, the

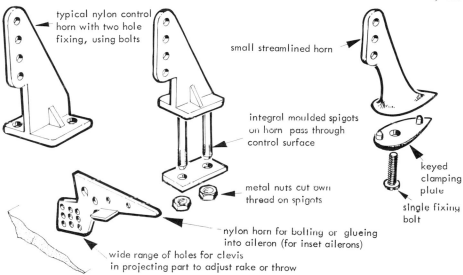

typical nylon control horn with two hole fixing, using bolts

small streamlined horn

integral moulded spigots on horn pass through control surface

metal nuts cut own thread on spigots

keyed clamping plate

single fixing bolt

nylon horn for bolting or glueing into aileron (for inset ailerons)

wide range of holes for clevis in projecting part to adjust rake or throw

Fig. 151

Although there is a plethora of commercial mouldings of all types, without doubt the widest selection is for control horns!

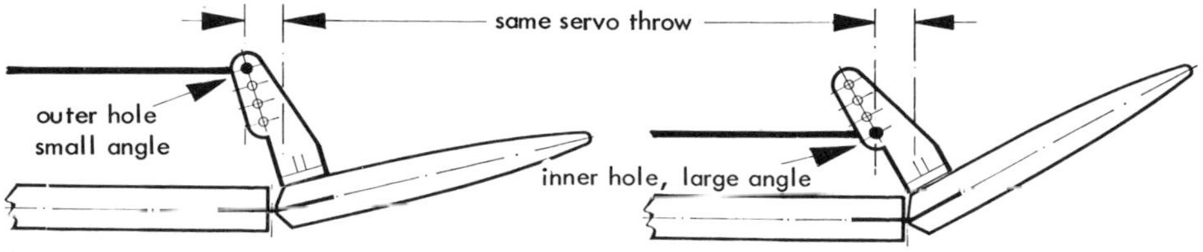

same servo throw

outer hole
small angle

inner hole, large angle

Fig. 152

greater the movement for a given servo travel, and vice-versa – Fig. 152. The majority of rudder and elevator control surfaces call for this type of horn, which incorporates a mounting plate for bolting on to the control surface. If the balsa of the control surface is very soft, it is often a good plan to inlay a small plywood plate ($\frac{1}{16}$ or $\frac{1}{32}$in. ply) about $\frac{3}{4}$in. square, each side of the surface where the horn is fixed, to spread the load and ensure that the horn does not sink into the balsa when the bolts are tightened – Fig. 153.

Horn geometry

The basic geometry of any pushrod system, to achieve equal travel of the control surface in either direction, is that a line taken from the hinge line to the hole in the control horn, must be at 90° to the line of movement of the pushrod. If this is not so, then there will be more movement in one direction than the other. (This fact can sometimes be used to advantage, as is explained in Chapter 16, but here the concern is with general principles.) The important thing is not the angle at which the clevis attaches to the horn, but the line of movement of the pushrod in relation to the horn. It is easy to confuse these, but a study of Fig. 154 will make it clear.

Horns are usually made, however, to provide only for the pushrod working parallel to the surface, and this is generally achieved by forming a crank in the

Fig. 153

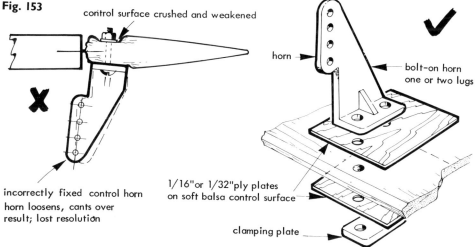

control surface crushed and weakened

horn

bolt-on horn
one or two lugs

incorrectly fixed control horn
horn loosens, cants over
result; lost resolution

1/16"or 1/32"ply plates
on soft balsa control surface

clamping plate

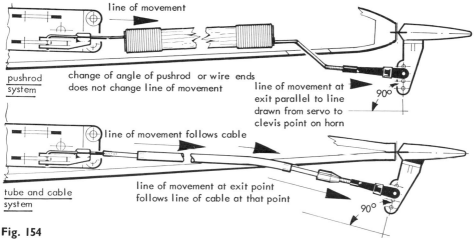

line of movement

pushrod
system

change of angle of pushrod or wire ends
does not change line of movement

line of movement at
exit parallel to line
drawn from servo to
clevis point on horn

90°

line of movement follows cable

tube and cable
system

line of movement at exit point
follows line of cable at that point

90°

Fig. 154

pushrod wire end, as shown in Fig. 155a. It is not always possible to arrange for pushrods to exit in this way, however, and other provisions for correct geometry may have to be made. Some modellers, while careful to fix the horn at 90° to the centre-line of rudder or elevator, fail to realise that the geometry can be upset by using a linkage system (particularly in the case of cable linkages) which comes out of the fuselage at an acute angle – Fig. 155b. In cases of this kind, the horn may be raked forward by adding a wedge of hardwood packing, to retrieve the necessary right-angle – Fig. 155c.

Fig. 155

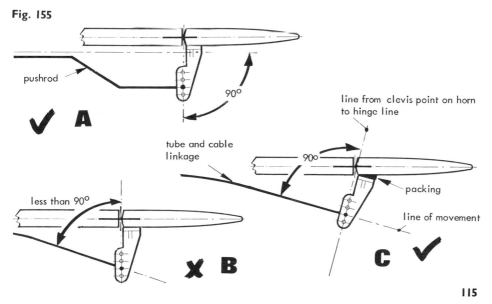

pushrod

90°

✓ **A**

tube and cable
linkage

line from clevis point on horn
to hinge line

90°

packing

less than 90°

line of movement

✗ **B**

C ✓

115

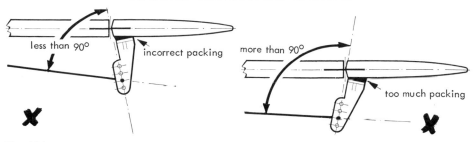

Fig. 156

A certain amount of care is necessary in this operation, however, as adding too much (or too little) packing would again cause the angle to be incorrect – Fig. 156.

With a fairly thick control surface, of solid wood, it is possible to rake the horn by chamfering that part of the surface to which the horn is to be attached – Fig. 157 – but this should only be done in cases where it will not weaken the structure. If a control surface is sharply tapered in cross-section – as it would be with a thick airfoil – a

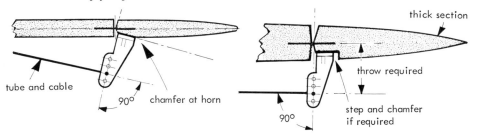

Fig. 157   **Fig. 158**

recessed step cut in the surface will accommodate the horn in a level position relative to the centre-line of the control surface, which is what is required – Fig. 158. This is usually more satisfactory than packing a horn up to compensate as in Fig. 159.

Another point apparent from Fig. 158 is that a horn mounted on a thick surface will afford less throw, with the clevis in the same relative hole, than the same horn on a thin surface. This is because any given linkage hole will be farther from the actual

Fig. 159   **Fig. 160**

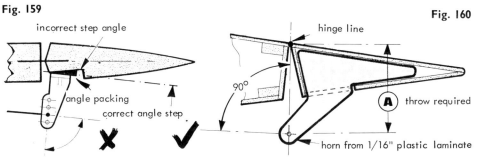

hinge point on the thicker surface so, in order to preserve the same amount of throw, a hole farther inwards on the horn must be used.

Aileron horns

Whilst it is quite common practice to use bolt-on horns of the type already described, some models will require "purpose-made" aileron horns, which are usually built into the control surface itself. If a commercial type such as shown in Fig. 151 is not suitable, then a "home-made" one can be cut from tufnol or paxolin (plywood is a poor substitute and should not be used). The former is preferable, as it provides a harder wearing surface, and it is fixed in place with contact adhesive, having been cut to a shape that fits inside the aileron – Fig. 160. If the aileron is top hinged, the horn will project very little since, to achieve the correct angle of deflection, a similar length to that of an elevator horn is used. This length ("A") may be checked by measuring the distance between the clevis hole and the hinge. A thick wing section will mean that the hole may be barely $\frac{1}{4}$ in. from the lower surface for correct working.

With strip ailerons it is normal to use a torque rod type of linkage with built-in horn, and reference to Chapter 11 will show the various types and methods of mounting.

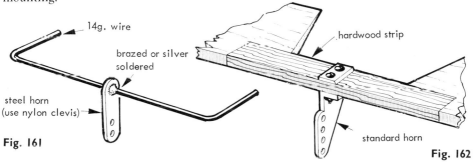

Fig. 161

Fig. 162

Split-elevator horns

Some models have "split", or two-piece elevators – usually to allow a "vee" cut-out for rudder movement. Stout wire joiners (nothing less than 14g.) are commonly used, and these are commercially available, incorporating a central control horn which will actually be concealed inside the fuselage of the finished model. These horns are either of metal, brazed or silver soldered to the wire, or of moulded nylon with a set-screw bedding on to a "flat" on the wire.

The former type are quite easily made – Fig. 161 – if facilities for silver soldering are available. Ordinary "soft" solder is unsuitable as it probably will not withstand the loads and could lead to disaster. Naturally, with such a metal horn, a nylon clevis, or a nylon grommet, to obviate metal-to-metal noise should be used, and the position of the hole for clevis attachment must be decided, by experiment, before building-in the assembly.

An alternative method of joining elevators is to use a length of hardwood of rectangular cross-section (say, $\frac{3}{16} \times \frac{3}{4}$in. for $\frac{3}{16}$in. sheet elevators) and bolting a nylon horn to this as shown in Fig. 162. Drilling holes for the bolts, however, will tend to

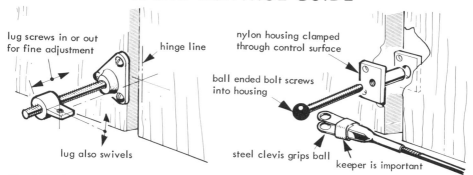

lug screws in or out
for fine adjustment

hinge line

nylon housing clamped
through control surface

ball ended bolt screws
into housing

lug also swivels

steel clevis grips ball

keeper is important

Fig. 163

Fig. 164

weaken this, but a much larger piece of hardwood will necessitate rather an unsightly gap in the rudder to allow for elevator movement, so it is a matter of individual judgement on particular models.

Adjustable horns

Instead of having several holes to allow for different amounts of "throw", some horns feature a fine screw adjustment. This type comprises a threaded rod, on which a nylon coupling is screwed. The position is altered simply by threading it in for large deflection, or out for small deflection, for a given servo travel, as depicted in Fig. 163. This kind of horn is especially useful when coupling a raked or swept-back control surface, as it will accommodate an angular change by permitting the nylon coupling to twist on its thread, automatically maintaining the correct geometry.

Universal joints

Ball-and-socket horn/clevis units are available in the shops, and these have been specially designed to cater for raked or swept-back control surfaces and where ready detachability is required. One type maintains its connection purely by the springiness of the metal clevis, and thus will detach in the event of a crash. Many fliers are reluctant to use this type on highly stressed surfaces, such as might be found on a very

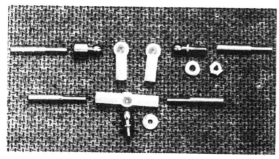

Extremely neat commercial ball-and-socket clevis set, for attachment to various types of pushrod end; also one for aileron use.

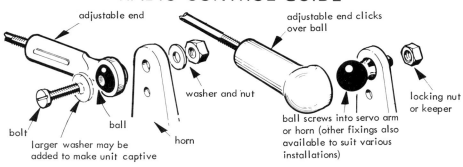

adjustable end

adjustable end clicks over ball

washer and nut

ball screws into servo arm or horn (other fixings also available to suit various installations)

locking nut or keeper

bolt

ball

larger washer may be added to make unit captive

horn

Fig. 165

fast model – or indeed, most medium to large power models, as they might unclip in flight. They come into their own on gliders, where they have also been used successfully for aileron connections, this being dealt with elsewhere. Fig. 164 shows a typical commercial unit – note how by screwing the ball in the mounting bush the throw may be adjusted.

Alternatives, which have proved more secure against vibration and shock loads and hence make the best choice for use with power models, are shown in Fig. 165. Indeed, with helicopters, where the head movement makes very special demands, this latter type of ball and socket clevis have proved especially successful. Both are also ideal for throttle connections.

CHAPTER 14

HINGING
CONTROL SURFACES

NO matter how precise is the resolution and centring of the servos, or how accurate
and slop-free the linkages, unless the control surface hinging is equally precise,
all else will count for naught. The ideal hinging will be so accurately aligned and fixed
that, subject only to any natural resilience in the material used, the control surface
will "fall" under its own weight.

One of the prime mistakes everyone makes – once – is to hinge all the control
surfaces before painting the model, and then find that the paint has gunged up the
entire works. Therefore, wherever possible, control surfaces should only be hinged in
place after the finish of the model is completed. Obviously there are instances where
this is not possible, and here, especially, care will have to be taken to keep the hinge
free of paint.

The most important rule of all is to ensure that the bending axis of the hinges
and the hinge line of the control surface(s) are exactly coincident, both vertically and
horizontally. Even a small misalignment can lead to appreciable binding and rapid
wear. Also, with the mylar or stitched type of hinge, it is important that the gap
between the surfaces is as close as possible, to prevent the introduction of unwanted
movement into the control surfaces, as shown in Fig. 166. Further, such excessive gaps

Fig. 166

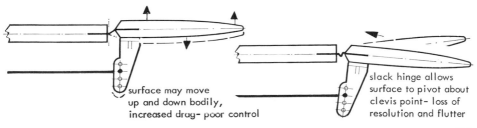

surface may move
up and down bodily,
increased drag- poor control

slack hinge allows
surface to pivot about
clevis point- loss of
resolution and flutter

cause aerodynamic turbulence but, far more important, often lead to control surface flutter, which is a destroyer of aeroplanes!

Virtually all methods of hinging are covered by the four following basic types:

Cross stitch

This is just about the simplest and cheapest hinge available and its method of operation is shown in Fig. 167. The thread hinge is especially useful for attaching the surface after finishing, and it has been successfully used on all types and sizes of model. The best material is braided nylon fishing line of about 9lb. breaking strain, although monofilament is almost as good and a lot cheaper. Household thread, however, is not suitable as it will quickly fray and break.

Similar in principle is the cloth hinge shown in Fig. 168. This is very popular and widely used, binding tape (not bias binding), available from any millinery shop, being the best material. Strips of nylon covering material should not be used as this is too flimsy and will quickly tear in use. With this system the hinges must normally be fixed before final covering and finishing. Glue must not be allowed to get into the material where it bends, because not only will it stiffen the hinge action, but will also lead to early fracture.

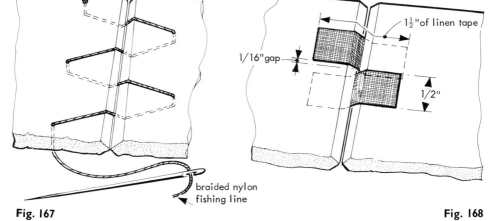

Fig. 167   **Fig. 168**

Mylar, nylon or polypropylene inserts

This is probably the most widely used of all hinging systems, as strips of suitable material, or packs of ready moulded hinges of this type are available at any model shop. Also it is easy to install, remove and replace, without seriously marking the finish of the model. To install the hinge it is usual merely to cut a slit (not a slot) in the control surface with a modelling knife or chisel, so that the hinge is a tight push fit. Although it is usual to smear the hinge with a contact type adhesive, this alone must not be relied on to hold the hinge in place, the material should be pierced with a cocktail stick or similar piece of hardwood, held in place with a dab of glue – Fig. 169. The hinge material should be pre-drilled slightly under-size before inserting the peg.

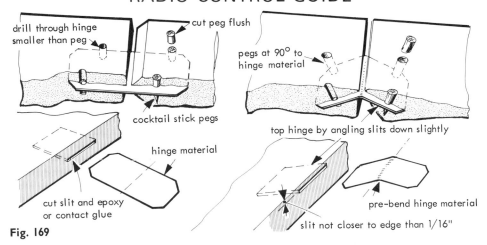

drill through hinge smaller than peg

cut peg flush

cocktail stick pegs

hinge material

cut slit and epoxy or contact glue

pegs at 90° to hinge material

top hinge by angling slits down slightly

pre-bend hinge material

slit not closer to edge than 1/16"

Fig. 169

There is a degree of mechanical stiffness in this type of hinge, which will prevent the surface falling under its own weight, as mentioned earlier, but which has the advantage of giving a certain amount of mechanical centring. This slight degree of stiffness will have no effect on the centring of the servo.

Adhesive film

The introduction of heat activated adhesive film has led to the use of a new type of hinge, which is simple to make and effective in use. Effective mechanically in that it is extremely free, and aerodynamically, because there is no spillage of air and hence a minimum of turbulence at the join. Fig. 170 shows the construction quite clearly – "A" showing the application of the first strip of material; "B" the control surface doubled back on itself and the second strip ironed in place; and "C" the completed joint. On

Fig. 170

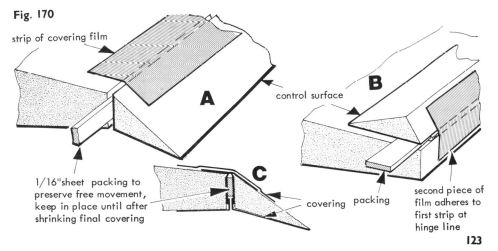

strip of covering film

control surface

A

B

C

1/16"sheet packing to preserve free movement, keep in place until after shrinking final covering

covering   packing

second piece of film adheres to first strip at hinge line

123

larger models a "belt and braces" job, made by attaching the control surface as shown and then ironing the final covering over the previous joint is advised, so that there is a double thickness of material at this stress point.

Mechanical

There are a number of commercially available hinges of the leaf and pin (door hinge) pattern. These are very free acting and with some types the model can be completed with the halves of the hinge inserted, after which the control surfaces are attached merely by inserting the pin, when the finishing of the model is complete.

The "tongue" of the hinge is fixed to the model in the same way as described for the mylar type except that a slot, rather than a slit, must be made. Care should be taken to insert the body of the hinge so that the pin hole is as near as possible to the face of the join to ensure that that gap is kept as small as practicable. Fig. 171 shows various commercial types.

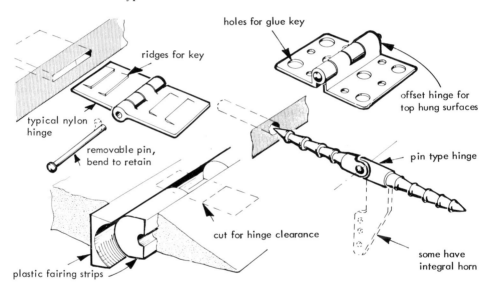

Fig. 171

Gaps and clearances

As will have been obvious from the preceeding paragraphs, it is important, in order to achieve the most effective control response, that the gap between the control surface and the model should be kept as small as possible and, in this respect, plastic film hinges are the most effective, because there is no gap at all!

The various sketches in this chapter have indicated the type of bevel or chamfer which is necessary to accommodate the movement of the various control surfaces. Especial attention must be paid to this at the construction stage, with the surfaces temporarily hinged in place to ensure the angles are correct. If there is insufficient

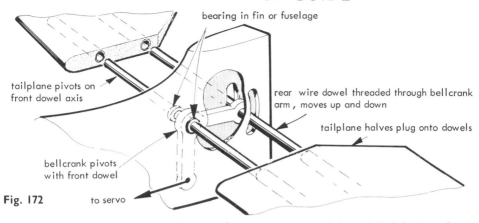

bearing in fin or fuselage

tailplane pivots on front dowel axis

rear wire dowel threaded through bellcrank arm, moves up and down

tailplane halves plug onto dowels

bellcrank pivots with front dowel

Fig. 172   to servo

bevel, the servo will be stalled before the full travel is reached, but while it is, therefore, preferable to err on the side of too great a clearance, this should be kept to a minimum to ensure aerodynamic efficiency.

To take this gap-reducing to the nth degree, special plastic fairings are available, as shown at the foot of Fig. 171, but these are only suitable for centre-hinged surfaces. In general, ailerons are top or centre hinged (usually the former); elevator top or centre hinged (usually the latter); but a rudder is always centre hinged.

All the methods described thus far have been for the general type of control surface, where the moveable part is hinged to the fixed part of the same unit. There are, however, more specialist requirements, the most common of which is, undoubtedly, the all moving tail, which has become quite widely used, especially for gliders.

The two fundamental problems with the all moving tail, whether it be mounted on the fuselage or in a T-tail configuration, is that the hinging must be sufficiently rigid to hold the tailplane secure, both laterally and longitudinally, and that, as the degree of movement is much less than with a normal hinged elevator, the system must be entirely free from backlash and slop, or the unwanted movement will cancel out delicate control movements.

For fuselage mounting, the system shown in Fig. 172 is very popular and

Various types of commercial hinges are illustrated here. This is only a selection of the many types available, so it must be possible to find something to suit every requirement!

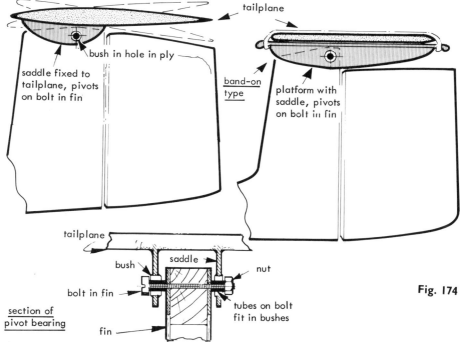

tailplane

bush in hole in ply

saddle fixed to
tailplane, pivots
on bolt in fin

band-on
type

platform with
saddle, pivots
on bolt in fin

tailplane

bush   saddle   nut

bolt in fin

tubes on bolt
fit in bushes

section of
pivot bearing

fin

Fig. 174

Fig. 173

successful, with the additional advantage that the tailplane is removeable in two halves
for transport. T-tails present more of a problem, but the saddle type of hinge –
Fig. 173 – is probably the best, in combining easy dismantling for transport with
slop free action. A variation of the latter is to have a fixed platform permanently
hinged to the fin, and then to attach the tailplane to this with rubber bands or tie
down bolts – Fig. 174.

CHAPTER 15

SPECIAL PURPOSE LINKAGES

SO far all the linkages have been relatively straightforward and uncomplicated with all the control runs straight, and hinge lines at 90° to the pushrod. Not all models are so obliging, however, so now to consider the linkages required when the fins, elevators, or wings, are swept back, then describe the special installation and linkage problems for knock-off and two-piece wings, elevons, "V" and "T" tails, flaps, air brakes, wheel brakes, retracting undercarriages and so forth.

Swept-back fins

This is the problem most likely to be encountered, and Fig. 175 shows how, if an orthodox horn and clevis are used, the action of the rudder will try to twist the horn either up or down, as left or right are signalled. It is possible to use a tube/cable pushrod angled as in Fig. 176, although this is not recommended unless the disposition of the cable is such that undue drag, and hence imprecise centring, is avoided. It is

Fig. 175   **Fig. 176**

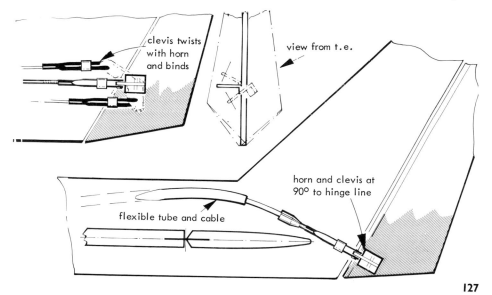

clevis twists with horn and binds

view from t.e.

flexible tube and cable

horn and clevis at 90° to hinge line

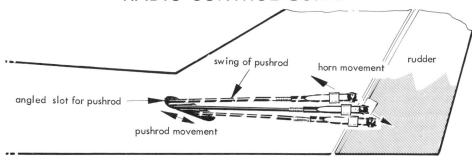

swing of pushrod

horn movement

rudder

angled slot for pushrod

pushrod movement

Fig. 177

far better to use one of the ball-and-socket clevises available – Figs. 164 and 165 – or, alternatively, one of the screw-threaded types with nylon end-connectors, illustrated in Fig. 163 provided that the latter is sufficiently free on the thread to pivot easily with the swing of the rudder. Also, the rise and fall of the pushrod must be allowed for as shown in Fig. 177. A closed loop system may, of course, be used with no problems at all.

Swept-back tailplanes

In general, the degree of sweep on a tailplane and the amount of control movement, is far less than for a rudder. In such case, although there is some twisting movement, it can be accommodated by the normal flexibility of a standard horn. A separate pushrod end to each elevator half is also necessary and Fig. 178 shows a convenient layout. With this system, unwanted movement and differential can easily be introduced by the pushrod moving from side to side; therefore the guides that hold it central are essential. If the sweep-back and movement are such that standard horns are not practical, the only solution is to use the universal type as recommended for rudder. Ball-and-socket types must have a secure keeper (normally a piece of neoprene fuel

Fig. 178

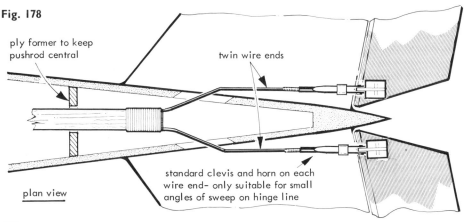

ply former to keep pushrod central

twin wire ends

plan view

standard clevis and horn on each wire end– only suitable for small angles of sweep on hinge line

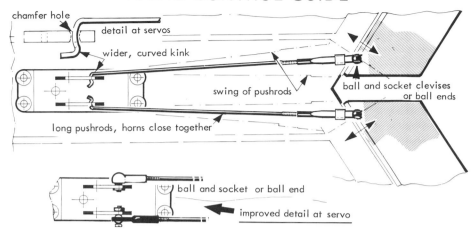

chamfer hole

detail at servos

wider, curved kink

swing of pushrods

ball and socket clevises or ball ends

long pushrods, horns close together

ball and socket or ball end

improved detail at servo

Fig. 179

tube, slid over the arms of the clevis as explained in Chapter 10) because vibration and shock loads have been known to cause the clevis to "jump" from the ball and, while this is only inconvenient on rudder (if aileron control is available!!) it is disastrous on elevator! Once again the closed loop system may be used perfectly satisfactorily.

Swept-back wings

The problems here are not dissimilar to those encountered with fins and tailplanes, in that the action of the pushrod imparts a twisting motion to the horn. Fig. 179 shows the use of a ball-and-socket clevis/horn and how the pushrod ends should be curved to allow the pushrod to "ride" in the servo output, to accommodate not only the rise and fall of the pushrods, but the sideways swing caused by the oblique hinge line. This is necessary even if the holes in the output arms are horizontal. The only good mechanical solution is to use ball ends at both servo and horn points.

An alternative is to use a tube and cable system as in Fig. 180 but it is preferable to avoid such relatively tight bends on a vital function such as aileron, and use bell-

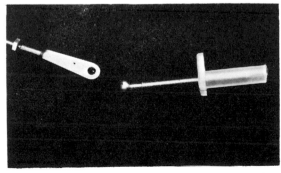

A typical ball and socket horn and clevis. The throw is adjusted by screwing the ball into or out of its mounting. A 'keeper'—see text—should be used on the clevis.

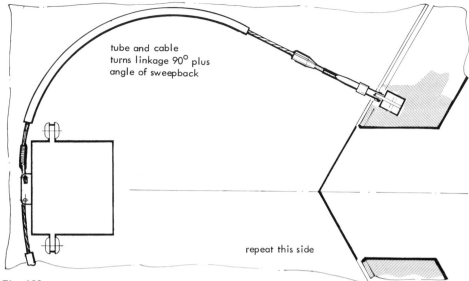

tube and cable
turns linkage 90° plus
angle of sweepback

repeat this side

Fig. 180

cranks as in Fig. 181. If there is insufficient space in the model for either of these linkages, then Fig. 182 shows a much more compact system, using a bellcrank and rotary (or linear) output servo, while Fig. 183 shows how a rotary output may be coupled directly to the surfaces without using a bellcrank at all.

Fig. 181

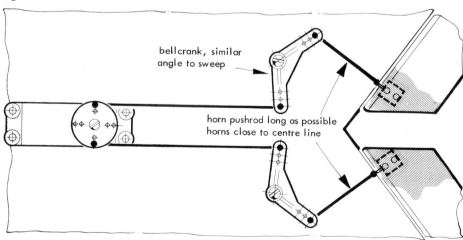

bellcrank, similar
angle to sweep

horn pushrod long as possible
horns close to centre line

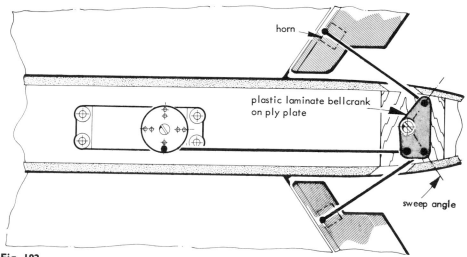

Fig. 182

Yet again, it may well be found that the closed loop system can be adapted to provide an excellent solution to some of these problems.

Knock-off wings

Some models, notably high aspect-ratio gliders, often have two-piece or plug-in wings, with which it is not practical to use the normal linkage with the aileron servo fixed in the wings. In this case it is necessary to mount the servo in the fuselage, and have some form of linkage which can be uncoupled when the model is de-rigged.

Fig. 183

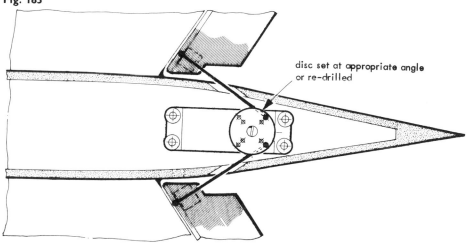

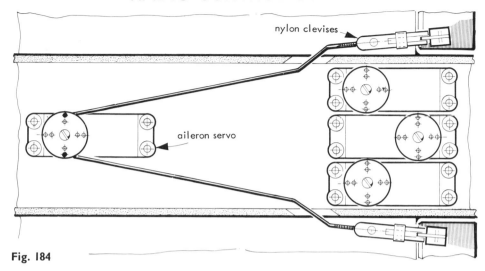

nylon clevises

aileron servo

Fig. 184

Fig. 184 shows one of the simplest systems for use with strip ailerons, but in-set ailerons must be coupled into the operating linkage in the wing. Fig. 185a and Fig. 185b show this with both a one- or two-piece wing. On some models the outer panel is removable and here the system shown in Fig. 186 is popular, the servo, of course, being mounted in either the centre section or fuselage.

Obviously flaps may be operated in the same way. Fig. 187 suggests a system using bellcranks, and a light spring ensures the flap is retained in the fully closed position, so that the connection to the clevis can be via a slide-on keeper which just "clicks" in place, thus giving simple detachability.

Fig. 185 a

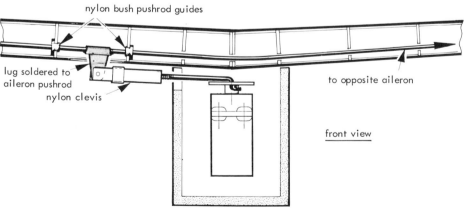

nylon bush pushrod guides

lug soldered to
aileron pushrod

nylon clevis

to opposite aileron

front view

RADIO CONTROL GUIDE

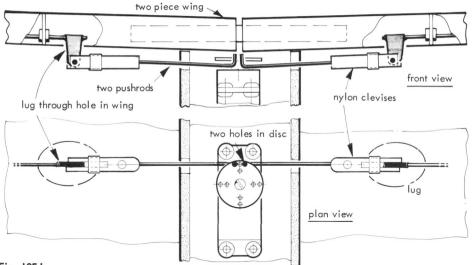

two piece wing

two pushrods

lug through hole in wing

front view

nylon clevises

two holes in disc

lug

plan view

Fig. 185 b

The ready dismantling of the model, and the knock-off ability of all these systems, is improved by using a ball-and-socket type connector, provided it is sufficiently secure only to come apart in a crash and not in the air!

"T" tails

Because they are often flown from rough terrain, gliders are especially prone to

Fig. 186

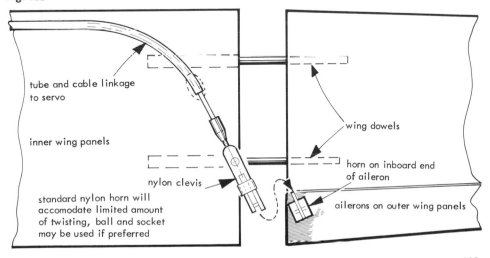

tube and cable linkage
to servo

inner wing panels

nylon clevis

standard nylon horn will
accomodate limited amount
of twisting, ball and socket
may be used if preferred

wing dowels

horn on inboard end
of aileron

ailerons on outer wing panels

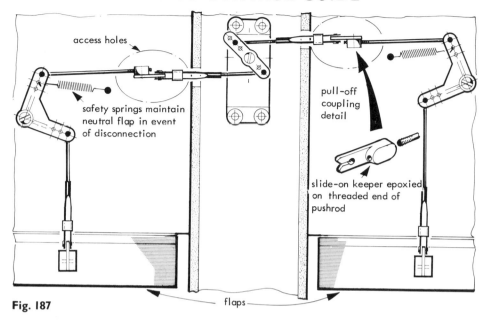

access holes

safety springs maintain
neutral flap in event
of disconnection

pull-off
coupling
detail

slide-on keeper epoxied
on threaded end of
pushrod

Fig. 187

flaps

damage in landing, the tail-plane probably being the most vulnerable part. For this reason "T" tails are popular, but they do pose some linkage problems.

Tube and cable, as in Fig. 188, is a simple way of operating the elevator or, if bellcranks are preferred, Fig. 189 shows the system, and also how the sense of the

Fig. 188

Fig. 189

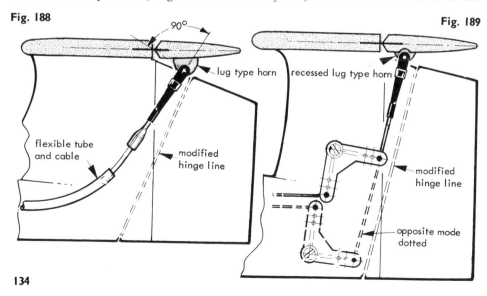

90°

lug type horn

recessed lug type horn

flexible tube
and cable

modified
hinge line

modified
hinge line

opposite mode
dotted

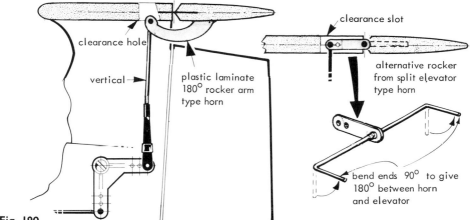

clearance slot

clearance hole

vertical →

plastic laminate
180° rocker arm
type horn

alternative rocker
from split elevator
type horn

bend ends 90° to give
180° between horn
and elevator

Fig. 190

Fig. 191

servo travel can be reversed. Obviously the linkage will be enclosed within the thick fin used with "T" tails, so with these two systems it will be necessary to use an angled rudder as indicated by the dotted lines. An alternative system, therefore, is shown in Fig. 190 and this, itself, can be modified to use a standard split elevator wire horn, with the ends bent (carefully so as not to impair the soldered joint) at 90°, as shown in Fig. 191. Finally, more complicated but the only possible method with some installations, is the double bellcrank system shown in Fig. 192.

It is not intended here to go into matters of construction, but it will be seen that

Fig. 192

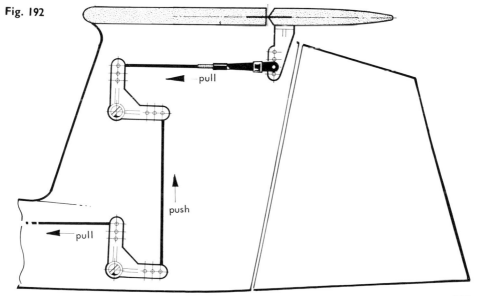

pull

push

pull

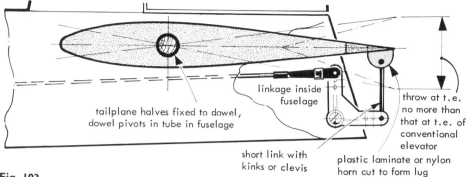

linkage inside
fuselage

tailplane halves fixed to dowel,
dowel pivots in tube in fuselage

throw at t.e.
no more than
that at t.e. of
conventional
elevator

short link with
kinks or clevis

plastic laminate or nylon
horn cut to form lug

Fig. 193

all these systems readily lend themselves for use with a detachable tailplane although, in this case, a ball-and-socket clevis would be worthwhile incorporating.

All-moving tailplanes

These are now widely used, especially on scale models and gliders, and it is important to note that a normal control horn method of actuation cannot be used, because the required movement is so small. The system shown in Fig. 193 has proved very satisfactory in use, and it is simple to adjust the throw by repositioning the pushrods in the bellcrank.

On gliders, the all-moving tail is often employed in conjunction with the "T" tail configuration. In this case the linkages shown in Figs. 188 and 189 are commonly used in conjunction with the hinging methods shown in Fig. 174.

Elevons

With tailless models, such as deltas, unless there is a central elevator with tip ailerons, it is necessary for the ailerons to act simultaneously as elevators (or vice versa) and these are known as elevons. This is not so frightful as it sounds and there are various methods of achieving this action, possibly the simplest being that shown in Fig. 194 where the aileron servo is itself moved fore and aft by the elevator servo. Provided the servo moves freely, but without slop or wobble, then the system is very effective.

Fig. 194

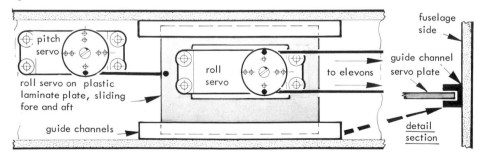

pitch
servo

roll servo on plastic
laminate plate, sliding
fore and aft

roll
servo

guide channels

fuselage
side

to elevons

guide channel
servo plate

detail
section

RADIO CONTROL GUIDE

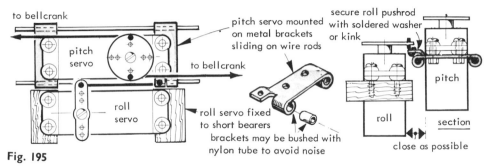

to bellcrank

pitch servo mounted
on metal brackets
sliding on wire rods

secure roll pushrod
with soldered washer
or kink

pitch
servo

to bellcrank

pitch

roll
servo

roll servo fixed
to short bearers

roll

section

brackets may be bushed with
nylon tube to avoid noise

close as possible

Fig. 195

Certain models require the use of transverse pushrods and, for such installations, the elevator servo is driven by the aileron servo, either on rods as in Fig. 195 or on a swinging plate as in Fig. 196. The 90° geometry between the static pivot and the

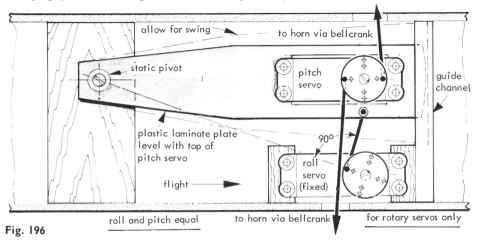

allow for swing

to horn via bellcrank

static pivot

pitch
servo

guide
channel

plastic laminate plate
level with top of
pitch servo

90°

roll
servo
(fixed)

flight

roll and pitch equal

to horn via bellcrank

for rotary servos only

Fig. 196

aileron servo disc is vital on the latter method, which is, incidentally, only suitable for use with rotary servos.

Should a system where the servos are fixed be preferred, then Fig. 197 suggests a

Fig. 197

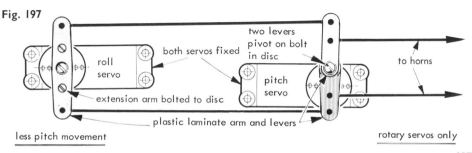

both servos fixed

two levers
pivot on bolt
in disc

roll
servo

pitch
servo

to horns

extension arm bolted to disc

plastic laminate arm and levers

less pitch movement

rotary servos only

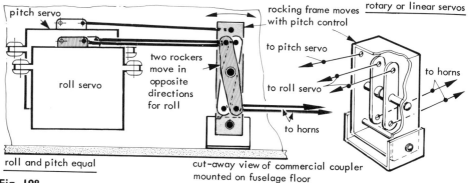

pitch servo

rocking frame moves
with pitch control

rotary or linear servos

to pitch servo

two rockers
move in
opposite
directions
for roll

roll servo

to roll servo

to horns

to horns

roll and pitch equal

cut-away view of commercial coupler
mounted on fuselage floor

Fig. 198

method for use with rotary servos. Fig. 198 shows an alternative system, which can be used with either linear or rotary output servos.

It may be necessary to mount the servos in the wing and, in this case, the system shown in Fig. 199 is applicable. Models with swept-back wings will require a slight modification to this system to use 120° bellcranks, as shown in Fig. 200.

Flaperons

A relatively recent innovation, very popular in slope soaring gliders, is to couple aileron and flap together, to give "flaperons". Any of the elevon linkages in Figs. 194 to 199 may be used, but it must be remembered that the flap servo is positionable, not self-centring, so the neutral must be positioned to suit the type of model. For example,

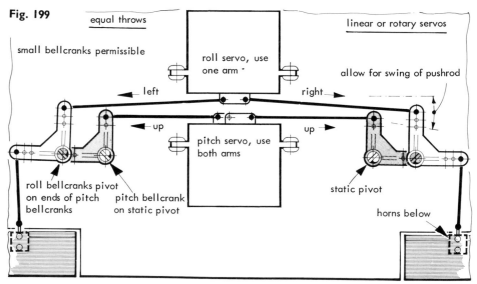

Fig. 199

equal throws

linear or rotary servos

small bellcranks permissible

roll servo, use
one arm

allow for swing of pushrod

left

right

up

up

pitch servo, use
both arms

roll bellcranks pivot
on ends of pitch
bellcranks

pitch bellcrank
on static pivot

static pivot

horns below

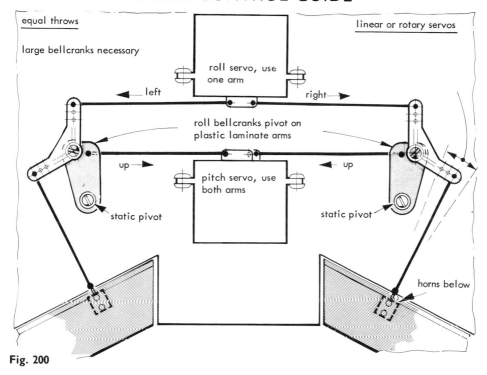

equal throws

large bellcranks necessary

linear or rotary servos

roll servo, use one arm

left

right

roll bellcranks pivot on plastic laminate arms

up

up

pitch servo, use both arms

static pivot

static pivot

horns below

Fig. 200

a general purpose soarer would have neutral at one extreme of travel, but an aerobatic machine would have the neutral at centre, so that the flaps could be used during inverted flying.

"V" tails

If a "V" tail, to combine the functions of rudder and elevator is being used, then problems similar to those just described exist, and are overcome in the same manner. The sliding servo method in Fig. 194 is to be preferred, because it has the simplest linkage, but, the methods shown in Figs 197 and 198 may also be adapted. The function of the servo, as noted in these drawings, may not be as specified. Therefore, the installation must be made up before it is determined which servo must be used to suit both function and sense.

Flaps

After all this, straightforward, common or garden, flaps present few problems! Most manufacturers will provide a special servo, with a greater-than-normal total throw, to operate flaps, spoilers, undercarriage, and so on. Allowance must obviously be made for this extra movement, and this is one of the applications where a linear servo is at an advantage over a rotary output type, in that the extra throw can introduce problems

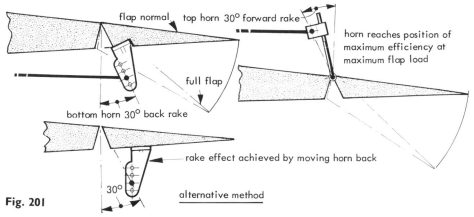

flap normal   top horn 30° forward rake

horn reaches position of
maximum efficiency at
maximum flap load

full flap

bottom horn 30° back rake

rake effect achieved by moving horn back

30°   alternative method

Fig. 201

of lost motion at either extreme of travel with the latter. The actual linkage from the servo to the flap can follow the pattern already described for aileron linkage, except that the horn should rake back if below, or forward if above, the surface, some 30° to ensure that it does not over-ride its centre at extremes of travel – Fig. 201. A linkage similar to that shown in Fig. 187 may be used but, if the servo is permanently in the wing, the detachable clevis/keeper joint may be omitted, also the springs, as the servo will hold the flaps securely closed.

It must be remembered that both flaps are either up or down at the same time (unlike aileron where it is one up – one down), so the take-off must be one from each

Fig. 202

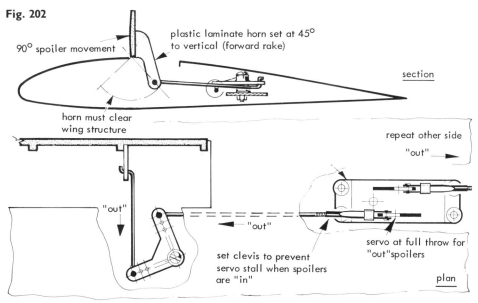

90° spoiler movement

plastic laminate horn set at 45°
to vertical (forward rake)

section

horn must clear
wing structure

repeat other side

"out"

"out"

"out"

set clevis to prevent
servo stall when spoilers
are "in"

servo at full throw for
"out" spoilers

plan

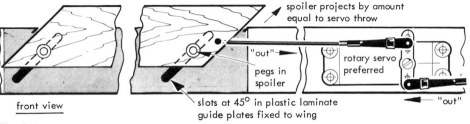

spoiler projects by amount
equal to servo throw

"out"→

pegs in
spoiler

rotary servo
preferred

front view

slots at 45° in plastic laminate
guide plates fixed to wing

←— "out"

Fig. 203

side of the servo disc, or from each of the linear arms as appropriate, unless it is preferred to use a pushrod with a bifurcated end – as in Fig. 178.

Spoilers and airbrakes

These are now widely used on gliders, where precision of landing is often of vital importance, either because of obstructions on the slope, or lack of space or, in the case of thermal soarers, simply to bring them down out of lift. The effect of even relatively small spoilers is most noticeable. Fig. 202 shows a popular type, and it will be seen that, to achieve the necessary throw, a special servo, such as is used for flaps, is preferable, so that the mechanical advantage of using the longest possible horns can be exploited. It is important that the blade should fit tightly and flush with the wing, to avoid unwanted drag in the closed position, so some form of slipping linkage, as described for use with throttle, could be usefully incorporated, so that the spoiler is held securely retracted, but without stalling the servo.

It will be seen that to raise a spoiler such as shown in Fig. 202, against the airflow of a fast moving model, could require considerable power. Therefore, the sliding motion type shown in Fig. 203, offers advantages in that this load is almost non-existent. Again, so as not to impair the flying performance, it is important the spoiler retracts flush with the wing, so some form of positive stop, combined with a slipping link to the servo is to be preferred.

The parallel action airbrake shown in Fig. 204 is obviously most effective, in that

Fig. 204

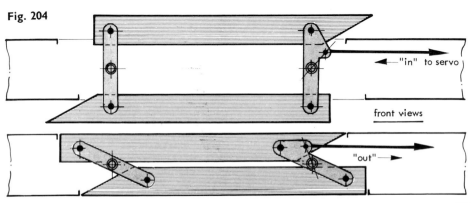

←—"in" to servo

front views

"out"—→

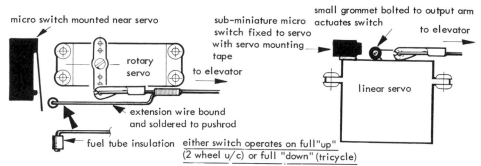

micro switch mounted near servo

rotary
servo

to elevator

extension wire bound
and soldered to pushrod

fuel tube insulation

sub-miniature micro
switch fixed to servo
with servo mounting
tape

small grommet bolted to output arm
actuates switch

to elevator

linear servo

either switch operates on full "up"
(2 wheel u/c) or full "down" (tricycle)

Fig. 205

Fig. 206

not only is the airflow over both surfaces of the wing spoilt, but drag is also greatly increased. Naturally, previous comments on the importance of the blades fitting flush, but not stalling the servo, apply.

Retracting undercarriage

The comments in the previous paragraphs concerning the amount of travel and the importance of not stalling the servo, apply to all mechanical retracting undercarriages. Equally important is to select a unit which over-rides and locks into both the up and down position, so that no shock load is transmitted to the servo.

If an electrically operated undercarriage is being used, then all the servo has to do is to switch the unit on and off, and how this is done would depend on the type of switching recommended by the manufacturer of the undercarriage unit.

Fig. 207

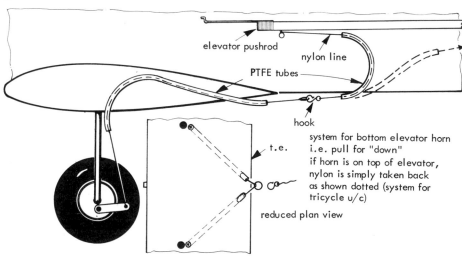

elevator pushrod

nylon line

PTFE tubes

hook

t.e.

system for bottom elevator horn
i.e. pull for "down"
if horn is on top of elevator,
nylon is simply taken back
as shown dotted (system for
tricycle u/c)

reduced plan view

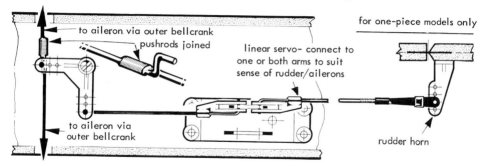

to aileron via outer bellcrank
pushrods joined

linear servo- connect to
one or both arms to suit
sense of rudder/ailerons

for one-piece models only

to aileron via
outer bellcrank

rudder horn

Fig. 208

Wheel brakes

Those modellers lucky enough to fly from runways often have problems with the model "taxiing" when they want it to stand still! Some form of braking is the answer, and it is usual to operate this from the elevator servo in the full "down" position, with a tricycle undercarriage, or the full "up" position with a two-wheeler. The simplest brakes to install are the commercially available electrical types, and two simple ways of switching these are shown in Figs. 205 and 206. At full down (or up) the servo operates the micro-switch, which is "automatically off" as soon as the servo is released. It is normal to have a separate battery supply, because the current drain of an electrical brake is quite high and, when flying aerobatics, for example, full elevator control is selected many times during a flight!

Mechanically operated brakes are also commercially available and, here again, full elevator movement is the means of control for selecting them. Fig. 207 shows a popular method of connecting to the servo. Nylon fishing line of about 7 to 9lb. breaking strain is generally used, as this is pliable enough to follow the complex curves without undue drag, has enough inherent stretch not to stall the servo and will, depending on the efficiency of the braking system used, transmit enough power to lock the wheels.

Coupled aileron and rudder

This system, known as CAR, was very popular at one time, when it was often impossible to install four of the large servos then in use, in a small model or because it was possible to purchase an initially cheaper outfit and then extend its uses. In general, this duplication of controls from one servo is not recommended and, with a 3-channel outfit; it is preferable to use either rudder or aileron depending on the model. There are, however, exceptions, such as high aspect-ratio gliders, where positive control is not transmitted by ailerons alone as with most models, but rudder and aileron have to be used simultaneously, as in full size practice.

With a one-piece model, the linkage is fairly simple, Fig. 208 showing a typical installation. Usually, however, the wing is removable and this introduces complications. Fig. 209 suggests one method using a linear output servo and breaking the connection

RADIO CONTROL GUIDE

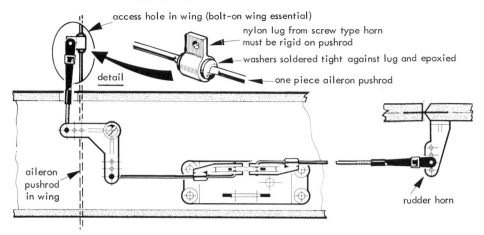

access hole in wing (bolt-on wing essential)

nylon lug from screw type horn
must be rigid on pushrod

washers soldered tight against lug and epoxied

detail

one piece aileron pushrod

aileron
pushrod
in wing

rudder horn

Fig. 209

at the clevis, while Fig. 210 shows the same idea applied to a rotary output. Both these systems assume the servo to be in the fuselage, but it is often more convenient that it be fixed in the wing, so Fig. 211 shows how to connect up to an outboard aileron and Fig. 212 to a strip type. In both cases the rudder pushrod goes through the side of the fuselage, so that it is a simple matter to couple and decouple to transport the model. If it is decided to use any of these systems, a study of earlier suggestions for linkages for knock-off wings will be helpful.

Incidentally, to avoid clubroom argument, both aileron and rudder must give the same control – i.e. right aileron – right rudder!

Fig. 210

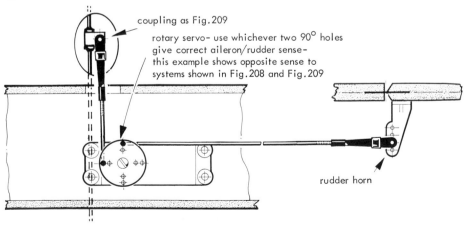

coupling as Fig. 209

rotary servo- use whichever two 90° holes
give correct aileron/rudder sense–
this example shows opposite sense to
systems shown in Fig. 208 and Fig. 209

rudder horn

RADIO CONTROL GUIDE

extra bellcrank used as connection
between aileron servo, aileron pushrods
and coupling point for rudder pushrod

pushrod joint as Fig.208

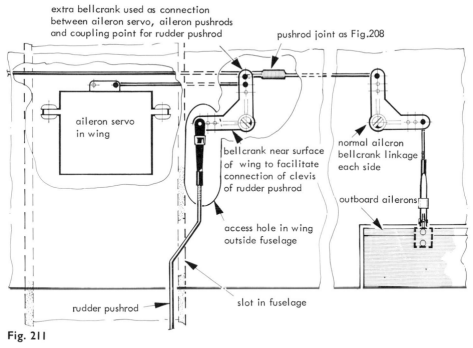

aileron servo
in wing

bellcrank near surface
of wing to facilitate
connection of clevis
of rudder pushrod

normal aileron
bellcrank linkage
each side

outboard ailerons

access hole in wing
outside fuselage

rudder pushrod

slot in fuselage

Fig. 211

Fig. 212

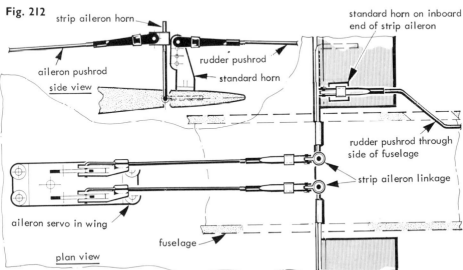

strip aileron horn

standard horn on inboard
end of strip aileron

aileron pushrod

side view

rudder pushrod

standard horn

rudder pushrod through
side of fuselage

strip aileron linkage

aileron servo in wing

fuselage

plan view

CHAPTER 16

DIFFERENTIAL LINKAGES

IN Chapter 13, while discussing the geometry of control runs, it was pointed out that, unless the angles were correct, differential movement could be introduced. What then, is differential movement? The most quotable definition is that "the centre is not the middle", or, to put it more prosaically, the control surface will move more in one direction than in the other, even though the servo travel remains equal in each direction – Fig. 213.

Some designs call for differential movement of the controls, in order to equalise the diameter of inside and outside loops for a given amount of control stick movement; to make the model "roll in a straight line" or even to make it respond to aileron at all. Therefore the methods of obtaining differential will be described in practical terms, for it is not the purpose of this book to digress into theoretical aspects – only to make sure readers know how to obtain differential if convinced it is needed!

The principle

This is that the transference of a circular to a straight push-pull movement (or vice versa) can, if the connecting point is offset from a position 90° relative to the line of

Fig. 213

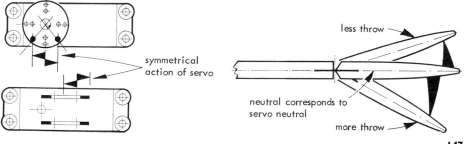

symmetrical action of servo

less throw

neutral corresponds to servo neutral

more throw

147

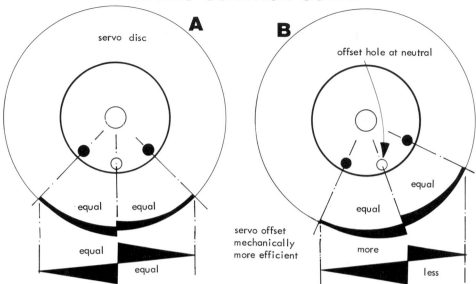

Fig. 214

motion when at neutral, result in the movement transferred to the control surface being greater in one direction than in the other. Fig. 214 shows the simplest system using a disc output servo; "A" shows the normal condition and "B" the differential condition, while Fig. 215 shows the principle applied to the control horn end of the model. Fig. 216 shows how bellcranks may, if it is more convenient, be used to achieve

Fig. 215

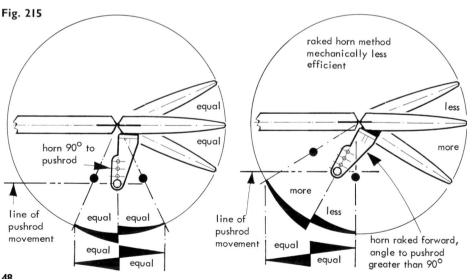

RADIO CONTROL GUIDE

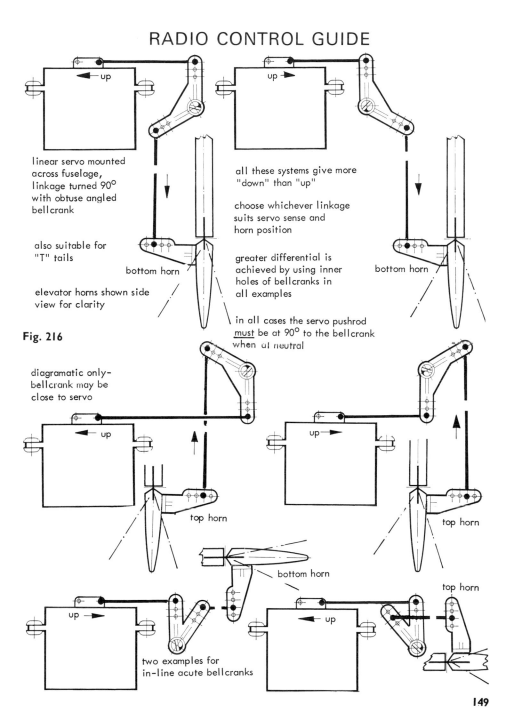

linear servo mounted
across fuselage,
linkage turned 90°
with obtuse angled
bellcrank

also suitable for
"T" tails

elevator horns shown side
view for clarity

all these systems give more
"down" than "up"

choose whichever linkage
suits servo sense and
horn position

greater differential is
achieved by using inner
holes of bellcranks in
all examples

in all cases the servo pushrod
must be at 90° to the bellcrank
when at neutral

Fig. 216

diagramatic only-
bellcrank may be
close to servo

up

up

bottom horn

bottom horn

up

up

top horn

top horn

bottom horn

up

up

top horn

two examples for
in-line acute bellcranks

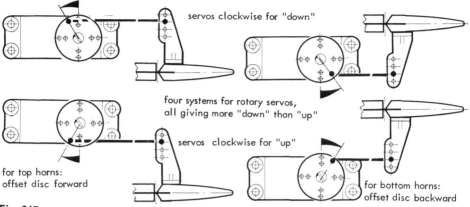

servos clockwise for "down"

four systems for rotary servos,
all giving more "down" than "up"

servos clockwise for "up"

for top horns:
offset disc forward

for bottom horns:
offset disc backward

Fig. 217

the same result. With a linear output servo, either of the last two systems must be used.

Differential elevator control

As this is the easiest to understand in practice, it will be described first even though, with proportional equipment, the demand for it, in practical terms, is not great. This is because the proportional use of the transmitter control stick enables the size of inside and outside loops to be equalised, so there is seldom need to resort to mechanical devices. However, it is easy to grasp and this will simplify understanding the more complex aileron systems.

The best practical way to obtain this differential is via the disc of a rotary output servo. This way the control horn may be set up to be geometrically correct at neutral, as in Chapter 13, then a series of holes drilled in the servo disc (many servos are now supplied with such holes pre-drilled; alternatively, on units with splined output shafts, the disc may be moved in increments so that the required hole positioning is readily obtained), will provide the differential as shown in Fig. 217. With this system trial and error tests, until the required differential deflection is obtained, are extremely easy to make.

If, however, a linear output servo is to be used, there is no practical alternative to raking the horn, as in Fig. 218, which is just as effective, but more tedious in practice,

Fig. 218

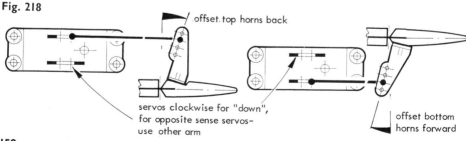

offset top horns back

servos clockwise for "down",
for opposite sense servos-
use other arm

offset bottom
horns forward

150

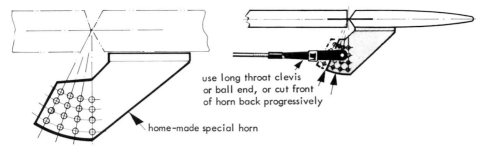

use long throat clevis
or ball end, or cut front
of horn back progressively

home-made special horn

Fig. 219

unless a special horn is made up as in Fig. 219. From reference to the illustrations it will be seen that, in order to achieve more down than up (the most common require-ment) with the horn underneath the elevator, it must be raked forward, or the pushrod connected aft of the 90° position on the servo disc. If the horn is on top, then it must be raked back, or the servo connected forward of the 90° position on the servo disc. The opposite of the foregoing applies if the requirement is for more up than down.

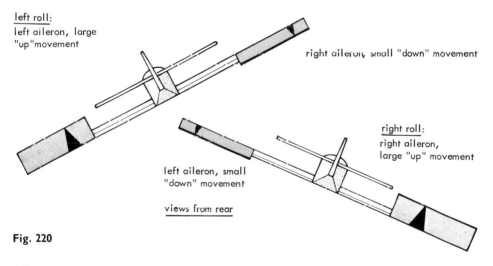

left roll:
left aileron, large
"up" movement

right aileron, small "down" movement

right roll:
right aileron,
large "up" movement

left aileron, small
"down" movement

views from rear

Fig. 220

Ailerons

The required differential here is that the up-going aileron should travel a greater distance than the down-going one, and this applies to both ailerons – Fig. 220. The theory, in very basic terms, is that, with various designs and under various conditions of flight, the drag of the down-going aileron can be greater than the lift it creates to do its work. In some extreme conditions it has been known for the model to refuse to respond to aileron control at all because of this drag.

Strip ailerons are the easiest to set up for differential, and Fig. 221 shows how

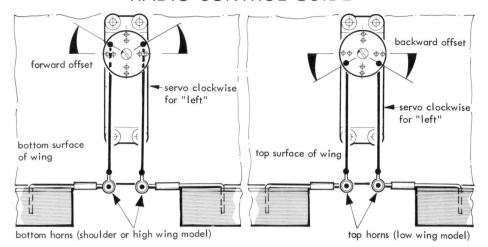

forward offset

servo clockwise
for "left"

bottom surface
of wing

bottom horns (shoulder or high wing model)

backward offset

servo clockwise
for "left"

top surface of wing

top horns (low wing model)

Fig. 221

off-setting the position of the pushrods aft in a servo disc will be correct with horns on the top of the wing, and off-setting them forward is correct if the horns are underneath the wing. With a linear output servo, however, the horns themselves must be raked forward if on top and aft if underneath as in Fig. 222.

Inset ailerons can be more difficult. A typical problem is when a ready-to-use wing with built-in 90° bellcranks and horns, or tube/cable linkage, has been bought, and here, without doubt the simplest way to introduce differential is, once again, via the servo disc. Fig. 223 shows how to connect the pushrods to the disc for either servo sense and top or bottom mounted horns. If, however, a linear output servo is to be used with 90° bellcranks or a tube/cable, then there is no alternative (apart from a

Fig. 222

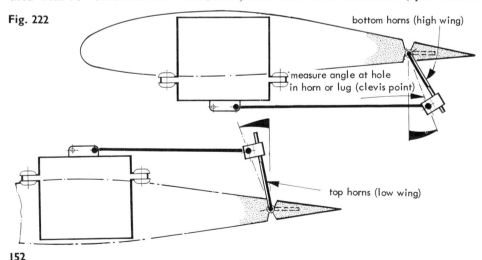

bottom horns (high wing)

measure angle at hole
in horn or lug (clevis point)

top horns (low wing)

RADIO CONTROL GUIDE

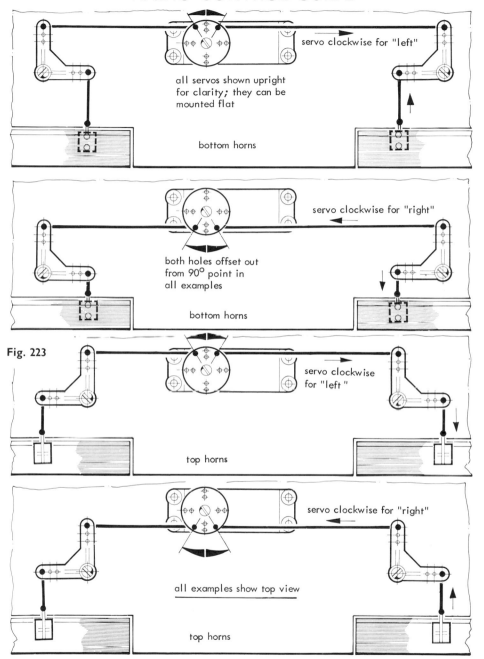

servo clockwise for "left"

all servos shown upright for clarity; they can be mounted flat

bottom horns

servo clockwise for "right"

both holes offset out from 90° point in all examples

bottom horns

Fig. 223

servo clockwise for "left "

top horns

servo clockwise for "right"

all examples show top view

top horns

RADIO CONTROL GUIDE

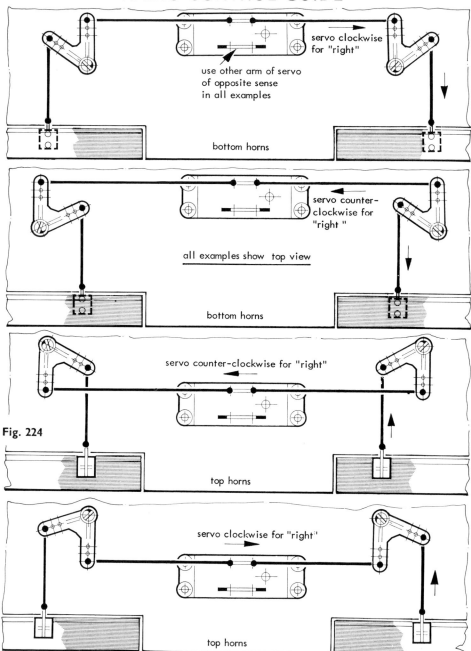

servo clockwise for "right"

use other arm of servo of opposite sense in all examples

bottom horns

servo counter-clockwise for "right "

all examples show top view

bottom horns

servo counter-clockwise for "right"

Fig. 224

top horns

servo clockwise for "right"

top horns

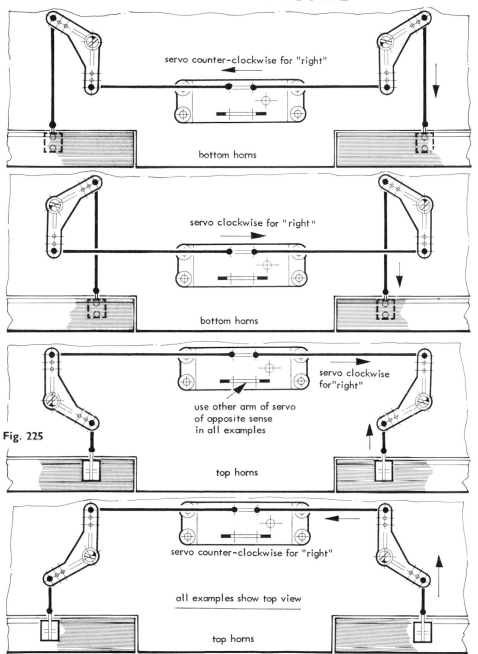

servo counter-clockwise for "right"

bottom horns

servo clockwise for "right"

bottom horns

servo clockwise for"right"

use other arm of servo
of opposite sense
in all examples

Fig. 225

top horns

servo counter-clockwise for "right"

all examples show top view

top horns

special horn as in Fig. 219) to raking the horns. The connecting holes should be aft of the hinge line if the horn is underneath, and forward of the hinge line if it is on top.

Should, however, a wing with a pushrod/bellcrank system, be under construction, then the differential can be obtained with either acute (60°), or obtuse (120°), angled cranks. Figs. 224 and 225 show the various combinations necessary to accommodate both the alternative servo senses, and whether the horn is on top or underneath the ailerons.

Other ideas

The inventive mind will by now have dreamed up several alternative methods of obtaining differential in a gimmicky way. For example, off-setting transmitter trims and then mechanically re-centring the control surface; introducing a stop to limit the travel of the transmitter control stick, interfering with the servo pot track and so on. The best advice is to have nothing to do with such schemes. If the advice in this chapter is followed and the required differential built into the model, then equipment may be interchanged without fear of affecting the trim, and this is how it should be.

CHAPTER 17

BOATS
AND CARS

Chez When, seen here, is a really attractive 36 in. near-scale yacht for those with a more leisurely approach to modelling.

THERE is no doubt at all that, no matter what protestations are made, the following comments are bound to appear condescending or derogatory, or both – if such be possible. Nonetheless, as was stated much earlier in this book, there can be no question but that the requirements for trouble-free operation and a long working life for an aircraft, are far more stringent and demanding than any other model. This is because an aircraft is 3-dimensional in its operation and hence, to a much greater degree than with boats and cars, is susceptible to crashing and consequent damage, should there be any shortcoming in the equipment, installation and linkages.

This is not, however, to say that a slapdash installation in a boat or car is acceptable. If satisfactory performance is expected then the installation, and the subsequent checks described in succeeding chapters, must be planned and executed with all the care prescribed as essential for an aircraft.

All of which said, there are requirements for boat and car operation which do not exist with an aircraft, the main additional concern being to protect the equipment from the depredations of water, or dust and grit. A boat does not have to be dunked to become water-logged. Spray has a habit of entering unforeseen places and the mess

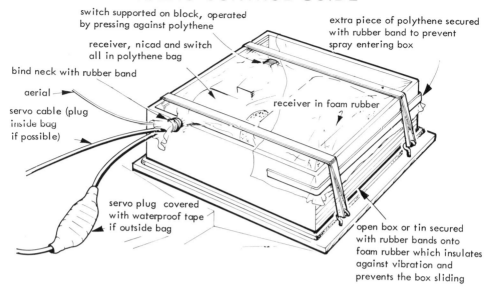

switch supported on block, operated
by pressing against polythene

extra piece of polythene secured
with rubber band to prevent
spray entering box

receiver, nicad and switch
all in polythene bag

bind neck with rubber band

aerial

servo cable (plug
inside bag
if possible)

receiver in foam rubber

servo plug covered
with waterproof tape
if outside bag

open box or tin secured
with rubber bands onto
foam rubber which insulates
against vibration and
prevents the box sliding

Fig. 226

resulting from a flywheel whirling round in a mixture of bilge water and oil, has to be seen to be believed! Even cars operated on an apparently clean, dry track, rapidly accumulate liberal quantities of oily dust, so it can be seen that environmental hazards are never to be underestimated.

Power boats

It was noted earlier that many manufacturers have available waterproof servos and obviously, for marine use, these should be selected. (Sometimes a "water-resistant" servo is advertised and while it is preferable to use such, in preference to a standard aircraft unit, unlike a fully "waterproof" one it must be mounted in a waterproof box — as will be detailed in a moment — for full protection.) With a fully waterproof servo, however, no additional protection will be needed, so it may be mounted in the most convenient position to allow simple control runs. It must be remembered that vibration in a boat is probably worse than an aircraft, so all the precautions to insulate against this, as described in Chapter 8, must be observed.

It is not, however, only the servos which are susceptible to damage from moisture, as any penetrating into the receiver, switch, plugs and sockets can also cause complete loss of control. Therefore, as there are no waterproof versions of these components available, they have to be insulated in a different manner.

The easiest way to do this is to place them, well protected with rubber packing, in a suitably sized plastic box. This can then be waterproofed with a "lid" of polythene, through which the wires will exit via a sealed hole — Fig. 226. With a flexible "lid" such as this, there is no need to make provision to operate the switch via a

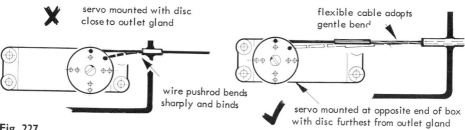

servo mounted with disc
close to outlet gland

flexible cable adopts
gentle bend

wire pushrod bends
sharply and binds

servo mounted at opposite end of box
with disc furthest from outlet gland

Fig. 227

pushrod as it may, of course, readily be turned on or off by gripping it through the polythene.

If waterproof servos are not available, then probably the most effective, and certainly a very widely used system, is to mount them, together with the other components, in a waterproof box, it being relatively easy to seal the small openings necessary to allow exiting for the pushrods, aerial, switch operating rod, and so on. Although it will often be found that airtight (and hence watertight!) plastic food

The Survey Vehicle is a most interesting amphibian scaled from a geological survey vehicle. It is equally at home on land or water. 21 in. long it requires three electric motors and four-function radio.

Designer's photo

containers, sold at multiple stores, may readily be adapted, most specialist shops sell a purpose made waterproof casing.

Without doubt linear servos are best for such an installation as, in a box of this type, space is often limited and the swing of a rotary output can cause problems. If, however, rotary output units are to be used, then they must be installed so as to give the maximum possible allowance for the swing – Fig. 227.

Again the importance of ensuring that there is proper insulation from vibration must be emphasised. Therefore, the servos must be properly mounted and the receiver and nicad protected with foam, in a similar manner to the aircraft installation shown

159

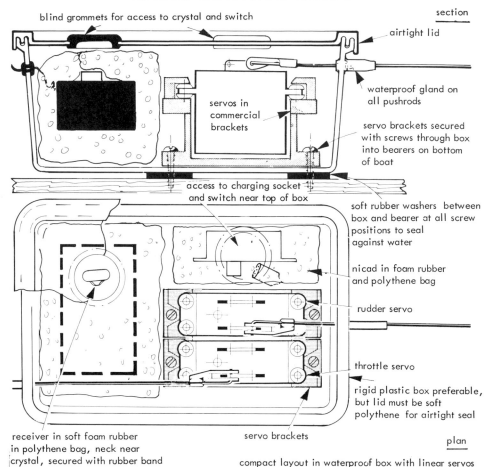

blind grommets for access to crystal and switch

section

airtight lid

servos in
commercial
brackets

waterproof gland on
all pushrods

servo brackets secured
with screws through box
into bearers on bottom
of boat

access to charging socket
and switch near top of box

soft rubber washers between
box and bearer at all screw
positions to seal
against water

nicad in foam rubber
and polythene bag

rudder servo

throttle servo

rigid plastic box preferable,
but lid must be soft
polythene for airtight seal

receiver in soft foam rubber
in polythene bag, neck near
crystal, secured with rubber band

servo brackets

plan

compact layout in waterproof box with linear servos

Fig. 228

in Chapter 8. Figure 228 shows a typical layout of components in a box, and it will be
noted that clip mountings are often preferred as offering a system simple to install,
with good vibration insulation qualities.

Having installed the equipment, the exit holes for the pushrods, control cables
and wiring, including the aerial, must be made watertight. An effective method of
sealing a pushrod is by passing it through a piece of brass tube in which it is an easy
sliding fit. This tube is then epoxied into the wall of the box. The seal is formed by a
piece of silicon rubber tube, which is just tight on the pushrod wire, but a really tight
fit on the brass tube. Tube and cable ends can be sealed in a similar manner. The
glands so formed must be tight enough to exclude water – a smear of Vaseline inside

the silicone tube may be a necessary added precaution – but not so tight as to restrict the free operation of the servos. In all cases the gland should be on the outside of the case.

Harness wires passing through the case should be glued with silicon rubber into a soft grommet, of sufficient size to allow the plugs or sockets to pass through the hole in the box. If the hole is accurately cut, so that the grommet is a really tight fit, it will be found that it will provide a waterproof seal without recourse to silicone compound at the grommet/box joint. A single wire, such as an aerial, should be glued with silicone into a thicker wire sleeving which is itself a tight fit in a small grommet. All of these joints are shown in Fig. 229.

A pack of Silica-Gel should be placed in the case to absorb the condensation which will almost inevitably be present, but this itself can soon become saturated, so the installation must be inspected regularly, opening the case as necessary, to give the works an "airing". Despite having complete faith in the waterproofing of the unit, the added precaution of spraying the plugs, switch and so on with one of the protective sprays available for the protection of car electrics, is a worthwhile added precaution.

Having mounted the equipment in its box, this must now be secured in the boat. Its actual position will be determined by the disposition of the motor, the required control runs and the need to achieve the correct balance. Once the position is determined, the box unit has to be mounted securely. With a box containing only the receiver, nicad and switch, it may be placed on a flat platform and secured with rubber bands, as was shown in Fig. 226, or similarly wedged in place. A box con-

Fig. 229

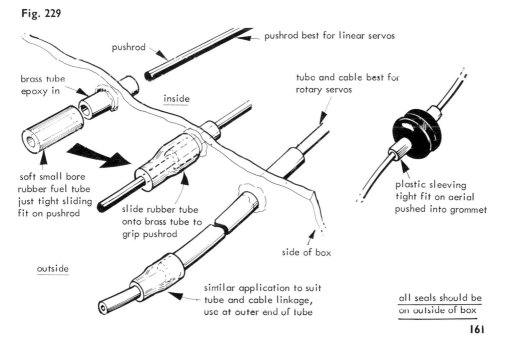

pushrod best for linear servos

pushrod

brass tube epoxy in

tube and cable best for rotary servos

inside

soft small bore rubber fuel tube just tight sliding fit on pushrod

slide rubber tube onto brass tube to grip pushrod

plastic sleeving tight fit on aerial pushed into grommet

side of box

outside

similar application to suit tube and cable linkage, use at outer end of tube

all seals should be on outside of box

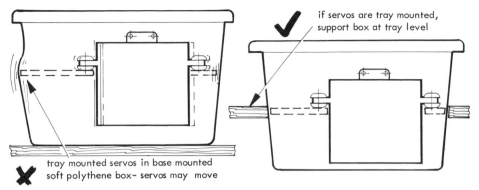

if servos are tray mounted, support box at tray level

tray mounted servos in base mounted
soft polythene box- servos may move

Fig. 230

taining servos must, however, be much more securely mounted, as vibration, plus the pull of the servos, will rapidly dislodge it with consequent loss of control.

Also, there is a danger that, if the box is mounted without consideration being given to the possible twisting motion imparted as the servos are operated, thin walled polythene will become distorted. Therefore, if the box is mounted on a flat platform, the servo mounting screws should pass through the base of the box and into the platform, the hole being sealed to ensure watertightness. This also is shown in Fig. 228.

If, however, the servos have not been clip mounted, but secured to an aircraft type tray, which is itself mounted to the walls of the box, this should not be screwed to a flat platform, as it may distort as shown in Fig. 230, which also shows the correct way to mount such an installation.

Linkages

It may not be convenient for the pushrod to pass direct from the box to the rudder or throttle and, indeed, it is often useful to have some sort of external bellcrank to permit simple operational adjustment, or to operate, say, a twin rudder set-up as in Fig. 231.

Fig. 231

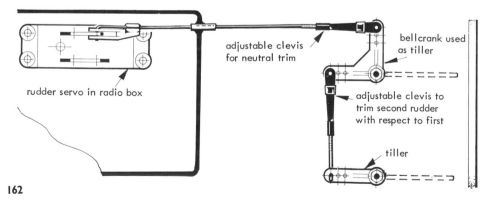

adjustable clevis
for neutral trim

bellcrank used
as tiller

rudder servo in radio box

adjustable clevis to
trim second rudder
with respect to first

tiller

RADIO CONTROL GUIDE

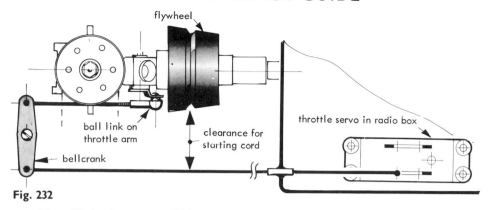

flywheel

ball link on
throttle arm

clearance for
starting cord

throttle servo in radio box

bellcrank

Fig. 232

More likely, however, will be the necessity to provide adequate clearance round the flywheel of the motor, to enable the starting cord to be inserted and operated without risking damage to the pushrod, and Fig. 232 shows a typical, simple, solution.

Yachts

Sailing craft are subjected to much the same conditions as power boats except for vibration and the ingress of oil, but there is an important "extra" – a sail winch. This will need a really firm mounting, particularly in larger craft where the effort necessary to haul in the sheets while under sailing conditions, could well be in excess of 10lb.

Waterproofing of the equipment may be carried out as just described, but the points where the sheets leave the deck need a gland which does not bind on the lines yet, at the same time, is waterproof to a fair extent. To this end a hard grommet, such as is used on fishing rods, is placed in the deck to take the wear and, if required, a small bore plastic tube is bonded to the inner face to provide further waterproofing.

Cars

With cars, the enemy is not water but dirt! This isn't going to affect the electronic parts too much, but it will play havoc with pot. tracks, electric motors (the things that drive servos!), switch contacts and so on. Therefore, although not as stringent as waterproofing, the requirements are not dissimilar. Space, however, is generally far more limited in a car, and it is usually impossible to make a "box" installation. Therefore, careful attention to sealing all the seams in the servo cases with a strip of adhesive tape will pay dividends. Also, if it is at all possible, each unit should be placed inside a polythene bag, which will not inhibit either mounting, or operation of the pushrod – Fig. 233 – but will certainly keep out the grit from the road surface. Once again the importance of watching out for condensation must be emphasised.

Pushrods and linkages

It is doubtful if ever any call will be made for a balsa pushrod in a boat or car, the plain wire, or tube and cable types, being far more suited to the short runs generally encountered. The actual method of connecting and supporting pushrods was dealt with earlier, also methods of coupling the brake and throttle together, switching

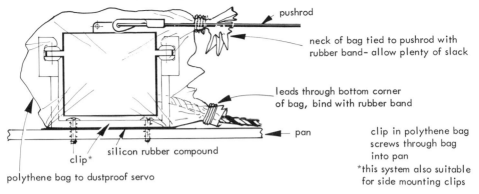

pushrod

neck of bag tied to pushrod with
rubber band- allow plenty of slack

leads through bottom corner
of bag, bind with rubber band

pan

clip in polythene bag
screws through bag
into pan

*this system also suitable
for side mounting clips

silicon rubber compound

clip*

polythene bag to dustproof servo

Fig. 233

electric motors and so on, were described, but a car steering linkage presents very special problems.

The jarring from an aircraft nosewheel is gentle, compared to the continual juddering that occurs at the front end of a model race car! If the steering mechanism were connected directly to the servo, it would subject the latter to stress far in excess of that for which it was designed. The imposed vibration would rapidly wear the gear train and pot. while a really hard knock on the front wheels could strip the gears. It is, therefore, important to isolate the servo with a shock absorbing linkage, and three are shown in Fig. 234.

Aerials

Apart from a yacht, where it can often be attached to the mast, the receiver aerial often proves an embarrassment in a power boat or car; therefore, the whip aerial is

Fig. 234

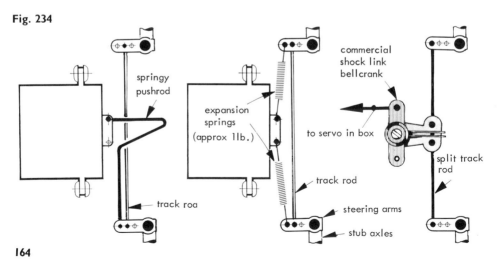

springy
pushrod

expansion
springs
(approx 1lb.)

commercial
shock link
bellcrank

to servo in box

split track
rod

track rod

track rod

steering arms

track roa

stub axles

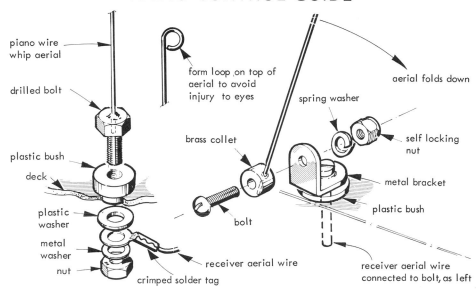

piano wire
whip aerial

form loop on top of
aerial to avoid
injury to eyes

aerial folds down

drilled bolt

spring washer

brass collet

self locking
nut

plastic bush

deck

metal bracket

plastic
washer

bolt

plastic bush

metal
washer

nut

receiver aerial wire

receiver aerial wire
connected to bolt, as left

crimped solder tag

Fig. 235

very popular. In fitting one of these, however, it is very important that the total length of the aerial is unchanged. For example, if a 24in. whip aerial is fitted, then 24 inches must be cut from the flexible aerial fitted to the receiver. It is often convenient for the whip aerial to be removable or to fold flat and Fig. 235 shows two popular installations.

*　　*　　*

This completes the installation information and the time has come to move on to the first pre-operational checks.

Actually the next chapter is entitled "Pre-flight Tests" but, having read the introduction to this chapter, it will be appreciated what is meant! It cannot be emphasised too strongly that all the relevant tests prescribed for an aircraft, are just as important to boat or car users if trouble-free operation is expected. Also, the subsequent advice about flying field etiquette, and especially transmitter control, is the only guarantee that a model upon which many hours have been lavished, will not be damaged through loss of control caused by interference, so *all* model operators should read – and take note!

CHAPTER 18

PRE-FLIGHT CHECKS AND FLYING FIELD ETIQUETTE

THE model is now complete and ready for the big day. Firstly, however, a final and comprehensive check over of every part must be made. One complete evening should be allocated to this procedure, so that there is ample time to rectify any small faults which show up. This way there is no question of having to take a chance on its being "all right on the day", because, as far as is humanly possible, it *will* be all right.

First the fuselage is placed on its "cradle" in the middle of the lounge carpet, so that there is completely free access to it from all angles. Then, starting with elevator (because it is usually the least complicated linkage and hence unlikely to give trouble), the pushrod is disconnected from the control surface to check that the latter is still "free". (This procedure may be thought redundant, because the check was made during the installation stage. It is, however, surprising how frequently surfaces "tighten up" subsequent to installation, so this check must not be missed). Next the pushrod is uncoupled from the servo, checked to see that it is not binding anywhere, then re-connected to the control horn; again a check is made that both are free, before they are re-connected to the servo. This check should be made to every control, including engine, and treating the rudder and nosewheel linkage separately.

*This historic Battle of Britain **Hurricane** is very popular. At 68 in. wingspan it is for .61 motors, four-function r/c and the more experienced pilot, under whose control it becomes a most realistic sight in the air.*

RADIO CONTROL GUIDE

*This Slingsby **Sedburgh T21** side-by-side trainer glider seen here with designer Mick Morritt, turns all heads at the slope. At 109 in. wingspan it is more than impressive and, being full-house plus spoilers, requires four function radio.*

It takes only a few minutes, unless any unsuspected tight spots have to be traced and relieved, and if this happens then it was well worthwhile!

Next the radio link is switched on and each control carefully checked by moving the transmitter control stick slowly over its entire travel, including trim, while listening carefully for any "hardening" of the noise from the servo, which indicates a tightness somewhere. If this happens, the pushrod should be disconnected from the servo to make sure the unit itself is not at fault, and then the movement of the pushrod checked again before re-connecting and tracing to find that, for example, it is the "swing" of a rotary output which is causing the trouble. An additional check with the throttle control, is to ensure that the pushrod will not vibrate against the engine, insulating it with a strip of plastic sleeving if this is thought likely. When the fuselage controls are completely checked as A–OK, the wing which, with its relatively more complex linkages, is more prone to cause trouble, should be put through the same procedure.

Now the model is assembled, with the wing fixed on securely as for flying, and placed on the carpet in take-off position ready for the final check. The servos usually make a totally different noise when the model is assembled; also, turning a nosewheel

RADIO CONTROL GUIDE

For the vintage enthusiast, the very practical construction and superb flying characteristics of this Bristol **D-Scout** *make it a firm favourite. At 51 in. wingspan it requires a .61 motor and four-function radio.*

Designer's photo

against the drag of an Axminster carpet, can cause protesting noises from the servo. If this happens the nosewheel should be lifted clear and the control tried again before the conclusion is reached that something has gone wrong!

First the "sense" of all the controls is checked – stick forward, throttle open; elevator stick back for up; rudder stick right, rudder and nosewheel right; aileron stick right, right aileron up as viewed from the rear. All the trims (except throttle, which is set-up as explained in Chapter 12) should now be placed at centre and the clevis on each control surface adjusted, until this also is at centre or neutral. This set-up will allow the maximum amount of trim movement in any direction, and this may be needed if the model is badly off trim*. With many designs an immediate visual reference that the control surfaces are at neutral is possible. For example, with inset ailerons, the trailing edge of the wing and aileron must line up but, with strip ailerons, one piece elevators and so on, although all sorts of elaborate jigging systems have been devised, experienced modellers always end up aligning them by "eye", and often the old adage "if it looks right it is right" has proved many a jig and graph to be wrong!

The question of "how much control movement?" is impossible to answer categorically. With power models, both aileron and elevator can initially be set to

---

*Although it has already been said and will be said again in the chapters on flying, it is relevant here to again emphasize that the trim control is only used to adjust the model in flight. When it is trimmed out "straight and level" the various amounts of trim deflection are transferred permanently to the control surface by adjusting the clevis, and the transmitter trim is returned to centre. For safe consistent flying it is essential that all trim levers (except throttle) are at centre, so that there is an immediate visual reference that they have not been accidentally moved.

move $\frac{3}{4}$ in., each way and then re-adjusted, if necessary, after flight trials. The amount of rudder movement on a full-house model is unimportant and is normally set for as much movement as possible, without introducing lost motion at centre because of poor mechanical advantage using the inner hole of the control horn. If, on the other hand, rudder is a primary control, then the arbitrary $\frac{3}{4}$ in. should prove satisfactory as a starter.

Many modellers think that a small amount of movement is "safer" initially, but this is not necessarily so, as sometimes quite drastic control deflections are necessary if there has been a serious error in pre-flight "guesstimation".

With gliders, however, all control movements are generally considerably greater than with power models and, as the shapes and areas of the control surfaces vary so much more, it is not possible to give figures in general terms – the book "Radio Control Soaring" should be consulted for detailed guidance.

When all the controls work freely, and in the correct sense, there is time available to indulge in the one vice which (apart from telly) more than any other, protracts the building of a model – standing back and admiring what's already done. Now, however, the model is complete, ready (apart from charging the batteries) to fly, so time, which previously would have been wasted in admiration, is put to good effect by "flying" the model round the room. Not only is the pleasure that all flights of fancy provide achieved but, of practical importance, familiarity with the model is being established, getting the edge off its newness, so that, when the time comes for the test flight, some of the worry associated with a completely new machine is already dispersed.

When the excitement of this has worn off, one final and vital check must be made – *is the correct frequency pennant displayed on the transmitter?* After this the batteries are put on charge, the tool box packed, and off to bed for the first time before midnight for weeks, ready to set off for the flying field at the crack of dawn!

CHAPTER 19

AT THE FLYING FIELD

THERE is a splendid section in the rules of golf which describes the etiquette of the game, and its sole purpose is to ensure that each participant's enjoyment is not marred by the bad (or thoughtless) manners or behaviour of others, and vice versa! There is no written code of etiquette for the flying field, the pattern of behaviour normally having evolved into an unwritten code among regular users. A newcomer to the hobby is, however, ignorant of this, so how can he be expected to conform? Well, by following this guide, it is not possible to go far wrong but, if in doubt, the wise modeller always asks himself how he would expect to be treated – and then does unto others . . . . .

Having said which, the first actions to be described are, unless carried out thoughtfully, a breach of etiquette! Very few modellers, however, have the facility to test and check a motor other than at the flying field so although, ideally, the following final checks should have been made at home, usually there is no choice in the matter, and this essential operation must be carried out with the minimum of inconvenience to other users.

The vibration from a motor can affect the operation of the equipment so, before ever the first flight is undertaken, all systems must be checked as "go" power-on, just as they were "go" power-off. Now, the worst breaches of etiquette, leading to the greatest number of ruffled feathers, concern engine running. Firstly, it is extremely difficult for anyone to enjoy his own flying if someone else is continually ground running an engine and, secondly, to monopolise a frequency for hours, while fiddling about with engine settings, is unlikely to make the culprit the most popular person on the field.

The answer is (1) for the flier to retire to the furthest corner of the field and (2) if a manual over-ride has not been fitted to the throttle linkage, this must be disconnected from the servo so that it may be operated by hand*. Obviously under these circumstances, the transmitter has become redundant so it must be deposited at the Tx control, or with another flier, so that there can be no accusations of "switching-on" and causing interference! (All this has assumed being at the local "free-for-all" area but,

---

*Ideally, during the preceding checks at home, the throttle linkage should have been marked to show the total throw, plus trim, when it was operated by the servo. This will then give the necessary reference for manual operation so that, when the servo is reconnected, the settings will be correct, but for final small adjustments.

of course, those who are privileged to use a "private" site, before doing anything, will have checked local requirements with the committee member in charge – right?)

However, to complete the pre-flight checks . . . The model is assembled in flying trim, exactly as when the indoor checks were completed, the engine started and adjusted to proper consistent running at all stages of throttle opening. This may well take some little time but is certainly not an exercise to be skimped, and if there is any difficulty in obtaining satisfactory running, or interpreting the instructions, then help should be sought at this point – not when the engine starts playing-up in the air! When the operation is 100%, the model is cleaned of all the exhaust spume and returned to where the transmitter was parked.

Now every flying site – public or private – should, for the protection of all, have some form of transmitter control. It is vital that everyone using the site is familiar with this and, if they are in doubt, they must ask. *Nothing must ever be assumed* on the score of transmitter control – the future of the model which has taken so long to prepare is at stake!

So, conforming with the local system, the receiver and transmitter are switched on and the motor started. The motor must not be started before switching on – there have been more stitches necessary through reaching through the prop to switch-on, than for any other reason! With the engine running, a check is made that the throttle response and settings remain as they were with the manual setting-up and, if not, adjusted accordingly.

The motor is opened up to full bore and an eagle-like watch made of each control surface in turn for at least 10-15 seconds, to see if there is the slightest sign of twitching. (It is easy to be misled at first by the inevitable "flutter" caused by the vibration from the motor and the action of the propeller slipstream, but this is readily distinguishable from a genuine "glitch" should this occur.) If everything is A–OK, each control is moved in turn, slowly and deliberately, through its extremes of travel, watched all the time for the least sign of an unsignalled movement and, if one is spotted, it will be necessary for a searching investigation to be made, as detailed in Chapter 21 – "Fault Finding".

Such is, however, seldom the case and usually no problems show up, so the model is ready for the very first flight, advice about which will be found in Chapters 23 and 24.

Naturally, there are many rules governing flying field behaviour, other than consideration when setting-up a motor. Obviously many of these are of purely local significance, but there are some general and vital requirements, which must be understood.

Firstly, and most important of all, is frequency control. As has been said, the local methods of ensuring this vary, but there are requirements common to all, and the most important of these is identification. It is vital not only that a frequency pennant is displayed, but that it is the *correct one!* Don't laugh! This is one of the most common causes of interference, especially where outfits with interchangeable frequencies are in use. It is so easy for the frequency to be changed and not the pennant. It is even easier for both to be switched and this not to be noticed by other fliers, to say nothing of the poor souls who are colour blind! If a pilot has been flying on a certain colour and decided to change for any reason, this must not be done quietly in a corner – but everyone must be told – loud and long! If not, Fred, who has been flying happily all morning, is quite likely to assume it is still safe to do so, not realising that someone else has changed to *his* frequency. At least one wrecked model will result. Guess whose it could be?

Other aspects of safety, behaviour and etiquette, such as fliers landing having precedence over fliers taking-off, not flying near other pilots – (not only will it annoy them, but their transmitter being nearer the offending model than its own Tx., could cause a crash) – not flying over spectators, not approaching to land over the model park, and so on, are really matters of commonsense and, as such, form the basis of the local code. So, every flier must find out about it, adhere to it and, if in doubt, remember that the best advice of all is to . . . do unto others . . .

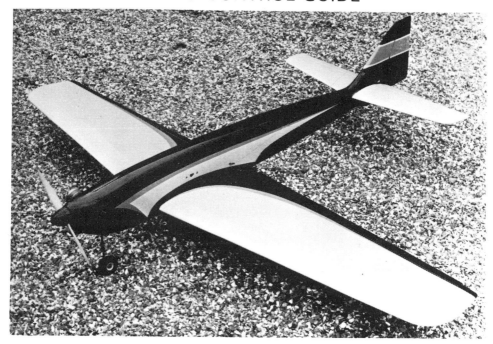

Two totally different types of model . . . above is **Déjà Vu III**, an aerobatic pattern model for the serious enthusiast, with optional retract u/c and requiring a .61 and four- or five-function radio, while below is **Roulet II**, an attractive 54 in. span parasol for .19 to .40 motors and two or three function r/c, which is an ideal intermediate trainer.

CHAPTER 20
ROUTINE MAINTENANCE

THE life expectancy of a model and the reliability of its equipment, are both proportionate to the proper and regular maintenance bestowed on them. Broadly, care and maintenance may be divided into four categories:–
1. Pre-flight
2. Between flight
3. End of session
4. After every 30-50 flights or 4-5 weeks
5. Laying up.

Pre-flight
This may be divided broadly into three parts, the first taking place before leaving home for the flying field. The equipment is switched on and a quick check made that the controls are working. The batteries will, of course, be fully charged (this will be dealt with later) and, if they have just been taken off charge, it may be found that the control surface neutrals have "moved" slightly. This is quite common with many makes of outfit and, once the initial surge of power is dissipated (normally after 2-3 minutes switched on), the servos will return to their normal centre. If the trim settings are changed to adjust for this "drift", they will almost certainly need to be "adjusted back" in the air during the first flight.

(Incidentally, the servo centring of some sets will, again, start to drift as the batteries become almost flat so if, after several flights, in-flight trim adjustment becomes necessary to maintain the proper trim of the model, the hint should be taken and terra firma headed for, voluntarily!)

Assuming all to be well after this first check, the model and all the equipment is packed in the car and a check made that nothing – usually transmitter, fuel or starter battery – has been left behind!

At the field, a check is made on what form the transmitter control takes and, if there is a pound, it is placed there immediately. It is important at this point, (especially with an outfit with interchangeable crystals), that a final check is made to ensure the equipment carries the correct frequency identification. (A table detailing the recognised frequencies appears elsewhere.) A strongly coloured flag, or wide strip of ribbon, are widely used methods for identification.

The model is now assembled and, conforming with the Tx control, switched on and a check made that all the controls are working smoothly without binding. After this, as the time to fly approaches, the model should be fueled up, so that the motor may be started without further delay.

With the engine running, a final check – just a brief flick is all that is necessary –

is made of each control. No prolonged fiddling should be necessary because, if something is not functioning, the motor must be stopped and the model taken back to the pit area for investigation. If ever anyone is seen indulging in interminable pre-flight fiddling, experienced fliers will be found hiding in their cars until the model is safely (or otherwise) landed again.

Between flights

After the model has landed and been taxied back to the pit area (well that's what the experts do!) the motor is stopped and first the receiver, and then the transmitter, are switched off. Never must the Tx be switched off first, because the receiver, not now being controlled by its own Tx, can sometimes respond to one on another frequency, and if this operates the throttle control the model will run amok and could cause injury.

Now all the soggy fuel must be wiped from the model (glider fliers ignore!) and a check made that the wing or tail has not been knocked out of true during the landing. The next check is that all the controls are OK, and this is done by gently trying each control surface for slack movement. If there is any excessive play, or one is not centred, investigation and correction will be required. If it is necessary to switch on the transmitter for an adjustment to be made, obviously it is vital that the Tx control system is conformed to.

Now is the time for the model to be fuelled up ready for the next flight, and this should be done before the transmitter is collected from the pound, so that everyone gets the maximum air time.

End of Session

This is like the end-of-flight check only more so. A good practice is for the model to be given a fairly perfunctory rub down at the field, followed at home by . . .

1. A thorough clean with spray-on detergent, especial care being taken that none is sprayed on the equipment. While the model is being wiped down a thorough examination is made of the airframe to make sure no stress cracks, or other damage, which could allow oil to enter are present and, if any are discovered, they should be rectified forthwith.

2. A check is made of the servo mountings and all clevises to see that they are as they were before flying started; also that the electrical wiring is secure and the packing round the receiver properly in place.

3. Engine mounting bolts checked for tightness; also the silencer.

4. The batteries are placed on charge.

5. The model is stored carefully in a suitable place, and so that it will not rest on any of the control surfaces. If there is any danger of this (a danger that applies equally when transporting the model) then the clevises should be disconnected so that the surface is free. Many makes of metal clevis have a lock-nut so that the setting is not lost.

After 4-5 weeks or 30-50 flights

The foregoing procedures are again carried out but, during No. 2 the various foam

Mongrel, as the name implies, is an interesting amalgam of several light aircraft, which combine to make a most attractive semi-scale model. It is 60 in. wingspan and designed for .40 motors and four-function radio.

packings are removed and the wiring examined very carefully, especially at the switch, plug and sockets, grommets and so on.

Now also is the time for the wing/fuselage junction sealing tape to be replaced if it has become oilsoaked, and a check made of the tank connections to ensure there are no leaks anywhere. The latter is a simple test to make – the needle is closed, one vent sealed with a finger tip and the other sucked through, sealing it with the tongue. If the vacuum is maintained there are no leaks!

Laying up

If the model is to be out of commission for some time, it is a good idea for the equipment to be removed for proper storing. Condensation is one of the biggest potential hazards and this can affect the equipment in a very short time, which is why it is recommended that, even from weekend to weekend the model must be stored in a suitable place. What then is a "suitable place?" Ideally it is a centrally heated room, but it is unlikely for this to be allowed, (even if it is available), so the average modeller must settle for a room which stays at a reasonably constant temperature, but certainly not in one heated by an oil stove.

It will probably have been noticed that condensation often forms on servo and receiver cases after taking the model into the workshop from a cold flying field, and this must always be dried off. Receivers wrapped in plastic bags are especially prone and if, for any reason, this procedure is followed, then a bag of Silica-gel should be placed with the receiver and dried out near an open fire, or replaced regularly.

It requires little imagination to foresee the effect of condensation going un-noticed when the model is stored, so unless it is possible for the model to be kept in a reasonably constant temperature, the gear should be removed and stored separately in the original makers' carton, especially if this is a polystyrene one, which is ideal.

When the equipment is removed from the model, each item must be checked thoroughly, the plugs and sockets being untaped and examined for chafing, loose connections, and so on, these being made good as necessary. If possible wear elsewhere is suspected (for example, one servo might be making more mechanical noise than the others) then the manufacturer should be contacted. While it certainly should not be necessary, indeed unwise, to strip each component, it is a good idea for the lid of the receiver to be removed, because oil can enter this via the aerial (capillary attraction) and soak the components. Finally, before everything is packed away, the batteries must be fully charged.

After checking and storing the equipment, the same should be done for the engine, tank and airframe. It should not be necessary for the motor to be removed, provided it is accessible enough to be washed in petrol and then receive a good squirt of thin machine oil in the exhaust stack, turning it over several times to ensure that this circulates. The tank should be filled about quarter full with neat methanol, shaken well and drained through the feed line to the needle valve. This will remove all the residual oil, which otherwise would clog everything before next season.

The airframe must be thoroughly cleaned to remove all the oil which, it will be found, defies even washing in detergent. If the model is capable of withstanding a "dunking", then the application of Gunk or Swarfega, followed by a thorough washing, can work wonders. If the covering is one of the commercially available polyester films, a rag soaked in cellulose thinners or neat methanol and rubbed over the model has an amazing effect. With a paint finish, however, unless there is absolute certainty about the fuel-proofing, White Spirit should be used – less effective but less amazing!

With the equipment out of the fuselage, it is easy for a check to be made that the fuel has not been seeping in unnoticed. If it has, then the ingress point must be found and sealed. Also, the soaked area should be cleaned as well as possible with methanol.

Finally the model must be stored safely. Something like 90% of all minor damage is caused when a model is being carried into or out of the house or car, or because something falls on it in the corner of the workshop, so precautions taken in storing safely are never wasted.

Charging the Batteries

There seems to be more mystique and more rubbish talked about this aspect of r/c operation than any other! Nevertheless it still remains the simplest "maintenance" of all to carry out.

Basically, all nickel-cadmium batteries are designated by their 10 hour discharge cycle, a 225 will discharge at 22.5 mA for 10 hours, a 500 will discharge at 50 mA for 10 hours and so on. Although, however, it takes 10 hours to discharge, to fully recharge the batteries they must be connected to the charger for 14 hours, at 22.5 mA, or 50 mA according to their rating. A lot of people try to calculate the amount of discharge the batteries have received and then calculate the required charge accordingly. This is totally unnecessary and a waste of effort.

It is difficult to think of any manufacturer who does not either supply or have available a charger for his equipment. All of these are designed so that, even if the battery is inadvertently left on charge for two, or even three times the stipulated charging time, no harm will occur. Of course, if it is left on for weeks . . .

The following system of charging is simple, practical, and has ensured trouble-free service from nicads over many years.

1. They are initially charged as the manufacturer instructs.

2. Immediately after use they are given an overnight charge, either with the manu-facturer's pre-set charger, or at the recommended rate – for example, 50 mA for 500 type. Under no circumstances is the normal charge rate exceeded.

3. If the radio is not used for more than seven days after this, a top-up charge is given overnight before flying, at about one-third of the normal rate (i.e. 15 mA for 500, and so on). With a non-adjustable charger, the *charging time* must be adjusted appropriately.

4. If the outfit is not used for 4-6 weeks an overnight charge is given at full rate.

Overnight charges tend to vary from 8-12 hours depending on circumstances, but this is not important provided the model is never flown beyond three-quarters of the known discharge time for the equipment in use. For those folk who use the batteries to their maximum, however, (mostly this seems to be the soaring fraternity) it is essential that the full re-charge time be allowed.

Some authorities state that it is necessary to "cycle" the batteries. That is, fully discharge and then recharge them. If the manufacturer recommends this it is wise for it to be done, and it will be found that many model shops stock a special unit to carry out this operation properly.

Certain types of equipment take an unequal drain from a centre-tapped battery pack. Thus, one part of the pack may be subject to, say, 50 mA discharge and the other part to 100 mA. Obviously this will result in half of the pack being discharged, while a partial charge remains in the other half. It is not necessary to worry about this at all, however, unless the manufacturer has given specific instructions on the point, in which case, again they must be followed.

A good question at this juncture is "how long is it safe to fly?" Obviously this is impossible to answer in general terms and without knowing the current drain of the particular outfit except, once again, to advise following the manufacturers' instructions. Often these state that a full charge will allow "x" flights. Unfortunately, the duration of each flight is often unspecified. It is, however, reasonable to assume that all modern sets will give a "full day's" flying, generalising that a "flight", including ground testing and so on, is 10 minutes and most weekend modellers consider 8-10 flights a "day's flying". If this does not seem adequate (and slope soarers do tend to stretch a flight to an hour or so!) the wise man will invest in a spare set of nicads and arrange the model and harness so that these may be plugged-in easily. To be safe, however, both the transmitter and the receiver batteries must be replaced at the same time.

Even though all manufacturers have a proper charger for their equipment, some being built into the transmitter and some separate units, it is a sound idea for modellers to invest in one of the adjustable dual-purpose units on the market. This enables the trickle (or one-third rate) type charge described earlier, to be given while simultaneously recharging the glo-plug accumulator. There has been some confusion about the description of these units as "dual chargers", but this means that a nicad and an accumulator may be charged simultaneously. It is not, generally, possible to charge more than one nicad at a time except with the more sophisticated units. These metered chargers are designed for all types of nicad, as they normally have a simple control potentiometer which is adjusted until the meter reads correctly (e.g. 22.5 for a 225 pack) for the charge required.

Finally a word of caution – it is vital that it is ensured that the batteries are actually on charge! Normally, equipment with a built-in charger, indicates charging is taking place via the RF meter or a lamp in circuit, similarly with all but the cheapest commercial units. Having, however, checked that charging is taking place, it is important that no outside agency will then switch off the mains! The classic example of this is the character, whose gear was continually back at the manufacturer's because he always crashed on his second or third flight. His trouble was finally diagnosed by the manufacturer, who insisted the gear was not being fully charged, and it transpired he was charging it at work and did not realise the main power was switched off after he left at night, but was switched on again before he arrived in the morning! Similarly, it is not unknown for people to put the model on charge in the garden shed workshop, then come indoors and switch the power off! To say nothing of the character who put the equipment on charge via a mains plug where the fuse was blown, a fault which would have been discovered immediately by checking the meter.

CHAPTER 21

FAULT FINDING

AN intermittent twitch in the air could be anything! If, however, this is experienced, the first priority is for the model to be landed; not flown around to see if it will happen again – landed! With the model safely on the ground, the following checks, which are roughly in order of the frequency of the fault, should be carried out.
1. The battery voltage checked.
2. An inspection made to see if there are any loose connections.
3. A check made that the foam rubber is properly in place round the receiver.
4. The servo mountings checked to see if they are too tight or too loose.
5. An inspection made to see if there are any possible metal-to-metal joints that are causing electrical noise.

The cure to all these is pretty obvious, but to check them a certain amount of trouble is involved, so the temptation is for another flight to be chanced. As has been said earlier, however, temptation exists to be resisted so . . . to check the faults in order.

1. It is unlikely that a voltmeter will be available to check the batteries under load so, assuming that when flying started they were fully charged and that enough flights have not been made to reach the limits of charge, then the airborne battery is checked by trying the servos for two or three minutes (this allows for the battery reviving after being switched off). If they are faster one way than the other, or slower than usual in each direction, there is no need to look further. The wise flier will pack up and go home, charge the batteries properly and, if there is still doubt, consult the manufacturer.

The transmitter batteries are more difficult to check. It is possible that the meter will give an indication by reading low, in which case there is the answer but, if not, the only other course is a range check. This is why one should always be carried out, using the manufacturers' recommendation, before flying with new gear, to establish the parameter for future reference. If range is now decreased, the same advice applies as for the airborne unit. If, however, no fault is apparent then a check must be made on . . .

2. This is pretty self evident, but can involve checking every joint. Most likely are a loose aerial on the transmitter, a receiver aerial broken inside its sleeving by being pulled too tight, a faulty plug/socket connection, or intermittent switch connection. Each should be checked with the equipment switched on, but it is not enough that the fault is located, before further flying can take place it must be rectified.

3. It is wise that this should be re-packed, even if it does look O.K.

4. As was explained in Chapter 8, by placing a finger firmly on a servo, it should be

RADIO CONTROL GUIDE

possible to rock it so that it can just be seen to move on its grommets. Excessive pressure needed to do this indicates a tight mounting and hence continual transmission of vibration, causing an intermittent fault. Too loose a mounting can have the same effect, as the servo can move about and come into contact with the framework of the model, or an adjacent servo.

5. Unless there is a long run of wire, such as is normally only found with the throttle linkage, metal-to-metal noise is unlikely to upset any modern equipment. However, a throttle link often runs alongside the receiver, so it should be bonded, especially where it joins the throttle arm. In Chapter 12 methods of bonding against metal-to-metal noise were explained.

If it is believed that the fault has been detected as either 3, 4 or 5, and rectified appropriately, or it is not possible to find a fault at all, it is unwise for the take-off area to be headed for forthwith. Instead, a couple of willing helpers should be recruited for a further check. After the engine is started, the two helpers should lift the model clear of the ground, by holding it each by one wing tip. This is as near to actual flying as it is possible to get, and several minutes "flight" should be made using all the controls and with the engine at various speeds. If, despite maintaining an eagle watch for a repeat of the trouble, everything seems O.K. then it may as well be assumed that the fault is cured or that it *was* interference. Now is the time for the model to be given another flight. After all, it has got to be flown again some time and it is easy to run out of willing helpers if this last procedure is persisted in! Of course, if there is a repeat of the uncommanded signal while testing, the only thing is for the model to be packed up and the manufacturer consulted.

A different type of fault, which shows up with some regularity, is where for example, up-elevator is signalled (naturally it happens more often with down!) and the servo does not immediately neutralise on the release of the signal. This is almost invariably a fault in the servo. If there is no doubt the model did not follow the command (i.e. it was not a gust of wind which appeared to cause the model to continue to climb) then, if the equipment is not fitted with plugs and sockets, even if it now appears to be perfect, it must be returned to the manufacturer. If, however, the servos are fitted with plugs so that they can be interchanged, an attempt should be made to duplicate the fault by following the test procedure described earlier – if there are still volunteers about! If there is a repetition, then the servo should be interchanged with one from a less important function. For example, if the trouble is on elevator, then this servo should be interchanged with the engine one. Another "ground flight" must be tried and, if the elevator now functions satisfactorily, indicating that the fault was in the servo and not the receiver or harness, it is at least possible to carry on flying for the rest of the day with "hesitant" throttle, but the faulty unit must be repaired before the next session.

Let it be assumed that, instead of being hesitant in centring, the servo did not centre at all. If the aircraft is landed safely, the servo should be tried in a different output, for example, rudder and elevator should be interchanged. If the elevator servo still does not work in the rudder function, then the fault is in the servo. If the elevator servo now works and the rudder one sticks, the fault is in the receiver, or harness, plug and socket.

RADIO CONTROL GUIDE

*Extremely practical and attractive, this 61 in. wingspan Messerschmitt **Me. 109e** requires a .61 motor and four function radio. It makes a perfect 'opponent' for the **Hurricane** and **Spitfire**.*

In order to complete a day's flying it is possible, if the fault is in the servo, to exchange this unit with the throttle one, but the faulty unit must not be plugged into the throttle output, as it might well draw excessive current and could cause the model to run out of electrics in the air.

So far the assumption is that any twitches, glitches and crashes are as a result of the equipment malfunctioning, but this is not necessarily so. Any manufacturer will tell of the many times he has painstakingly reconstructed a wrecked outfit, and discovered no fault at all except crash damage. Obviously something caused the model to crash but what? Interference is the most likely claim and, indeed, there are many cases of this. By far, however, the more common cause of unexplained crashes is mechanical failure in the aircraft — broken pushrods, severed clevis pins, pushrods binding together, clevises coming undone, servos coming loose and so on — or, even more common, failure of the operator!

But, for all the exceptions that are interference, how can this be detected and what can be done when it is experienced? Regrettably, if interference occurs during a flight, unless it is just a twitch or two, there is nothing that can be done except pick up the bits. There are, however, many excellent and relatively inexpensive monitors on the market, so the wise man or club will have invested in one before ever attempting to fly. A super-regen monitor is useless except to indicate either that the air is clear, or that there is interference somewhere on the band (badly designed super-regen monitors have themselves been known to generate enough radiation to cause interference), so, to be effective, a superhet monitor is required. From this it is possible, for example, to learn that, although it is quite safe to fly on four or five of the spots, the other one or two may have interference on them. This is often the case in specific areas and, if it is noticed that all the local fliers are on red, blue, green and yellow,

RADIO CONTROL GUIDE

enquiries should be made as to why this is, before flying on brown or orange to have a "clear" frequency!

Quite often the monitor will pick up apparent interference on one spot, yet people have (usually in ignorance) been flying quite safely on this frequency, even when the interference was there. Obviously the interference was not of a nature to affect the model receiver but as to how, apart from "sucking and seeing" this can be determined . . . One suggestion is to conduct a long distance range check or one with the aerial retracted, to see if the receiver responds to interference when the transmitter signal is relatively weak. This, however, can only be done effectively when there are no other transmitters (even if they are on a different frequency) switched on, because a receiver can respond to a transmitter on a different frequency when the signal is markedly stronger than that from its own transmitter. The converse is interference which is not picked up by the monitor, which is at ground level, but which gets to the model when it is 200 to 300 ft. up. Here, with luck, the model will fly out of the interference, and again respond to its own transmitter as it gets near the ground.

By far the most common interference, however, is from nearby commercial units, which can be so powerful that they just swamp the model band entirely. Modellers are privileged to share the medical, scientific and industrial band and are way down the list of priority users of it but, if there is such a problem from a permanent station, perhaps a hospital or factory, it is often possible to determine the transmission times, and arrange flying accordingly. Also, if there is reason to suspect that the transmission is too powerful, of too wide a band spread, or on an unauthorised frequency, the local officer of the Ministry of Posts and Telecommunications should prove helpful.

What, though, of mobiles? Police, ambulances, fire engines, army trucks, etc. have all proved to be sources of interference, either on 27 MHz, or at close range and at such power as to interfere with model control. In general, there is nothing that can be done about these, except to wait until they move on.

Before dissolving in a welter of gloomy tears, however, let the balance be redressed by stating that very, very, few modellers (touch wood – quick!) have ever crashed a model through extraneous interference*. Twitches, or glitches yes, but a complete blockout – never – well hardly ever! And this must surely be the general experience, otherwise no one could ever learn to fly!

*The term "extraneous" interference is used here, because there is also the "interference" when one flier is "shot down" by another, inadvertently operating simultaneously on the same frequency – probably the cause of more crashes than any other form of radio interference. All responsible fliers, even on "public sites" set up some sort of system to avoid such frequency clashes, which is why it is so vital to follow the earlier advice on finding out what system is in use – and abiding by it.

CHAPTER 22

WHEN REPAIR IS NECESSARY

A^T some stage or another equipment will have to be returned to the manufacturer, and it is important not only that he is told in detail, (but concisely,) exactly why it has been returned but also, if it is a crash repair, how the crash happened.

Packing

The original display box in which the outfit was packed should always be retained, because what better means can there be for storing or returning it to the manufacturer? (Also, it looks impressive if the outfit is put up for sale secondhand and it is still in its original wrapping!) If it is at all possible, the set should be returned personally or delivered by a friend. But, if it is necessary to use the post, then the wise man is doubly careful with the packing and also makes sure the parcel is fully insured.

It might be thought unnecessary to pack the equipment carefully if the set is being returned personally. Not so; it is always wise to do this, having first made sure that the various parts are clean and free from old pieces of servo tape and so on, and the batteries are fully charged. If the manufacturer has to waste time cleaning up equipment, charging batteries, or removing it from a model, guess whose bill the extra charge goes on. (Yes, some people even take the model along, so that the manufacturer can see for himself how his product has been abused. It is never the good models that get taken to a factory – they might get damaged!) Also, if equipment is returned in an obviously uncared-for condition, the manufacturer is unlikely to give much credence to claims that the installation, maintenance and pre-flight checks were impeccable, so that the fault must lie with his equipment.

What to say

The manufacturer's only interest is in the truth and the facts. An elaborate exercise in face-saving will only result in wasted time and a bigger bill. If it is known why the model crashed he must be told, even if it does not seem to put the flier in a good light because, once equipment is examined, the manufacturer can normally deduce what happened and, while he may not call his customer a liar, it is not nice to know he knows!

Therefore, accurate details should be supplied as follows:

1. Name and address.

.2. Details of exactly what has been returned, e.g. Transmitter No. .... Receiver

No. .... 4-Super Z servos, battery pack, etc. (Normally a complete outfit should be returned unless it is a simple routine job such as changing the sense of a servo.)

3. Date, time and place of crash.

4. How much use the equipment had had since its last charge.

5. If there had been any intimation of trouble – glitches, etc. – prior to the crash.

6. What actually happened.

7. What (if any) other frequencies were in use at the time.

8. What was the probable cause of the crash.

9. Any other helpful comments.

So far the worst was assumed in that the repairs were necessitated by a crash, because this is the sort of repair which gets all the publicity. In fact, by far the majority of sets returned to the factory are purely routine servicing jobs.

It is a wise precaution to have an outfit checked over periodically but the problem is to know when. Normally the first sign that a set needs servicing is when it ceases to work, and then it is too late. Many modellers like to have their outfits looked at after every 10-15 hours use, but this depends on circumstances. In general terms the radio link itself needs no attention; it is the mechanical parts – potentiometers; motors, gears, etc. – which wear, and this varies with the type of model and the quality of the installation. For example, in a glider, wear caused by vibration is non-existent; in a big trainer of sufficient mass to absorb the vibration, wear attributable to this is low but, in a pylon racer, the gear gets far more of a pounding and, perhaps, warrants a check over every 5-10 hours.

Regardless of this, however, if an unsignalled control is detected, or any sluggishness is suspected, for example, in a servo, the outfit should be looked at. It is better to pay for possibly unnecessary regular checks, than to have the expense and work of building a new model.

Which leads to one final point, aimed at the modellers – every club has one – who complain of the cost of servicing. Enquiries would tend to show that an average manufacturer's charge is less per hour than a local garage, despite having to employ highly skilled staff experienced in electronics. Money may be saved, initially by "self-servicing" but the end product will be far greater expense on repair bills in the long run. After all the man who made the equipment must be the best qualified to look after it!

CHAPTER 23

THE BASICS OF TRIMMING

WITHOUT doubt there is one thing this book cannot do with the degree of authority and detail that has characterised other chapters (if the advice they contain is followed, it will be almost impossible to go wrong), and that is to explain how to fly a model.

The reason for this is simple – each model is different. Even if it is built to the same design, subtle variations of material weight, constructional accuracy, and so on will result in a model which is as similar as two human beings. It may have two arms, two legs, one head – well wing, tail and fuselage – but there the similarity ceases. Therefore, the only way in which it is possible to be taught how to fly a particular model, is for the teacher to have handled it personally, and also to have been able to assess the ability of the pilot.

There are, however, certain basic rules and advice which are applicable to all models and which, if properly assimilated, come as near as is possible to "telling how to fly". In the next chapter Mr. Bowyer-Lowe has set these out in a concise, simple-to-follow manner and, if the advice is followed, then, with the services of an instructor available, success can virtually be guaranteed.

"Going it alone" is a rather different matter, however, because with the type of model which is categorised as a typical r/c trainer, there is an interesting paradox, in that it is only suitable for learning to fly with when it has itself been trimmed to fly, and it is certainly impossible for anyone to trim a model who does not know how to fly!

Of course, with an instructor to hand, this poses no problems in that he will trim the model. What, though, of the go-it-aloner? The answer, as was outlined in Chapter 7, is to start off with a model which will virtually fly itself, and which can be trimmed to do so without using the radio at all. In other words almost a "steered" free-flight model, and the ideal is a powered glider.

With such a model, initially the pilot is only "interrupting" its natural flight path with radio signals, so that if a real boo-boo is made it is only necessary to "let go", for the model to right itself. It really is surprising just how quickly it is possible to progress from interrupting the flight path to controlling the model.

A model of about 6ft. wingspan, weighing 2-3lb. and fitted with a power pod containing an engine of about 1.5cc., is the most docile trainer that could be found. Of course, such a model is restricted to fair weather operation but, at this stage, so is any instructional flying!

RADIO CONTROL GUIDE

model at gliding attitude

head clear of wing and tail

wings level

front view

WIND

Fig. 236

side view

Once a suitable design is selected and the construction completed as per the instructions, especial care being taken to ensure accuracy of alignment and balance, then it is a simple matter to trim it to fly "hands-off". Such a model will, in all probability, have rudder only or, at the most, rudder and elevator control, so once these are adjusted to be at neutral, all is ready to start trimming.

First the transmitter and receiver are switched on and a check made that, with the trims at neutral (centre), the control surfaces are also centred, then the receiver is switched off, followed by the transmitter. This sequence of "on" Tx, followed by Rx, and "off" Rx, followed by Tx, is important because, with some outfits, if the receiver is switched on before the transmitter, or off after it, this can cause the servos to "jump" a few degrees, which will give an entirely false neutral reading.

Facing exactly into wind and holding the model as shown in Fig. 236, the flier should run forward, accelerating gently, until the model is felt to start to lift. At this point it is released smoothly with a slight extra push – it must not be thrown nor decelerated – whereupon it should glide smoothly to earth in a straight line, at a gentle angle – Fig. 237. If it doesn't do this, there are three possibilities:

(1) It will have veered left or right;
(2) It will have dived more steeply towards the ground;
(3) It will have stalled.

Provided the variation from the desired flight path was not too vicious, a few more test glides should be made to make sure the deviations were not a result of the model –

a. being launched with the wings not level; b. being launched too slowly; c. being launched too fast.

Fig. 237

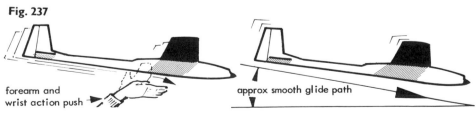

forearm and wrist action push

approx smooth glide path

188

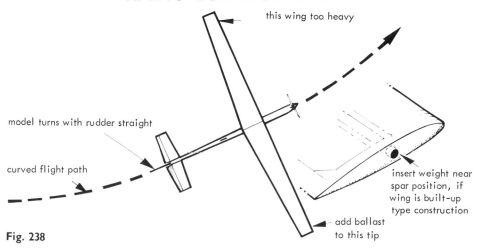

this wing too heavy

model turns with rudder straight

curved flight path

insert weight near
spar position, if
wing is built-up
type construction

add ballast
to this tip

Fig. 238

Assuming, however, that the deviation has persisted, then, if it is a turn as in (1), the rudder is adjusted in the appropriate direction. Between 1-3 turns of the quick link should be adequate but, if this does not effect a cure, it is possible that one wing is slightly heavier than the other and a little weight – a small nail should suffice – added to the opposite wing tip of the direction of turn – Fig. 238 – will correct the turn. If the trouble still persists, it must be assumed that the check for trueness of the flying surfaces was inadequate so a further look must be taken to see if the wing is warped.

If it is, it may be possible to straighten an open framework type as shown in Fig. 239. A foam wing, however, must never be treated thus! Here the only solution is to make up a small trim tab of celluloid and fix it to the wing so as to counteract the warp – Fig. 240.

If the model dives as in (2), then a small amount of up elevator – again 1-3 turns

Fig. 239   **Fig. 240**

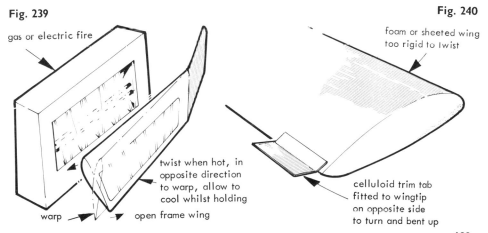

gas or electric fire

foam or sheeted wing
too rigid to twist

twist when hot, in
opposite direction
to warp, allow to
cool whilst holding

celluloid trim tab
fitted to wingtip
on opposite side
to turn and bent up

warp   open frame wing

189

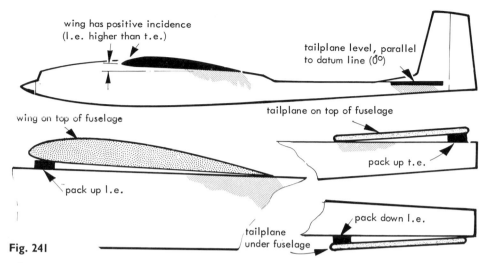

wing has positive incidence
(I.e. higher than t.e.)

tailplane level, parallel
to datum line (0°)

tailplane on top of fuselage

wing on top of fuselage

pack up t.e.

pack up I.e.

pack down I.e.

tailplane
under fuselage

Fig. 241

of a quick link – should suffice to correct the fault. If not, nose-heaviness must be suspected. If there is already ballast in the nose, a little of this should be removed but, if not, as a temporary measure, a little lead may be pinned to the tail. Such adjustments must not, however, under any circumstances move the c.g. aft of the recommended position. If they do, the ballast must be removed (or replaced) as it is probably the angles of incidence of the wing or tail which are incorrect. Fig. 241 shows these, and how adding a little packing $-\frac{1}{32}-\frac{1}{16}$in. should be more than enough – to the leading edge of the wing, or the trailing edge of the tailplane, whichever is the more convenient, should effect a cure.

Suppose, however, the model stalled (Fig. 242 shows that a stall is when the model rears its nose then dives to the ground) as in (3)? Once again a slight adjustment to the quick link, moving the elevator down, is the first step. Failing this, then the addition of weight to the nose should effect a cure. It should be remembered that, although the c.g. must never be moved aft of the stated position, no harm results from moving it slightly forward. Moreover, it is seldom advisable to adjust the angles of incidence to cure a stall – the simplest and safest way is always to add weight.

About half an hour's patience should see the model trimmed out to a straight consistent glide, and this is the stage at which it is tempting to switch on the radio and try some "control". At the altitude of a test glide however any signal from an

Fig. 242

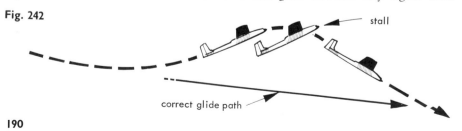

stall

correct glide path

inexperienced operator, whether to rudder or elevator, is liable to cause a "cartwheel" landing and this can cause a lot of damage! It is an established axiom that, when a model is approaching touchdown at a height of about 6ft., straight and level, then it should be left alone to continue on its way without interference! A model can usually land itself far better than the operator, except that he might add a little finesse, with just a touch of up elevator to flare the touchdown out at the last moment! Therefore, before it is possible to start "radio controlling", the engine has to be started (the next chapter gives advice on setting the engine and so on) and the model flown to a safe height.

By now, probably, and without conscious thought, the flier will have ceased to bother running until he could feel the model beginning to lift, and have become able, instead, to gauge the degree of "push" necessary for a successful hand launch, without moving more than a pace or two forward. Such a launch will be exactly suited to the first power release.

The model should fly smoothly from the hand and climb steadily away, the torque from the engine causing a gentle left turn. If this is so, then it must be let to continue on its way uninterrupted by a radio signal until a safe height is reached, whereupon it is possible to begin experimenting, and experience for the first time the thrill of *radio controlled* flying.

Of course, if during the initial climbaway it is obvious that something is wrong — too much turn, climbing too steeply (or not at all!) — then corrective signals must be sent at once. But, whatever happens, panic must be avoided. This model is docile, so a positive corrective signal which is held until the model is seen to respond, is necessary, then the pilot must also respond accordingly. If the initial hand launch trimming was carried out properly, there cannot be anything significantly wrong with the power-on trim, so the required corrective signals are sent until the model has reached a safe height, at which point the necessary control corrections are transferred to the trim levers, until the model is flying straight and level "hands-off".

When the time comes to land, it must be remembered that the model will, if set-up straight and level, land itself, so the aim is to let it do just that. Positioned at about 6-ft. altitude pointing into wind, with the wings level and the nose slightly down, if the control sticks are released it will do everything else itself! When the landing is complete the model is picked up, switched off — in the correct sequence — any trim adjustments transferred from the levers to the control surface, and all is ready for another flight.

Yes, it really is as simple as that, or at least that is how it will be remembered when, in a few weeks' time, it is wondered what all the anxiety was about!

Now the worry about the ability to fly is gone and busy plans are in hand for the next model, a final word of advice. Proficiency with a powered glider does not mean sufficient skill has been acquired to fly a scale *Spitfire*! What is needed next is a docile high or shoulder wing rudder/elevator trainer, preferably with motor control. This should be followed with a more advanced but similar type of model, then the first low winger, but a docile one, not a "hairy" aerobatic type, and then . . . ah then . . . the sky's the limit.

CHAPTER 24

ON LEARNING TO FLY

by Roger Bowyer-Lowe

AT last the first step has been taken and enough cash raised to buy a radio outfit and engine. With imagination fired with enthusiasm, that dream of a super scale *Spitfire, Lancaster* or other favourite subject seems reality, with such models being perfectly controlled. Thoughts of this nature are with everyone and there is no reason why these subjects should not be tackled when the necessary experience has been built up.

Here is the crunch; the operative words are "necessary experience" and, it is difficult to understand the problems involved and the risks attached to learning the art of radio control flying, until some experience has been gained. Of course, there are bound to be people who can claim to be the exceptions to the general rule, and who have successfully learnt to fly on a low wing type scale model with no trouble, but these cases are rare and the risk of serious damage to model and equipment is very high.

Possibly the biggest single factor influencing success in learning to fly, is the local club. It is strongly recommended that all would-be r/c'ers join their local club and gain the benefit of the wide experience and assistance which is normally offered, from within the membership. It *is* possible to learn to fly solo, but the long path can be littered with broken models, damaged equipment, frustration and possible eventual loss of interest.

For a raw beginner who attempts to build and fly a model without any assistance, the problems faced are many and various and the chances of successful first flights are very small. It makes no difference if it is possible to fly a full-sized aircraft, or reflexes are above average, so that it is thought possible to start at the top. Everybody starts with experience of model flying equal to a big fat ZERO and this fact must be accepted, or the optimist is soon brought down to earth with a bang!

The speed and ease at which it is possible to learn to fly depends mainly on three things:—

1. Ability
2. Instruction
3. Model

The first letters of these three requirements spell AIM and the Aim is to learn

193

to fly competently, with the minimum of effort expended on models and finance. Fig. 243 shows the basic steps to be taken.

There are two ways to progress up the ladder and these are shown as 1 and 2. The route chosen depends upon many things including ambition, modelling skill, financial position, local flying site, transport arrangements and whether it is intended to "go it alone" or to join a club. The diagram is, of course, a generalisation and it is perfectly possible to jump from one route to the other as interests develop.

The biggest problem is always the person who appears on the club scene with either a part-finished, or completely finished, model of a type totally unsuitable for a beginner to handle and, in many cases, incorrectly constructed. The best action is for the problems involved to be firmly explained and, if possible, for him to have a go on a trainer (possibly with "buddy box", for safety reasons) so that he can frighten himself with a few seconds trying to control its flight. This will leave a lasting impression, which should persuade him to build the correct model. Alternatively, he may go off on his own and try to fly the brute without assistance, with the inevitable result. This type usually returns to the club or disappears forever.

For the beginner to radio control who already has experience in other fields of aeromodelling, the problems of constructing the model are much reduced, and the chances of instant success in the flying stages enhanced, due to prior knowledge of the important points connected with aircraft, e.g. accuracy of construction, weight and balance problems, understanding of trimming procedures, operation of motors, control functions and the host of other details influencing flying performance. This type of person is obviously the most likely to succeed when "going it alone" because of his understanding of the model and its problems.

Go get your man

During the time the prospective pilot is building his selected model, it will become apparent from the flying sessions in the club which of the members are proficient and willing to give instruction to newcomers. Generally there is always somebody who undertakes this task in every club, and it only requires a few polite enquiries to discover the "willing horse". This person is not necessarily the keen competition flier, as that type is usually busy practising, or tuning his models, and may not have much spare time to devote to the beginner and his apparently simple problems. The instructor must be a competent flier, however, capable of handling advanced models and, possibly most important, seen to be a regular and safe flier at the club field.

Once this pilot has been found, an introduction should be effected and the position explained. The wise man will then make a courteous effort to get to know him; look at his models, and thus become generally confident of his ability to help. This does not mean he must be pestered with detailed questions all the time he's flying, or other unreasonable advantages taken of his good natured attempt to help.

The instructor who takes an interest and pride in teaching will make an assessment of the beginner's character, ability and modelling skill, and try to advise him in a way most suited to help with any particular problem of model, radio, construction or flying techniques. It is essential that the beginner has complete confidence in the instructor and is willing to follow his instruction. If, however, some particular point

194

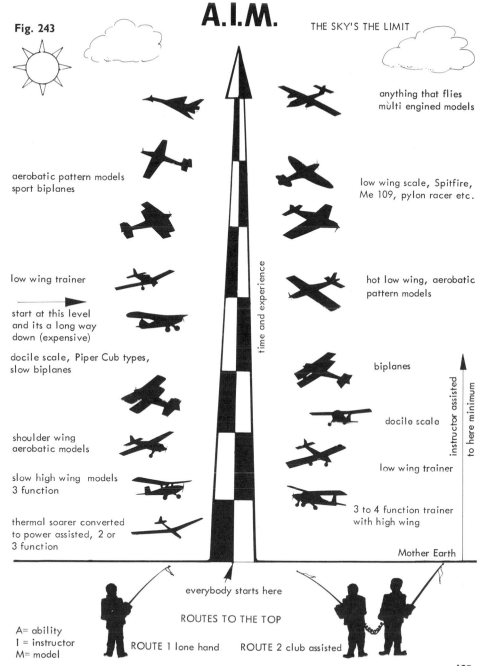

Fig. 243

A.I.M.

THE SKY'S THE LIMIT

anything that flies
multi engined models

aerobatic pattern models
sport biplanes

low wing scale, Spitfire,
Me 109, pylon racer etc.

low wing trainer

hot low wing, aerobatic
pattern models

start at this level
and its a long way
down (expensive)

docile scale, Piper Cub types,
slow biplanes

biplanes

docile scale

shoulder wing
aerobatic models

low wing trainer

slow high wing models
3 function

3 to 4 function trainer
with high wing

thermal soarer converted
to power assisted, 2 or
3 function

Mother Earth

time and experience

instructor assisted

to here minimum

everybody starts here

ROUTES TO THE TOP

A= ability
I = instructor
M= model

ROUTE 1 lone hand   ROUTE 2 club assisted

195

is not understood, an explanation should be sought at the time, or at a later date if time is short, as it is never wise for any doubts to be left unresolved.

The "confidence factor" built up between instructor and pupil, can have a profound effect upon the pupil's flying. When the pupil just reaches the stage of being able to complete a flight under his own steam, the presence of the instructor, offering the occasional word of advice, gives tremendous confidence and can take most of the nervous strain off the pupil, as the instructor is still able to take over control, should any unforeseen problem arise.

The instructor has to assess at what point the pupil is able to go it alone safely, and this can vary considerably according to the pupil's ability and choice of model. Equally, the pupil must accept that this period is potentially the most dangerous and be prepared for the odd minor scrape, or even a prang, resulting from the combination of inexperience and possible over confidence.

The poor old instructor has a lot to put up with carrying out these duties, and may well find that during the best flying weather he has insufficient time to enjoy flying his own model! Accordingly the pupil should try and appreciate the strain imposed on the instructor and always have his model ready to fly before asking for assistance, and also realise the instructor may not look too kindly on being asked odd questions whilst engaged in landing his latest scale model.

Learning with a Buddy box
During the first flights the use of a "buddy-box" system, where the instructor has full control of operations, can be invaluable, especially when the pupil is inclined to panic at the slightest sign of trouble. If the model is at a safe height it can be an advantage to let the pupil attempt to get himself out of trouble, in order for him to learn the actions required to cope with a similar situation, which may occur at a later date when he is on his own. The use of the buddy-box should not be too prolonged, however, as the pupil may get so used to the instructor taking over, that he may expect the same procedure when flying on his own, and not attempt to fly his way out of a pilot-error problem!

The man and his model
The choice of model for the initial flight training is an important factor in the progress of the beginner. If it is intended to join a club, this should be done before a model is selected, as the club members will be able to give practical advice on the model and radio combination most suitable for the local conditions, and which can be recommended from experience.

For those with limited finances and a desire to fly purely for quiet pleasure, the simple "single channel" type design (Route 1) fitted with 2- or 3-functions is a reasonably sure approach and, for the complete beginner, easy to build and small enough to handle comfortably. This type of model is well suited to the rougher flying sites, being easily hand launched, and can be operated single handed once trimmed out.

The basic flying techniques can be learnt with this type of model, including simple aerobatics and, once the pilot has fully mastered the control of this model, progress to the next stage should be easily achieved. The important thing to realise, when learning in this manner, is that each progressive step should be small and built up on the preceding one. For instance, having become proficient with a 3-function model, this does not mean that it is possible to jump to a fully aerobatic scale model, without an awful lot of assistance from an experienced instructor.

The alternative approach is Route 2, where the initial training is carried out on a more advanced 4-function model, capable of most aerobatic manoeuvres when the control movements are increased. This provides a single model which trains the pilot to a point where he can contemplate the large step up to low wing types, or the docile scale model, according to interest and ability.

At this point, in both routes, the pilot's ability will have shown through and started to govern his speed of progress, and the person who is slower to learn must not get discouraged when he sees another flier, who started later, flying more competently than himself. Even the person who has apparently "no hope" of learning can become proficient if he sticks at it and tackles the problem in the correct way, with patient help from his instructor, and a model particularly suited to his needs.

The buddy-box system is particularly useful for the slow or nervous learner as it inspires confidence and keeps the model in one piece which avoids lost time due to the need for repairs. Any long break in the initial learning period can cause quite a setback to the pilot's skill, inasmuch as he can forget what he has learnt previously and, when the model is back in action, has to start almost from square one again.

Many people have learnt to fly without the use of a buddy-box, of course, and it is by no means essential for a club to provide one for its prospective beginners. The only real problem attached to using a single transmitter is persuading the beginner to hand over the box when in trouble or, alternatively, preventing him from dropping it like a hot brick at the first turn!

A great deal depends upon the individual, and the instructor is the best judge of whether he has to take over control, or if he can leave the decision to the pupil when he feels out of his depth. The beginner's reaction to a model getting out of control can vary considerably from "freezing" to the transmitter, to blind panic and stirring the sticks round haphazardly, to letting go of the sticks completely, or even trying to remember the details of what should be done in this particular situation! Even the best instructor cannot retrieve the situation where the pupil refuses to hand over the transmitter, or only does so when the model is inverted at 3 feet half a mile away! There should be a clear understanding between pupil and instructor when to change over, if the pupil is inclined to act in this way.

It is under these circumstances the instructor's qualities of diplomacy and patience can be severely tested, especially if there is a shower of pieces to be collected. The cause of any such accident needs to be established, if at all possible, in order to avoid a recurrence although, in many cases, the reasons are a combination of small pilot errors and model problems, any one of which, on its own, would not be too difficult to counteract, but which are possibly aggravated by the pupil's efforts to regain control, giving the instructor insufficient time to recover the model.

The maiden flight
Anybody taking up radio control flying must be prepared to accept that his model may be damaged, or even written-off, during the training period and, indeed, at any time

afterwards; but, with a proven design of model, reasonably constructed and with reliable radio, the first flights should be successful, provided the test-pilot is an experienced flier.

It is normally recommended that the instructor flies the beginner's new model on its first flight and, if this is the case, he must be allowed to inspect the model and check over things like the c.g. position, correct operation of controls and so on and generally "clear" it for flight. It is surprising how many beginners have the motor or elevator stick action reversed, and it is not unknown for a model to have the aileron and elevator functions swopped over!

Provided the model is trimmable within the transmitter trim ranges, there is no reason why the proud owner should not have a "stir" at the sticks on the model's first flight. If the model requires large trim changes, however, or has other problems adversely affecting its flight performance, the beginner is well advised to let the instructor sort the problems out after landing, and continue this procedure until the model is flying satisfactorily.

Get those oily fingers on the box

When the model is trimmed, the instructor should be "collared" so as to get several flights in during each session, in order to consolidate what has been learnt. A single good flight may be very encouraging, but two or three flights will increase confidence and skill greatly, and also show up any particular weak points which the instructor can spot and help to overcome.

An important point to remember during this stage, is that it is not recommended to try to fly the model for too long a period during the flight. Most beginners are not able to maintain concentration on the model for more than a few minutes at a time, before becoming disorientated and getting into trouble. This is the time for the transmitter to be returned to the instructor, before things get out of control. After a short breather, it may be possible for control to be taken over again, assuming the instructor has kept the model in the air. This method of flying can be repeated until each period of flying approaches a full-length flight, take-offs and landings possibly still being undertaken by the instructor.

Golden rules for the beginner

A. The model should always be kept upwind. This will make life much easier, as most of the time the controls will be in the correct sense and, if there is disorientation trouble and the model is stable, it will tend to drift nearer to the pilot.

B. Reasonable height must be maintained. Not so high that there is difficulty in seeing the model or hearing the engine, but sufficiently high to give a margin of error for "overcooked" turns, or incorrect control movements. This height can vary greatly according to the model type and also the individual's eyesight. If there are any doubts or problems about seeing the model when apparently the instructor has no trouble, a visit to the optician is indicated, and if glasses are needed they will prove cheaper than breaking the model, and can have other benefits as well!

C. Hard concentration on the model is essential at all times and the "box" must be handed over as soon as this lags, but these short spells must be slotted in while the time, frequency and instructor are available.

D. All controls must be checked before take-off. It ensures that the receiver is switched on, and that none of the pushrods or links has become displaced after that last heavy landing.

E. If trouble is encountered, the answer is always to throttle back, as this gives slightly more time to react, and the model will be going more slowly if the ground comes up to hit it.

F. The take-off and landing is generally the most difficult to learn, so the instructor must be closely watched as he carries out these operations. The length of take-off run, the angle of climb out, and the height at which the first turn can safely be carried out must be impressed on the mind. Similarly, during landing, the height of approach and turn positions, and use of the throttle must be noted. There is, of course, no substitute for practice and once confidence in handling the model in the air is obtained, and it can be turned in a controlled fashion, the instructor should be asked to help with a take-off. He may even suggest this can be managed anyway, but he must be on hand to shout instructions should any problems arise!

Doing it the hard way

If the first flight is going to be "solo", with no skilled assistance, the model must be double checked for balance, warps, and correct sense of controls. Also, if the model is of a single-channel type design with a light wing loading, a few test glides will show up any major trim faults. It is often more practical to hand-launch this type of model, especially if the power unit is on the lower limit of capacity for the design. R.O.G. (rise off ground) under these circumstances can be uncertain and require a delicate touch on the controls.

If possible a colleague should launch the model so that it is possible to concentrate on the controls. It is vital that he understands what is required. As was explained in the previous chapter, there is no need for a "javelin" type run and heave – a couple of steps and a steady push will be sufficient for all but the most overloaded and underpowered models   placing the model in the air in a level, or very slightly nose-up, attitude and with the wings parallel to the ground. If the model is somewhere near trimmed it should accelerate steadily for a few feet and then begin to climb. The temptation to bang in a load of "up" to get the model climbing more quickly must be resisted, as it will already be perilously near the stall point.

If the model sinks slowly to the ground, the problem usually is lack of power or under-elevation, so a couple of notches of up trim should be given and another attempt made. If the result is the same, it points to under-power or overweight problems, although more trim might persuade it to fly, the model may be only marginally above stalling speed all the time, leading to difficulty in control, especially in windy conditions. If this is the case, the model will require some investigation in order for a decision to be made on what modifications are necessary. A simple prop change may be all that is required but, even in extreme cases, the use of a larger engine will not necessarily give the right answer, as it just adds even more weight to an already overloaded model. Some expert advice should be sought if this would seem to be the problem as all models have individual characteristics. (The previous chapter has also dealt with the problems of trimming in greater detail – N.B.)

Get that take-off right

It is important for the take-off to be carried out in a safe and orderly manner – not in a headlong rush straight from the pit area – and this is the correct sequence of procedure . . .

1. Before the radio is switched on the frequency peg must be obtained.

2. The motor must be running satisfactorily with the needle setting slightly on the rich side, two – or three – notches too lean and it may cut dead on climb out.

3. The motor is throttled back and the model guided to the take-off patch.

4. The wind direction is checked and the model is headed directly into wind.

5. A quick look round is taken to see if anyone else is about to land or take-off.

6. Anyone inclined to be nervous, should take a deep breath and settle himself.

7. The throttle is opened, the model released and as far as possible kept tracking into the wind. The instructor will advise if any rudder correction is needed to keep the model straight, as some designs need rudder deflection from the word "go".

8. The greatest temptation is to attempt lift off too soon; the model must be allowed to build up reasonable flying speed, especially if it is low powered. The instructor can advise here too. Most designs require application of up-elevator to lift off and, therefore, it is necessary to be prepared for a sudden jump and steep climb, especially in strong wind conditions. Any steep climb must be "killed" immediately with down elevator, otherwise a stall may develop, with little chance of recovery. The wind speed can make a tremendous difference to take-off performance and, again, "old greybeard" will advise as to what to expect on any particular day. The angle of climb-out depends mainly on the power/weight ratio of the model, but a general guide is an angle of 15 to 30 degrees up to a safe height for the first turn.

9. No attempt must be made to turn the model immediately after take-off, unless an obstruction has suddenly appeared, as this may initiate a loss of height near the ground, followed by possible incorrect panic reactions by the pilot.

10. If the motor cuts out during take-off, the model must be kept heading into wind, unless there is insufficient room to land. A quick stab of down elevator is normally required when the engine cuts, to get the nose down into a normal glide attitude. The model must never be turned down wind unless it has already attained 30 to 40 feet altitude, sufficient for a 360° turn. If it is necessary to fly round something, the turns must be kept as gentle as possible, with a view to heading the model into wind as it approaches the ground.

11. Once the model has attained reasonable height, the elevator is trimmed to cope

with the current weather conditions, and so that the model is holding a slight climb. Any model fitted with maximum size engine, may become easier for the beginner to handle with the engine throttled back to about $\frac{3}{4}$ power.

There are no signposts in the sky

It is at this point with the model successfully airborne, at a fair height and pointing nicely into wind, that the mind goes blank, and the aircraft is watched serenely flying off into the blue, while the pilot is paralysed, not knowing what to do next. Was that a hollow laugh? O.K., so it doesn't happen to everyone, but how many beginners fly the model in a controlled pattern, and how many just let it wander around, following the turns it starts of its own accord?

This is acceptable for the first few nervous flights, but the idea is for the pilot to fly the model where he wants it to go – not for the model to fly him! Therefore there are several basic patterns which will help achieve this, using gentle turns as a basis:

A. Large, approximately circular, circuits round the field.

B. Large square sided circuits, good for practising flying straight, cross-wind.

C. Square and round figure-of-eights, with the cross-over upwind of the pilot.

D. Holding straight flight into wind.

Most people find they can fly more easily in one particular direction, but they must not fall into the trap of only flying that way as, sooner or later, they will be forced into turning the opposite way, ending up with disorientation problems. So a point must be made of flying the simple manoeuvres in both right- and left-hand directions, and it is surprising how quickly it becomes easy to judge the amount of control to apply.

If an instructor is available he will initially be able to call the turns, until it becomes possible to judge the turn points without assistance. The most common mistake, during this phase of learning, is for the model to be allowed to go too far down wind before a turn is initiated. This is especially so in windy weather, when the model can quickly get blown away, if the turn is not positively controlled.

It must be remembered who is in control of the model! If it starts to drift off in a different direction from the intended one there must be no hesitation in giving a positive correction, which may possibly mean using a stab of full stick movement.

The art of judging the amount of stick deflection required can only be learnt from experience. Most models, with correctly set up control surfaces, require only gentle pressure on the stick for normal circuit turns. It is necessary, however, for especial care to be taken when applying down elevator, as the model can build up considerable speed after a short dive and, if it is directly overhead, it is difficult for its altitude to be judged.

Most beginners tend to over control by giving large stick deflections and quickly returning to neutral, causing a jerky flight pattern. This technique can, however, be ineffective in controlling some designs, which have "soggy" control responses as a result of a deliberate attempt to produce an ideal trainer. The result may be confusion on the part of the pilot, thinking that his gear has failed, or that the model needs more control surface movement, when all it really needs is a steady application of stick deflection. This type of model is most suited for the "go it alone" man, as it gives protection against over-control problems.

Under the guidance of an instructor, however, the model can be of a type with more positive reactions to control movements, without necessarily being "twitchy". This may be found easier, as it is possible to see straight away the result of any stick movements.

This way for terra firma

Once a few take-offs have been completed, and the model can be handled comfortably throughout its normal flight time, a landing may be considered. Landing is the most difficult operation and does require quite a lot of practice to achieve consistent results. The object initially is to achieve safe, and not necessarily close, landings. Smashing the model at the pilot's feet is not considered a good landing!

An instructor at the elbow can be a great asset in that he can prompt the various actions to take and, if a buddy-box is being used, he can progressively "hand-over" more of each landing. While the model is being flown normally, a few dummy approaches should be tried, using a square circuit pattern to bring the model over the landing area into wind – Fig. 244.

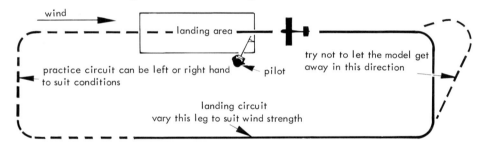

Fig. 244

The downwind and crosswind turns must not be allowed to degenerate into one large turn, as it is much easier for the rate of descent to be controlled with the model going straight. The best practice for the beginner is to keep on carrying out the dummy approaches, slowly bringing in the use of the throttle control to reduce height during the square circuit, until the model is approaching ground level on the upwind pass. Then, on one of these passes as the model is in exactly the right position, a further reduction of the throttle will let the model land. As it gets to within a few inches of the ground, the throttle should be chopped completely and the model flared-out by a gentle application of up-elevator.

As landing approaches are practised a routine procedure should be formulated in order that any repeated errors which may occur can be corrected. If a different landing pattern is used every time, it will be found difficult to see what is going wrong. The following is the correct landing procedure:

A. The wind direction is checked – it may have changed.

B. Height is reduced until the model is ready to enter the landing pattern. This is difficult to judge initially and also depends on the model, so a check should be made with the instructor.

C. On the downwind leg of the approach, throttle is reduced to approximately $\frac{1}{3}$rd and the process of losing height is begun. This leg should be parallel with landing strip, and about 200 ft. out. Small amounts of trim should be introduced to keep the nose up.

D. A 90° turn crosswind is then made with height still being lost. The model must not be allowed to slide too far downwind in this turn.

E. Height is lost gently crosswind, and it may possibly be necessary to reduce the throttle by another couple of notches to achieve this.

F. A 90° turn is made upwind to line up with the landing area. The turns must not be too tight, as the model will be flying near the stall point when in the turns.

G. The model is held into wind and, if it looks like undershooting, the throttle is opened to "stretch" the glide. If the model appears to be overshooting, down elevator must not be applied as this will only increase flying speed – the model must simply be allowed to land further upwind.

H. As the model nears the ground, it is flared out with elevator and the throttle is then chopped completely as the wheels touch. The aim is to reach touchdown with the model level, or slightly tail down.

J. If the model is not too close the first few times, there is no cause for concern as all that is needed for consistent close landings is practice.

It may be found with some models that the correct application of up trim will allow it to land itself and all that is necessary is to steer it into wind. Generally most trainers will land themselves quite well, and require only the minimum of correction once pointed into wind.

If it is preferred to land "dead stick", and this is popular with many beginners, the same procedure applies but, in all cases the model must not be slowed up too much, or attempts made to extend the glide, when undershooting, by use of a lot of up elevator, as that old enemy the stall is not far away!

When a model is being landed for the first time solo, a small amount of up trim must be introduced before the approach is started as this will reduce the airspeed. The model must, as far as is possible, be held into wind as it nears the ground, and the last upwind turn must not be cramped by doing it at too low an altitude, thus giving insufficient time on the approach to correct and settle the model for landing. A correctly trimmed light model may not need any flaring out with the elevator at all, and may be left to settle on the ground with no assistance from the pilot.

It may be found helpful if the throttle servo is set so that it is possible to stop the motor with the trim control – as was described in Chapter 12. This will give the option of landing dead-stick, or of cutting the motor during the flight should anything go wrong, or just allow a quiet glide down if this seems like a good idea!

When the model is down, the advice in the previous chapter must be remembered — that is to switch off Rx before Tx. If the Tx is switched off first the Rx will possibly pick up other signals on different frequencies, and may open the throttle, with dire results if the motor is still running – the model shooting off uncontrolled into pit area, car park, or even taking-off!

Time to think

With a feeling of satisfaction welling up inside, the time has almost come to start to think of the next flight, but first there are some important things to do. After calming down, the first thing is to take a look at the transmitter. Are the trims offset? If they are, the surfaces of the model must be trimmed via the clevises so that the transmitter trims can be returned to the central position – with the exception of throttle that is. This way it can be seen at a glance if the transmitter trims have been moved off-centre accidentally, or it may be found on the next flight that the wind has increased, and more down trim is needed, whereupon it is discovered that all the trim movement has been used up already.

Thinking back over the flight; were any of the controls unnecessarily sensitive or slow, or did the turn control trim vary with model speed? Was the engine happy all the time or did it tend to slow with the nose up?

If the controls were over sensitive, the links should be moved out on the horns (or in on the servo) to reduce surface movement, and the neutral position checked afterwards. Over-sensitive elevator control may be due to a tail-heavy condition, so the c.g. should be checked and, if necessary corrected with weight in the nose. In any case it is always safer for the model to be a little nose-heavy for the first flights, as it makes it much more stable. If the turn trim varied with speed, a warped wing is indicated which can be corrected or compensated for as described in the previous chapter.

An overall inspection must be made of the model to check to see if anything has moved or come loose. Are the engine mounting screws and silencer screws still tight; servo mountings OK; has the Rx battery moved; are the push-rod keepers still in place? All these small troubles are likely to show up after the first few flights, and any one could cause a big problem.

Keep up the good work

Once the stage of managing a complete truly solo flight has been reached, all that is necessary is to keep practising. As much flying as possible in the early stages is necessary to consolidate what has been learnt, even reasonably windy conditions must be no deterrent because, provided the instructor is on hand to assist, they should not cause any trouble. There will be rapid progress to a point where it will be wondered why it all seemed so difficult in the first place, and at this point it is necessary to be careful, because it may well herald a period of over-confidence.

There is no reason at all why the control throws should not be increased and a start made on learning basic aerobatic manoeuvres, but adequate height must be maintained, and the manoeuvres flown away from the pit area, spectators, cars and so on. During this period it may well be that the model gets into unfamiliar altitudes and this will start off panic actions to recover. There is no need for these – with sufficient height it is only necessary to throttle back and let the model sort itself out. Most trainers will be able to recover and come out the right way up, so it is only necessary to determine the point where it can be assisted by applying elevator or turn controls, once it is possible to recognise what is required. This is the reason for starting at a reasonable height!

If an instructor is available, he should be asked to "talk the way through" the manoeuvres until there is confidence in the ability to complete the manoeuvre safely, even if it is not necessarily perfectly formed. All that is now necessary is to keep practising until it is possible to fly the model to the limit of its performance and then land accurately every time. When this happens the time has come to go on to that more advanced model which has been built in the meantime.

It is vital not to get over-confident and push the model beyond its designed limits. Some trainers are not stressed for high speed aerobatics, so the speed must be kept down by use of the throttle and by not making any prolonged steep dives with sharp pull-outs, as the wings might just decide to applaud such efforts!

At this stage, everyone thinks he can fly. This is *true* – but he can only fly this one model, in this particular way and at this site! Therefore, he should go to a different site and suddenly his flying will seem to deteriorate, probably because turns and approaches have been judged by subconsciously using landmarks around the field, like the odd tree, house or hill on the horizon. Therefore, the pilot must be absolutely sure of himself and his model, before popping along to that nice little recreation field just down the road for a quick flight!

If, at any time, a genuine error of judgement is made, there must be an attempt to analyse what went wrong, in order to try and avoid a recurrence. In other words, it is essential to learn by mistakes and not blame crashes on some obscure failure in order to save face.

Now go to it
Now that all the foregoing advice has been read and, it is hoped at least part of it remembered, it is very easy to be fooled into thinking that this knowledge will suddenly make a proficient flier! Once the model gets into the air most readers will promptly forget everything they've read, so, in the end, it still comes down to solid practice and the ability to learn by experience.

All the same, the elated feeling that follows a successful day's flying really makes it all worthwhile!

CHAPTER 25

RUNNING-IN ENGINES

by Peter Chinn

THE manufacturer's instruction book for a new car always advises treating the first thousand miles or so as a "running-in period". For example, under this heading, the owner's instruction manual for the Rover V8-3500 states: "Progressive running-in of your new car is important and has a direct bearing on durability and smooth running throughout its life. The most important point is not to hold the car on large throttle openings for any sustained period. To start with, the maximum speed should be limited to 50 to 60mph (80 to 95kph) on a light throttle and this may be progressively increased over the first 1500 miles (2500km)."

At speeds of 50-60mph, the Rover's eight-cylinder engine is using only about 20 of its available 160 brake-horsepower, so it is clear that motor manufacturers take very seriously the need for treating an internal combustion engine gently during the first part of its working life. This being so, is there any reason to believe that model i.c. engines do not deserve similar consideration when new? When a new engine is fitted into a model and is started up and flown at full bore immediately, is this any different from flooring the accelerator pedal on a brand new car and driving it flat out?

The truth is that (as will be explained in a moment) a two-stroke model aircraft engine is often operating under less favourable conditions than a (four-stroke) car engine and, in spite of what some people might say, it is foolish if considerable caution is not exercised when a new engine is first operated. Failure to observe a few simple rules at the beginning of an engine's life may, or may not, cause immediately recognisable damage, but it will almost certainly result in (less obvious) deterioration that will reduce performance and require premature replacement of essential working parts.

Friction and heat

If the working parts of a modern good quality model engine are examined, they usually appear to be very accurately and smoothly finished. In fact, no matter how well these parts are made, their surfaces are microscopically "rough" when new. It is part of the running-in process to smooth out the high spots on these working surfaces as they rub against each other. However, this is not the whole story. When the engine is running, certain parts, and even different areas of those parts, become distorted to varying degrees, according to the thermal and mechanical stresses imposed on them. These movements cause additional "high spots" which must also be smoothed out so as to maintain adequate running clearances between the surfaces.

All this initial bedding-in of the working parts causes increased friction. Greater friction means increased heat which, in turn, means greater expansion and, in the case of the piston and cylinder assembly, this will usually mean that the clearance between the piston skirt and cylinder wall is reduced, thereby further increasing friction. The pattern is now set: more friction = more heat = reduced clearances = more friction; a spiral which, if something is not done about it, will, at best, cause excessive wear or, at worst, bring the engine to a grinding halt.

Happily, there is a simple solution to this problem. It is not a matter of following full-size practice and running the engine at a reduced throttle opening (this would, in any case, be difficult with the non-throttle equipped engines used for pylon racing, as well as with free-flight and control-line motors). The answer is simply to (a) open the needle-valve so that the engine is running on an excessively rich fuel/air mixture and (b) operate the engine in a series of short runs with cooling-off periods between each.

Running the engine on a very rich needle setting actually has a threefold beneficial effect: the engine not only runs slower but, much more important, remains cooler and is better lubricated. In fact, what actually happens is that, instead of *every* charge being ignited, the engine fires every *other* charge. In other words the engine runs like a four-stroke motor instead of a two-stroke.

First, therefore, "four-stroking" reduces the amount of heat generated by halving the number of power strokes in a given time. Secondly, the unburnt fuel, in passing through the engine, is evaporated and, in so doing, actually cools the engine. Thirdly, the oil content of the unconsumed fuel is deposited on the engine's working surfaces to further aid lubrication. The wide needle setting, of course, also means that an ample supply of oil is flowing through the engine at all times.

Choice of fuel

Unless one of the very small glow engines such as the "Half-A" size American Cox and McCoy .049 motors, (which require minimal running-in and can be safely operated on recommended nitro fuels from the beginning) is being used, the best fuel for running-in is a straight mixture of methanol and castor-oil. The use of fuels containing nitromethane or nitropropane is wasteful and undesirable since increasing power is not the concern at this stage and such additives increase running temperatures. Petrol should not be used in the fuel either.

A good all-round running-in fuel consists of 1 part castor-oil to 3 parts methanol. Castor-oil should always be used in preference to synthetic oils. The latter tend to increase running temperatures and, despite some claims to the contrary, they do not improve lubrication.

"Four-stroking"

A fuel and air mixture will burn only when the ratio of air to fuel remains within certain limits. If, therefore, a condition arises within the combustion chamber whereby there is either not enough, or too much, air to support combustion, the mixture will not ignite and the engine will misfire or stop.

"Four-stroking", with a two-stroke engine, is, therefore, actually intermittent misfiring and it is brought about as follows:

Let it be assumed that the needle-valve is opened to a point where the mixture strength is increased to just below that at which it is too rich to burn. In a "clean" cylinder, the mixture will, of course, fire but, as some traces of burnt gases remain in

Many racing engines have been ruined by being run flat-out after inadequate running-in. Some, such as the K&B SR-II shown below, now use chromed brass cylinder liners which have expansion coefficients nearer to those of aluminium. This maintains a more constant piston/cylinder-liner clearance and also ensures better heat transference to the surrounding cylinder casting. Recommended running-in time for the K&B SR-II is approximately 30 minutes, of which 15-20 minutes is bench-running on a '4-stroke' needle setting.

The manufacturer approves the use of in-flight running-in with the powerful O.S. 60FSR (left), provided that the first 2-3 flights are with a '4-stroke' needle setting and the next 4-6 flights are on a rich 2-stroke.

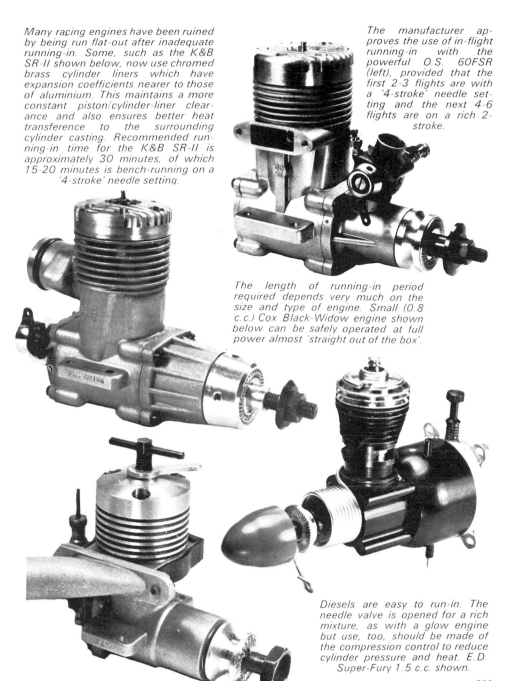

The length of running-in period required depends very much on the size and type of engine. Small (0.8 c.c.) Cox Black-Widow engine shown below can be safely operated at full power almost 'straight out of the box'.

Diesels are easy to run-in. The needle valve is opened for a rich mixture, as with a glow engine but use, too, should be made of the compression control to reduce cylinder pressure and heat. E.D. Super-Fury 1.5 c.c. shown.

209

the combustion chamber during the following cycle, the second charge of mixture will be contaminated and will fail to ignite. The wasted second charge does, however, have the effect of sweeping out most of the residual exhaust gases so that the third charge enters a now relatively clean cylinder and is duly fired. In this manner the engine continues to run, alternately firing and misfiring.

Basic running-in procedure

The engine must not be overloaded by fitting too large a prop for running-in. Generally speaking, with modern glowplug engines, the prop can be the same as will be used when the engine is fitted to the model – unless it is planned to use the engine with an extra large prop (e.g. on a scale model), in which case use the size that would be more appropriate to an aerobatic model, such as a 10×6 for a .35 or .40, or an $11 \times 7\frac{1}{2}$ for a .60.

There is not much point in throttling the engine down. To do so will simply lengthen the running-in time. It is better to open the throttle wide and to use a rich mixture to reduce heat build-up. The throttle will, nevertheless, be useful in an emergency: for instance, it may be used to reduce speed and heat build-up quickly if the engine shows signs of overheating and slowing up.

The running-in process is begun by giving the engine a minimum of six rich "4-stroke" runs of about one minute each with a cooling period of about two minutes between each. This is followed by another six runs (more for bigger motors) of 2-3 minutes each, again with cooling-off periods between each. Now the engine is restarted

Engines requiring the longest running-in time are generally the medium and large size lapped piston types such as this early model McCoy 40 shown left. Current model (right) has ringed aluminium piston and needs far less protracted running-in.

'Professional' bench mount for all sizes of model motors, is of machined steel with blued finish. Combination of Allen cap screw and grub screw enables clamps to be adjusted for wide range of lug thicknesses.

and the needle-valve screwed in until it just breaks into 2-stroke operation. If it starts to slow up, the throttle must be closed and the needle-valve opened, then the throttle can be re-opened and the engine given another six runs, or as many as may be required to reach the point where it will hold an even speed when the needle is adjusted for 2-stroke operation.

A falling engine note must never be ignored. A drop of a couple of hundred rpm may not be important and may simply be the result of a slight loss of power due to a reduction in charge density as the engine warms up. A bigger drop is more serious and invariably indicates that the engine is overheating and tightening up and, within seconds, it may slow right down to an abrupt stop. It may even stop so suddenly as to kick its prop loose. If it is suspected that this is going to happen, the throttle must be closed immediately.

In-flight running-in

This advice also applies most emphatically if the model is being flown. Bench running is still the safest method of dealing with the initial running-in period, but many modellers living in urban areas and with near neighbours may be unable to do this because of the noise problem. One answer is to mount the engine, tank, etc., on a portable stand on which it can be run-in, or at least partially run-in, on the flying field, well away from where fellow modellers or other people might be annoyed.

If the engine has to be run-in in a model, the basic procedures previously laid down must be followed. Obviously, it will be best if, before the model is actually flown, the engine is run sufficiently to be sure that it can safely two-stroke without tightening up. Then, when the model is flown, the needle-valve should be adjusted so that it is just four-stroking on the ground. This should ensure that when the model breaks into a two-stroke cycle in the air, it will still be on the rich side. The engine note should be listened to carefully, so it is advisable to avoid flying when there are other models in the air, and the throttle must be closed quickly if the engine sounds at all distressed. In any case, it is a good idea if the engine is throttled back every minute

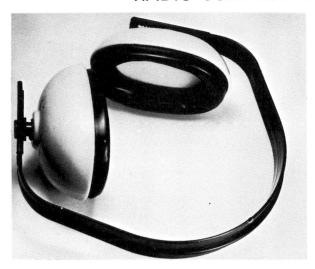

When running-in the larger and more powerful engines, ear protection, such as is provided by these ear-defenders will make the process more tolerable.

or two to allow it to cool off a little. It must be remembered, however, that with the needle-valve set rich, the engine will not run so well at low speeds, so if an attempt is made to throttle down to an idling speed it may stop.

Incidentally, a beginner who is doubtful about his ability to distinguish "2-stroking" from "4-stroking", need have no fear. When an engine switches from 4-stroking to 2-stroking, the sudden change in the engine note to a higher pitch is obvious and this is accompanied by an increase in power and a much less smoky exhaust.

Carrying on the good work

Ideally, once an engine is properly run-in, it should be in such good condition that it will withstand a limited amount of misuse without damage. It is quite common to hear about an engine being ruined through a "lean run", meaning that, while in flight, it has become overheated by running on too weak a mixture. On the other hand, a well run-in engine will often tolerate a slightly weak setting and will simply cut out if the mixture is excessively weak.

However, there is no doubt that overheating is a major cause of operational engine damage and the possibility of the engine running on too weak a mixture is always something that should be guarded against. Better that the needle be set too rich and a flight spoiled, than it be too weak with the risk of spoiling a good motor.

Keep runs short

The best way to run-in a model engine is to split the running time up into short runs with cooling-off periods between each, rather than to let the engine run continuously. With some motors, notably the larger lapped piston types, this is the *only* satisfactory solution. There have been instances where certain lapped cast-iron piston motors in the 5cc.-7.5cc. group have been run on a rich setting continuously for periods as long as 10 hours and, at the end of that time, the piston/cylinder fit has still been too tight, when hot, to allow the engine to deliver full power for more than a minute or two. In contrast, the same type of engine, run-in with a controlled series of short runs totalling only one hour, has freed off quite sufficiently for continuous full throttle running thereafter.

The reason behind this phenomenon is that the piston and cylinder have to go through several heating and cooling cycles in their working environment before expansion and contraction settles into a constant pattern that can be accommodated within normal clearances. It has been suggested that the initial instability is something that is brought about during the actual manufacture of the engine due to the stresses that are set up in the parts as they go through the processes of production. It has to be remembered, also, that the piston and cylinder are not heated uniformly when the engine is running. A piston, for example, is no longer round when hot but tends to expand to an oval shape in the direction of the gudgeon-pin axis. The cylinder and piston are also hotter on the exhaust side and to the rear, and cooler on the transfer side and to the front.

The theory is that molecular stability in the metal is achieved only after the component parts have been subjected to a series of "heat treatment" processes. In other words, each time a new engine is run, the piston and cylinder suffer microscopic changes of shape and have to be bedded-in again until, finally, when molecular movements have ceased and parts have acquired the necessary clearances, the engine is found to be adequately run-in.

All this is something that applies mainly to the larger lapped piston engines, as previously noted. Happily it is less of a problem nowadays for the r/c modeller because nearly all motors of more than .35cu.in. (5.7cc.) capacity now use ringed aluminium pistons or, in a few cases, have ringless pistons with chromed brass cylinders that have a coefficient of expansion closely matched to that of the piston to avoid the loss of vital clearances if the engine should overheat. The smaller lapped piston engines, in general, are also reasonably trouble free as they dissipate heat more rapidly than large ones.

As a rule, it can be said that the smaller the engine's swept volume, the shorter the running-in period necessary.

For example, the American "Half-A" motors, such as the Cox .049 (0.8cc.) generally require only a few minutes running-in. In the case of the Cox, running-in is also aided by the symmetrical cylinder and piston design (i.e. a one-piece cylinder with diametrically opposed ports and a plain flat crown piston free to rotate as it reciprocates) which are less prone to distortion. For these baby engines, a few runs of up to one minute each, running rich, is all that is required before they are put into use.

Engines in the .09 to .21cu.in. (1.5cc. to 3.5cc.) groups generally require no more than about 30 minutes running-in, but motors in the 5 to 10cc. displacement groups (e.g. .29, .35, .40, .45, .50, .60cu.in. or even larger) usually need about an hour.

It must be remembered, also, that with suction fuel feed, some variation in mixture strength occurs through normal flight manoeuvres and as the fuel level in the tank falls. This variation may be reduced by pressurising the fuel tank and the best

Fuel should be filtered at least twice to prevent risk of partial blockage weakening the mixture and causing the engine to overheat. The Fox line filter shown can be dismantled for cleaning.

way of doing this with a standard r/c engine is for exhaust gas pressure tapped from the silencer to be utilised. This is better for the r/c engines than a crankcase pressure system since it automatically reduces pressure at low speeds and thereby avoids upsetting the idling mixture at the carburettor. (The alternative, of course, is a more complex pressure feed fuel system such as the "YS" or Perry Pump which maintains a constant fuel pressure at the carburettor at all times.)

As a precaution against the possibility of the fuel/air mixture weakening in flight through a partially blocked carburettor jet, fuel should always be filtered. A common method of doing this is to fit a line filter between the fuel tank and carburettor. There is nothing against using a line filter, but it should be understood that this alone is not enough. Fuel should always be filtered *before* it is put into the tank. The preferred method is to filter the fuel before it is poured into the field fuel container and to fit another filter in the delivery tube used to transfer fuel to the model's tank. In this way there is a minimal risk of particles of foreign matter building up in the model's line filter and reducing fuel flow to the carburettor.

Diesels

The vast majority of engines used by radio-control aircraft enthusiasts are glow-plug motors. This is understandable. Glow engines are much smoother running, have far better throttle response and, in any case, available diesels are confined to the smaller displacement sizes. Accordingly, all the foregoing was written with r/c glow-plug engine users mainly in mind. Much of what has been said can apply to diesels but, in fact, there is rather less to worry about with a diesel. The main thing is for use to be made of the compression control. With this, the diesel owner enjoys the advantage of being able to reduce cylinder pressure and operating temperature during the running-in period. The use of a larger diameter prop than would be used with an equivalent displacement glow engine is also recommended.

Photos in Chapters 25 and 26 by Peter Chinn

CHAPTER 26

SETTING-UP THROTTLES

by Peter Chinn

M ODEL AIRCRAFT motors, like full size internal-combustion engines, belong to that group of heat engines known as "gas engines". The amount of power that such a power unit develops depends, first and foremost, on the quantity of gas that is burned in the cylinder. Therefore, varying the power output would seem to be quite easy: all that should be required is a throttle-valve to regulate the amount of gas admitted to the combustion chamber.

Regrettably, this is not as simple as it sounds. Because the fuel burned by a modern i.c. engine is stored, not in a gaseous condition, but in a liquid form, it has to be atomised in air to form the gas that is burned in the engine's combustion chamber. This mixing with air is the function of the carburettor and to obtain a combustible mixture, the ratio of liquid fuel to air must be held within fairly narrow limits. The carburettor must be able, therefore, to correctly meter the quantity of fuel required in accordance with the volume of air admitted.

This is not difficult to achieve in the case of an engine designed to run at a constant speed, consuming air at a steady rate, such as a stationary engine, or, for that matter, a non-throttle equipped (e.g. free-flight) model engine. All that is required here is that the amount of fuel released is correctly adjusted to the operating speed of the

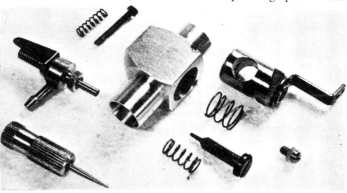

Heading photo shows the Merco 61 Mk. IV, an engine using a single-jet two-needle type carb. Shown in detail right, this is easier to adjust than the earlier and more complex Merco Micro-Flo carb.

engine (which, of course, is a function of the propeller size used) and all model engines are fitted with a simple needle-valve to enable fuel flow to be accurately metered to suit these requirements. The needle-valve also makes it possible to compensate for other variables, such as fuel delivery pressure and different fuels and atmospheric conditions.

With "full-size" carburettors, the main problem to be overcome is the alteration in mixture strength that occurs as engine speed is varied. As rpm are increased and the rate of air flow through the carburettor is raised, the air pressure in the choke is reduced, thereby increasing suction at the jet, with the result that the mixture becomes richer at high speeds. Most full-size carburettors therefore incorporate devices for automatically maintaining a more or less constant mixture strength, in the interests of fuel economy and performance.

With model aircraft engine carburettors, the situation is rather different and, in fact, is more serious. The problem here is not simply a matter of maintaining good performance without wastage of fuel, but of actually keeping the engine firing at all times. In other words, it does not matter if the mixture strength departs from the *economical* optimum fuel-to-air ratio, so long as it remains within the upper and lower limits at which it is still *combustible*. A combustible mixture strength ratio must be maintained not only throughout the speed range of the engine, from idling to full power, but also through the variations in fuel delivery pressure resulting from the wide variety of attitudes and manoeuvres occurring in flight.

In order to satisfy the first of these conditions, it is desirable to incorporate some form of mixture control linked to throttle movement. To satisfy the second, the simplest solution is to use a relatively small choke area that will exert a strong suction at the jet at all times, but since a small choke also has the effect of reducing the engine's potential power output, it is becoming increasingly common to use some form of assisted fuel delivery from tank to carburettor, instead of relying only on suction feed.

For r/c engines, the most widely employed method of doing this is to pressurise the fuel tank by means of the gas pressure generated within the exhaust silencer. Most silencers are fitted with a brass outlet nipple and a length of silicon fuel tube is used to connect this to a sealed fuel tank. This method of pressurising the fuel system is much better than the old method of employing crankcase pressure which, with a throttle equipped motor, tended to cause the carburettor to run over-rich at low speeds. With an exhaust pressurised system, this does not occur as the pressure of the gases within the silencer diminishes as power is reduced and fuel pressure is thereby quite closely matched to the requirements of the carburettor.

With an exhaust pressurised system it is feasible to use carburettor choke areas 30-50% larger than would normally be used with suction feed. Taking this a stage further, it is also possible to increase choke areas by another 30-50% (or to approximately double the "suction" size choke) by using a much more complex high-pressure system with a special regulator to meter the fuel supply to the carburettor. The American Perry-Pump and the Japanese YS Pressure Regulator, both used in conjunction with special carburettors, are examples of such an approach.

Basic carburettor types

Among the earliest forms of intake "throttle" used on model engines were simple

RADIO CONTROL GUIDE

One of the simplest types of barrel-throttle r/c carburettors was this early K&B with non-adjustable airbleed.

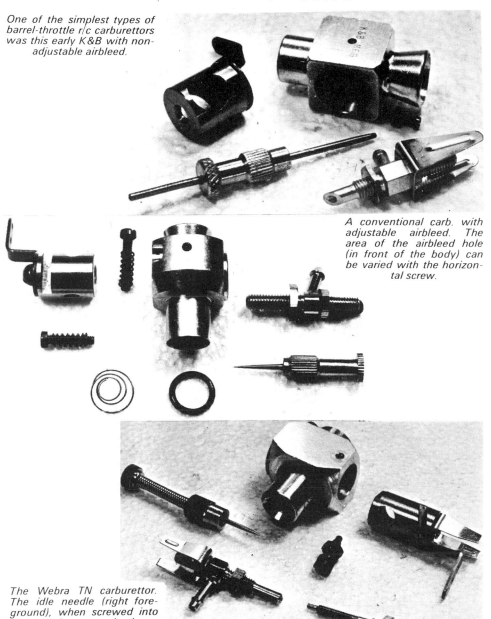

A conventional carb. with adjustable airbleed. The area of the airbleed hole (in front of the body) can be varied with the horizontal screw.

The Webra TN carburettor. The idle needle (right foreground), when screwed into the barrel, enters the jet at low speed to reduce the fuel flow.

pivoted flaps located in the mouth of the air intake. Such crude devices restricted only the amount of *air* reaching the carburettor and were effective in only partially reducing power. Closing the air valve beyond a certain point simply resulted in the engine's suction being transferred to the fuel jet (as occurs when the engine is being "choked" prior to starting) causing an excessively rich mixture on which the engine would not continue to run.

Barrel throttles

The throttle-valve most commonly employed by model engine carburettors since about 1960 has been the barrel throttle. This is generally in the form of a solid cylinder of brass or steel, located transversely in the carburettor choke and bored through diametrically to line up with it when the throttle is open. The barrel is usually drilled axially to take a spraybar or jet-tube so that fuel is discharged into its centre. Rotating the barrel reduces air admission on the "upstream" side and mixture admission on the "downstream" side.

In order to prevent too much suction at the fuel jet causing an over-rich mixture at idling speeds, the "upstream" opening may be made larger, or notched, so that more air is admitted. Alternatively, an airbleed hole may be drilled through the carburettor body so that extra air can enter the barrel when this is in the idling position.

Adjustable airbleeds

The basic barrel type throttle described above can be greatly improved by the addition of an *adjustable* airbleed. In this, the effective area of the airbleed hole (and thus the idle mixture strength) may be altered by means of a screw. Carburettors of this type are widely used, especially for the smaller and simpler types of motors.

Fuel metering systems

A well designed adjustable airbleed type throttle, properly set up, can be very reliable. It has, however, one distinct disadvantage, namely its fixed jet size. The fixed jet works well so long as fuel suction is primarily dependent on the depression created by the high speed air flow through the carburettor choke. However, as previously noted, when the air inlet is drastically reduced (i.e. during idling) the suction created in the engine crank chamber (a very efficient pump even at the lowest speeds) tends to draw an increasingly excessive amount of fuel from the jet and this strong suction is considerably reduced when air is fed in via the airbleed to avoid an over-rich mixture. To have to partially destroy suction in this way is a pity because it is when the engine is idling, especially when fuel level is low and model attitude changing, that it is necessary to maintain a steady supply of fuel at the jet.

The way to achieve this without resorting to an externally pressurised fuel system, is to maintain suction at a high level by eliminating the airbleed and to employ a device for reducing the *quantity* of fuel actually released through the jet.

This is the principle on which most of the larger model engine caburettors now operate. Mechanical design varies quite a bit and such carburettors, which, collectively, may be referred to as "automatic mixture control" (AMC) or "automatic fuel metering" (AFM) or "two-needle" (TN) types, go under a variety of proprietary names. They

The O.S. Type 4B carb. The mixture control valve (at right) is mounted in the barrel and slides over the spraybar, which is fixed in the body.

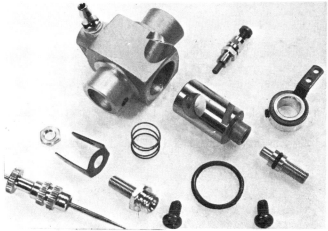

An O.S. Type 4B carb fitted to the O.S. Max 40F-SR engine. Recessed screw slot enables mixture to be adjusted while engine is idling.

Super-Tigre Mag variant of single-jet 2-needle theme, uses a sliding rod in the spraybar for idle mixture control.

include certain of the carburettors made by leading model engine manufacturers, such as HP, Merco, O.S., Super-Tigre and Webra, as well as those produced by accessory manufacturers such as Kavan and Perry.

Basic adjustments

It is impossible to deal in detail with the operation and adjustment of every type of carburettor, but the following information covers most of the more popular r/c carburettors in current use. It is generally recommended that an exhaust-pressure assisted fuel system be used, unless the engine or carburettor manufacturer specifically states otherwise. The fuel tank should be positioned as close as possible to the engine and with its centre-line level with, or slightly below, the height of the carburettor jet, and the engine should first be run-in in accordance with the manufacturer's instructions before any attempt is made to fix carburettor adjustments.

Airbleed carburettors

Setting up an adjustable airbleed type carb is a fairly straightforward procedure. The engine is started and the needle-valve set with the throttle wide open. The desired needle setting is usually $\frac{1}{8}$ to $\frac{1}{4}$ turn on the rich side of the setting at which the engine runs fastest. This will reduce maximum speed by perhaps 200 rpm but means that there is a safety margin in the event of the mixture weakening when the model is in a steep climb with an almost empty fuel tank. This can be checked by pointing the model's nose vertically upward with the engine running, after having made sure that the pressure line from silencer to carb is secure.

The motor is now throttled down to a reasonable idling speed. A "reasonable" idling speed is between one-quarter and one-fifth of the full throttle speed. In other words, with an engine that turns at 12,000 rpm on the chosen prop, the idling speed should be between 2,400 rpm and 3,000 rpm.

If the motor immediately stops on throttling down, it is probable that an attempt is being made to run it too slowly. If necessary, the throttle stop screw must be adjusted for a slightly higher idling speed. The other possibility here is that the mixture is too weak at idling speed. In which case, the airbleed screw should be screwed in, say, half a turn, to reduce the amount of air admitted and the engine restarted.

Nowadays, most r/c engines will start on their idle settings and, if the idle setting is too weak, it is possible gradually to enrich the idle until the engine starts and idles satisfactorily. If, on the other hand, the idle mixture is too rich, it is best for the airbleed to be opened and then the excess fuel remaining in the engine burnt off by opening the throttle, before the idle is again tried.

Generally speaking, it should not be necessary for drastic changes to be made to carburettor adjustments. Most of the better quality engines leave their factories with idling adjustments set quite close to the optimum and anyone purchasing a new engine is therefore advised to persevere for a while before making readjustments to the original settings.

Single-jet two-needle carburettors

One of the most widely used of the automatic mixture control carburettors is the single-

RADIO CONTROL GUIDE

The Hirtenberg 2-needle carb works on the same principle as the Webra TN, and is fitted to some HP 61 and 40 engines.

The well-known Kavan carburettor. The sleeve in the barrel rotates around the spraybar, partially covering the slit type jet at idling speed.

The Bernhardt HB 40 is one of many engines fitted with the Perry carburettor. Disc on side is for adjusting idle mixture.

jet two-needle type which had its origins in the Webra TN type first used in 1967 on the Webra 61. In principle, these carburettors are relatively simple barrel throttle units having a single jet, but with an extra needle which comes into operation to restrict fuel flow at part-throttle and idling speeds.

The main needle valve assembly is mounted in one side of the carburettor body. Its open-ended jet tube is concentric with the throttle barrel and protrudes into the centre of its choke. The barrel, inserted from the opposite side of the body, carries the idle-needle, which can be screwed in or out and also protrudes into the choke. The throttle barrel does not simply rotate when closed: instead it describes a helical path, moving axially inwards as well, so that, at just below half throttle, the tip of the idle needle enters the jet and reduces fuel flow as the throttle moves towards the idle setting.

Several other engines have carburettors that use this principle including certain Merco, HP, Taipan and OPS models. The Super-Tigre "Mag" carburettors are also of this type but, with these, the jet tube is in the form of a full-width spraybar with a longitudinal slit type jet. Instead of having a tapered tip, the idle needle is in the shape of a thin rod which is a close fit in the spraybar and gradually reduces the effective length of the jet as the throttle closes.

In general, all these carburettors work well and, since their operation is so easy to understand, adjusting them is quite simple. After setting the main needle at the full throttle position, the throttle is closed to the idle position and the idle needle is adjusted for the correct low-speed mixture.

The same basic procedure can be followed as has been described for air-bleed type carburettors but it must be remembered that the idle mixture adjustment works in the opposite mode: i.e., screwing in the idle needle weakens the mixture instead of enrichening it.

Other single-jet automatic carbs

Other single-jet AMC carbs include the Kavan, Perry and O.S. Type 4B and Type 7B carburettors. Of these, the O.S. retains the helical barrel movement of the TN type and has a full width spraybar with a longitudinal slit type jet like the ST Mag carb but, instead of an idle needle, it has a sleeve type mixture control valve which is a close sliding fit over the spraybar. This extends half-way across the choke bore at full throttle but moves along the spraybar reducing the length of the jet and also the effective area of the choke as the throttle closes. The mixture control valve is threaded into the throttle barrel and sealed against leakage or accidental movement by an O-ring. Adjustment is simple and positive via a recessed screwdriver slot and can be set while the engine is running. The Type 7B carb also has an optional choke insert giving a choice of choke areas for suction or pressure feed.

The Kavan carburettor, outwardly, looks like an orthodox barrel throttle carb with airbleed. The barrel does not move sideways. Instead, it incorporates a full length brass sleeve that rotates around a spraybar. The jet is in the form of a narrow radial slit in the centre of the spraybar and this is uncovered, at full throttle, by a circular hole in the sleeve. As the throttle rotates towards the closed position, the exposed length of the slit is shortened, thereby reducing fuel flow. The extent to which fuel flow is reduced at part throttle openings can be changed by slackening a screw retaining

Parts of the Perry carb. The reel shaped part in the centre of the photo, controls the idle mixture strength. This carburettor is made in three sizes.

A novel accessory is the Perry filter for fitting to the air intake. Useful in dusty conditions but a fuel filter is more essential!

the complete spraybar and needle-valve assembly and rotating it a few degrees: clockwise to weaken the idle mixture; anticlockwise to enrich it. An adjustable airbleed is retained for correcting the idling mixture.

The Perry carburettor, like the Kavan, uses rotational barrel movement, only, to meter the fuel but is of quite different design. The barrel is fitted with a fixed brass jet tube, the extended outer end of which passes through a small cylindrical chamber in the closed end of the plastic carburettor body and also carries the needle-valve. Fuel fills this chamber from an inlet nipple in the rear of the body and is transferred to the jet tube through a slot in the side of the latter after passing through a small slit in a reel shaped sleeve surrounding it. This sleeve, fitted with two O-rings, is an integral part of the *idle mixture disc* visible on the outside of the carb. Rotation of the disc alters the idle mixture strength, clockwise to weaken, anti-clockwise to enrich, but it is very sensitive to movement and needs to be turned only two or three degrees at a time.

223

The Enya 'G' type carburettor has non-adjustable automatic fuel metering via a groove in the throttle barrel surface. It also has an air-bleed for idle mixture control.

Unlike other carburettors, the Fox two jet type has metered mixture control at high-medium speeds and runs on a separate idling jet at low speed.

There are two important things to watch with the Perry carb. First, the metering slit in the idling mixture control is very fine and effective fuel filtering is therefore essential. Secondly, when the carburettor is cleaned, it is necessary to avoid *soaking* the plastic carburettor body. Petrol (in particular) and most of the usual solvents will ruin it. It is best for it just to be rinsed in glow fuel and dried off.

Non-adjustable AFM carburettors

All the automatic carbs dealt with so far have had provision for adjusting the low speed fuel metering. An exception is the Enya "G" series carburettor. Here, fuel is fed from the carburettor body to the interior of the throttle barrel (and then to an open-ended jet tube) via a hole in the surface of the throttle barrel which, in order to reduce fuel flow, gives way to a fine groove as the throttle barrel rotates towards the idling position. Like the Kavan, the Enya "G" series relies on an airbleed to overcome any richness at idling speed.

RADIO CONTROL GUIDE

Fox twin jet carbs

Finally, there are those carburettors which use separate jets for high speed and lower speed operation, specifically the carburettors fitted to the medium and large size Fox engines. At one period Fox carburettors included a triple-jet, triple needle type but, in the interests of simplified adjustment, the mid-range jet and needle assembly were eliminated in favour of a non-adjustable mid-range metering device.

Fox carburettors also differ from those previously described in that the throttle valve, while still a semi-rotary pattern, is not the usual barrel type, bored diametrically. Instead, it has a flat centre section so that, in effect, it operates as a butterfly valve. Operation is as follows:

Fuel enters the carburettor through an inlet nipple in the front of the body and takes two routes: (a) directly to an idling jet in the carb throat, the amount of fuel released being controlled by a small needle-valve and (b) to the main jet through a delivery hole in the left side of the carb body where it is picked up by a hole in the surface of the steel throttle valve, conveyed to its interior and discharged through the main jet located in the middle of the flat centre section. The amount of fuel released here is adjusted by a large needle screw installed in the left hand end of the throttle valve.

At part-throttle settings, the pick-up hole in the throttle valve is no longer aligned with the delivery hole in the carb body. However, a fine groove in the surface of the rotor (as in the Enya "G" series previously described) allows a reduced quantity of fuel to be admitted and this automatically adjusts mixture strength to part-throttle requirements. Further rotation of the throttle cuts off the fuel to the main jet entirely, so that the engine now runs on its idling jet only.

There is one important point to remember when a Fox twin-jet carburettor is being adjusted. Because the engine runs on the idling jet only at low speed but on both jets at intermediate and high speeds, it is necessary for the idle needle valve to be adjusted *first* and then the throttle opened to full speed to set the main needle-valve. This, of course, is the exact opposite of the procedure applicable to all the other carburettors discussed.

* * * * *

Many modellers have trouble in adjusting carburettors, simply because they do not understand how they work. It is hoped that the notes contained in this chapter will throw some light on the situation, particularly when read in conjunction with the manufacturer's instructions on individual carburettors.

Once a carburettor has been properly set up for a particular installation, it should not be necessary for any further readjustment to be made (except, perhaps, a slight change in the main needle-valve setting to cope with different fuels and atmospheric conditions) until such time as the effects of wear become apparent. The main thing to be borne in mind is that r/c carburettors, particularly those using slit type metering jets, will not tolerate unfiltered fuel. It takes only a minute particle of fluff or dirt to partially block such a jet and completely upset throttle operation. Therefore, at least two fuel filters should be used: one in the supply tube from the fuel container to fuel tank and one in the delivery line from tank to carburettor, and not only must they be used but also cleaned frequently!

APPENDIX 1
HISTORICAL SURVEY

THIS short historical survey is not intended to be exhaustive* so there is no point in anyone nitpicking at some of the sweeping generalities! The sole intent is to trace, briefly, the development of radio control equipment, from the earliest commercial units, to those of the present day, in the context of the effect this has had on the popularity of the hobby. It will also be interesting to note the effect the earlier bulky equipment had on model design, and how the layout of the transmitter controls has affected marketing to the present day, a point which was touched on when Modes were under discussion.

The first commercial r/c units were marketed in the late '30s in the USA where (as also with engines), their relatively limited direct involvement in the war, permitted development to continue at a rate impossible here. This led to relatively reliable outfits being generally available in the late '40s.

All these sets were single channel and – the transistor being unheard of – models had to carry bulky valve receivers, and an even bulkier and heavier complement of batteries, so that, in those days, a typical model was at least 6-8 ft. wingspan, and with a cavernous fuselage. Transmitters also were big, too big to hold in the hand, so that they stood on the ground, with the control button at the end of a flexible lead.

This button gave two controls, which were normally to rudder, and the sequence was push-and-hold – left rudder; release – centre; push-and-hold – right rudder; and so on, ad infinitum. This meant that it was necessary to remember which signal was sent last, in order to know which control would be triggered next! An alternative was, therefore, available, where push-and-hold – left; release – centre; push-release-push-and-hold – right signalled the appropriate control. The control itself was "all or nothing", in that the rudder went to its full extreme of travel and stayed there until the signal was released.

Obviously modellers were not satisfied with just the one steering control, and many were the schemes developed to give further controls to motor, elevator, and so on. These, normally, were triggered by the action of the main steering control, and it was common for the signals to get out of sequence, with exhilarating consequences!

Servos also were unheard of, and the controls were operated by an escapement or actuator, which was driven by a loop of twisted rubber. Later, motorised actuators – not dissimilar in appearance to the modern servo – became available and, despite

---

*A far more comprehensive and technical survey is in the R.M. Books Publication "Radio Control" by Paul Newell.

their bulk and lack of power, (a maximum of 2 oz. pull was typical) they were an advance over escapements. Further refinements included a system of "coding" the signal from the transmitter, so that the required sequence of "pushes" was interpreted mechanically, or electronically, as the operator moved a control stick.

All these early sets were super-regenerative, which meant that only one model could be flown at a time, which did have the advantage that the flier was the centre of attraction until it was someone else's turn to fly! It was, however, the arrival of the superhet unit, which roughly coincided with the development of the transistor and the introduction of the first "reed" outfits, which really revolutionised the hobby, and started the surge in popularity which continues today.

The reed outfit got its name from the fact that the signals from the transmitter was translated by the receiver into a tone, which vibrated a tuned reed (like that in a musical box), which then made electrical contact and operated the servo. This may sound crude but, in fact, reed outfits proved exceptionally reliable and this, in endowing models with a much greater potential life span, was what led many modellers, as opposed to radio enthusiasts, to take up this most exciting branch of the hobby.

The reed transmitter was not dissimilar in appearance to a proportional unit, except that there were four, five, or six, switches, as appropriate, to operate the various functions. Most common was the five, which gave full house control. Two switches on the right of the case moved horizontally to give rudder and aileron, and three on the left vertically to give elevator, elevator trim, and motor. (Now it can be seen why ex-reed fliers prefer to operate in Mode B.)

Despite having all these controls, however, they were still "all or nothing" in that, when held on, the servo moved to the limit of its travel and stayed there. Nonetheless, a degree of proportional response was possible by "pulsing" the control stick, and a practised reed flier could put to shame many of today's proportional efforts. Typically, the bulk and weight of the reed airborne units was about twice that of today's proportional but, despite this, as has been said, it heralded the era of practical, non-fiddling, bought over the counter, radio control for all.

Slightly preceding and running concurrently with reed development, was "galloping ghost", which was the earliest, albeit very crude, form of proportional control. In actual fact it was really single "channel" except that the rudder and elevator continually cycled from left to right and up and down and so on, but could be biased more one way than another upon a signal from the control stick of the transmitter.

The advent of today's true proportional, spelt the almost immediate end of both reeds and galloping ghost, although single channel lingered on for some years, because of its price advantage. In their heyday, to get airborne with reeds, would cost £180-£200 and about a quarter of this for G.G., while single channel was around £11 for super-regen, and £20 for superhet. If these prices are compared with today's, allowing for inflation it will be seen that modellers get a pretty good deal!

This book is devoted solely to proportional because, at long last, it is the only system of control in production. There are, however, hundreds of single channel outfits still in use and, an offspring of them, 1 + 1 and 2 + 1 proportionals. The offspring is the + 1 servo which, normally, in common with a single channel servo, rotates through

RADIO CONTROL GUIDE

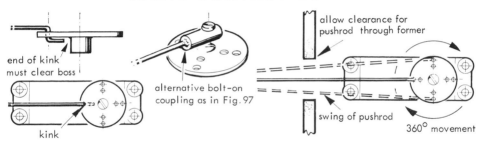

end of kink
must clear boss

kink

alternative bolt-on
coupling as in Fig. 97

allow clearance for
pushrod through former

swing of pushrod

360° movement

Fig. 245

Fig. 246

360° in each command cycle, unlike the true proportional servo, which moves to-and-fro some 160°.

Obviously, then, many of the linkages in this book cannot be used with a 360° rotational unit so, to prevent owners of these becoming dispirited, and to close on a note of instruction which, after all is the main purpose of this book, the two illustrations – Figs 245 and 246 show how to cope with a + 1 unit.

APPENDIX 2

INSTRUCTOR'S CHECK LIST AND TRAINING SCHEDULE

by Joe Coetzer

EARLIER discussion on the various aspects of "learning to fly" has put the emphasis on advice to the pupil, it being assumed that a competent flier will be aware of the many checks that a really conscientious instructor will wish to make before he test flies a new model. When, however, a beginner somewhat airily asks his instructor to give his model a "quick check over" he is showing his ignorance of what really is required. The end result of a "quick check" is almost invariably a quick return to the building board. What is needed is a *thorough* check, and just what this entails is described by Joe Coetzer, whose Instructor's Checklist first appeared in the South African Association of Radio Flyers' newsletter.

Although this list looks formidable at first glance, in fact, if all the advice in earlier chapters has been heeded, the various points will have been covered and all the instructor will need to do is to make a brief check to satisfy himself that nothing has been overlooked. Even so a "brief check" is not a five minute job, so it is no good someone turning up at the flying field with only an hour's flying time available, expecting to have the model test flown and also receive a lesson!

It is, of course, in some cases possible to arrange for many of these checks to be made at home, and hence save valuable flying time and monopolization of a frequency. Once, however, the flying field is reached, the instructor's first job is to obtain clearance for the appropriate frequency, and explain the system in use, and the importance of compliance with it, to the pupil.

Finally, before handing over to Mr. Coetzer, it is worth pointing out that, once a pupil has become a flier and is ready to test fly his own new model, many items on this checklist are an admirable *aide-mémoire*, and hence well worth running through before committing hours of work to the air! —*N.B.*

RADIO CONTROL GUIDE
INSTRUCTOR'S CHECKLIST

Pre-assembly check
1. Check wing(s) for warps
2. Check ailerons
   (i) method of attachment
   (ii) hinges (pinned etc.)
   (iii) movement (left/right/up/down)
3. Check centre section of wing for strength
4. Tailplane on straight/square
5. Fin on straight/square
6. Check method of attachment to fuselage
7. Check rudder and elevator hinges
8. Rudder and elevator movements
   (i) right direction
   (ii) amount of movement
9. Check method of mounting engine
   (i) type of mount
   (ii) type of screws
10. Check fuel tank
    (i) position
    (ii) fuel lines
    (iii) filter
11. Check front wheel (if applicable)
    (i) drag
    (ii) direction of movement
12. Check rear wheels
    (i) drag
    (ii) method of attachment to landing gear and axles
    (iii) tracking straight
13. Proceed with radio installation check.

Radio installation
1. Check servo tray/aileron servo attachment
   (i) screwed down tight
   (ii) servos in correctly
2. Check battery position and method of protection
3. Check receiver position and method of protection
4. Exit position of aerial and method of attachment
5. Linkages on servos
   (i) metal to metal?
   (ii) tube/cable (outer) glued down
   (iii) servo discs/arms screwed down
6. Foam packing where necessary
7. Servos plugged in properly
8. Linkages to elevator, rudder, ailerons, nosewheel and throttle
   (i) method of attachment
   (ii) throttle override
   (iii) nosewheel (shock absorbing system)
   (iv) clearances of aileron linkages with wing on fuselage
9. Check movement of servos
   (i) load
   (ii) binding
   (iii) movements in right directions in relation to the transmitter control sticks
       (a) elevator
       (b) ailerons
       (c) rudder
       (d) nosewheel
       (e) throttle
10. Proceed with assembly

RADIO CONTROL GUIDE

Assembly check
1. Method of attaching wing to fuselage
2. Wing square on fuselage
    (i) viewed from front
    (ii) viewed from back
    (iii) viewed from top
3. Check centre of gravity
4. Check wing incidence
5. Check tailplane incidence
6. Check thrust line of engine
    (i) viewed from side for down thrust
    (ii) check side-thrust by measuring to top of fin

Range check
1. Check range with transmitter aerial in and
    (i) other transmitters on
    (ii) other transmitters off (if necessary)
    (iii) engine running (if necessary)
2. Check reading on transmitter

Engine check
1. Propeller
    (i) right position
    (ii) right size for engine in use
    (iii) prop nut tight
2. Glow plug
    (i) right type
    (ii) tightened down
3. Carburettor
    (i) hold down screws tight
    (ii) air bleed position
    (iii) idle position

4. Fuel
    (i) correct type for engine used
    (ii) filter in fuel line (recommended)
5. Start engine
    (i) check high speed setting
    (ii) check for fuel foaming
    (iii) check idle
    (iv) adjust as required
    (v) re-check high speed
Note: Explain adjustments to pupil and let him participate in the necessary adjustments
    (vi) re-fuel if necessary

Pre-flight check
1. Re-check control movements
2. Taxi
    (i) straight?
    (ii) torque effect?
3. Nosewheel effective?
4. Speed (viz enough power for take-off)
5. Re-fuel if necessary

Flight check
1. Take off
    (i) more speed than usual
    (ii) keep climb-out flat
2. Check trims and adjust on transmitter (land if trim is way out)
3. Trim aircraft after landing

233

RADIO CONTROL GUIDE

4. Re-check trims in flight
5. Proceed with instruction

Ground instruction

1. Explain field etiquette and safety rules
2. Explain 'aerial theory' of orientation
   (i.e. the maximum range is obtained when the Tx. aerial is at 90° to the model and the minimum when the tip is pointed at the model. In practice this is academic unless the model is at the extreme of range or interference is experienced. – N.B.)
3. Explain 'stick towards wing that's down theory' of orientation
   (i.e. when the model is flying towards the pilot, if the Tx. control stick is moved towards the wing which is low, the correct control movement to level the model will be applied – in other words – prop up the wing which is low! – N.B.)
4. Explain stick movements
5. Explain position of hands and fingers on transmitter
6. Give commands and check pupil's response thereto viz left, up, down, right, etc.
7. Explain part 1 of training schedule to pupil (see training schedule)

Flight instruction

1. *First flight of pupil* (without buddy box)
   (i) model at safe height
   (ii) check pupil's hands on transmitter
   (iii) with hands over those of pupil demonstrate amount of movement required on sticks for gentle turns
   (iv) demonstrate part 1 of training schedule to pupil
2. *Second and later flights* (with buddy box)
   (i) proceed with training schedule (part 1)
   (ii) if pupil should get nervous at any stage, terminate flight and proceed after a few minutes

TRAINING SCHEDULE

Part I

Manoeuvre	Date passed	Instructor
straight flight		
left turn 90°		
right turn 90°		
left turn 180°		
right turn 180°		
straight climb		
straight dive		

Part II

Manoeuvre	Date passed	Instructor
360° circle left		
360° circle right		
horizontal figure eight		
one loop		
one roll		
one stall		

Part III

Manoeuvre	Date passed	Instructor
slow flight		
cuban eight		
approach pattern		
take-off		
landing		
solo flight		
recovery		

RADIO CONTROL GUIDE

Notes: To pass parts I and II a student pilot will have to accomplish each manoeuvre at least *three* times.

To pass part III a student pilot will have to accomplish each manoeuvre at least twice.

Notes to instructors: After passing a student on a manoeuvre the appropriate column must be initialled. This will indicate how many times a manoeuvre was accomplished satisfactorily

A student pilot may NOT progress to the next part of his training before completing the previous part.

SOME BASIC AEROBATIC MANOEUVRES

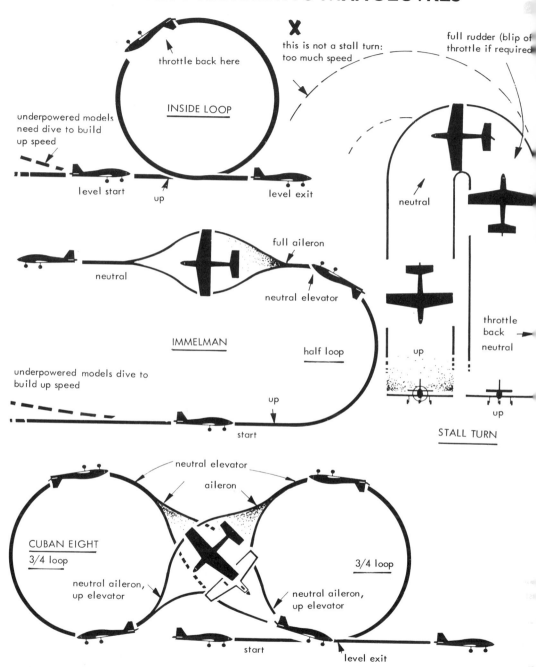

throttle back here

INSIDE LOOP

underpowered models need dive to build up speed

level start

up

level exit

X

this is not a stall turn: too much speed

full rudder (blip of throttle if required)

neutral

throttle back neutral

up

STALL TURN

full aileron

neutral elevator

IMMELMAN

half loop

underpowered models dive to build up speed

start

up

neutral

neutral elevator

aileron

CUBAN EIGHT
3/4 loop

neutral aileron, up elevator

3/4 loop

neutral aileron, up elevator

start

level exit

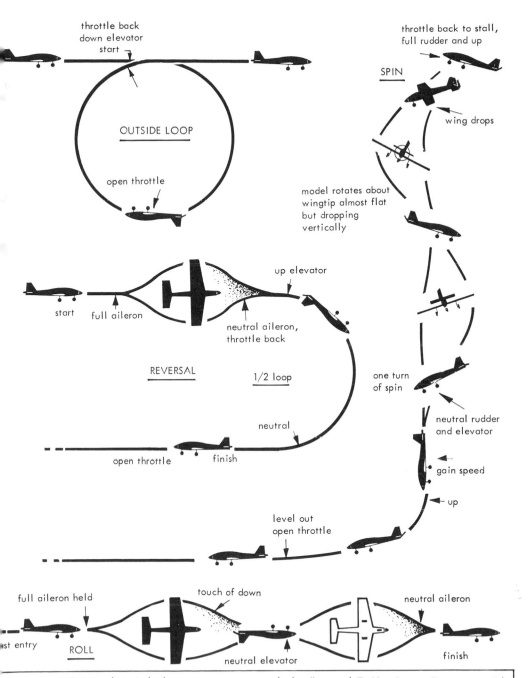

throttle back
down elevator
start

OUTSIDE LOOP

open throttle

throttle back to stall,
full rudder and up

SPIN

wing drops

model rotates about
wingtip almost flat
but dropping
vertically

up elevator

start   full aileron

neutral aileron,
throttle back

REVERSAL   1/2 loop

one turn
of spin

neutral

neutral rudder
and elevator

open throttle   finish

gain speed

up

level out
open throttle

full aileron held   touch of down   neutral aileron

st entry   ROLL   finish

neutral elevator

Everyone wants to graduate to basic manoeuvres as soon as he has "gone solo". Most intermediate type models
will loop and roll, so can perform the manoeuvres in which these are combined, but a more advanced design
will be necessary to fly the outside loop, axial rolls, and for real precision throughout

CONCLUSION

AND now all that remains is to wish every reader the best of luck with his radio controlled project. Theoretically luck should not be needed, because, if the advice in these pages is followed the radio will be reliable — the best there is will have been bought; the installation will be reliable — because it is mechanically perfect; flying field conduct will be impeccable, so the only thing on reflection, that is not needed is luck. Bad luck that is! A bit of good luck, though, never hurt anybody!

SCHEDULE OF RECOGNISED "SPOT" FREQUENCIES IN IN 27MHz and 35MHz BANDS

27MHz		35MHz	
Tx Frequency	**Channel code**	**Tx Frequency**	**Channel code**
26.970	Black	35.010	61
26.995	Brown	35.020	62
—	—	35.030	63
27.020	Brown/Red	35.040	64
—	—	35.050	65
27.045	Red	35.060	66
—	—	35.070	67
27.070	Red/Orange	35.080	68
—	—	35.090	69
27.095	Orange	35.100	70
—	—	35.110	71
27.120	Orange/Yellow	35.120	72
—	—	35.130	73
27.145	Yellow	35.140	74
—	—	35.150	75
27.170	Yellow/Green	35.160	76
—	—	35.170	77
27.195	Green	35.180	78
27.220	Green/Blue	35.190	79
27.245	Blue	35.200	80
27.270	White	—	—

The best of both worlds! Equally at home on land or water (or in the air of course!) This scale **Walrus** makes a most unusual and exciting model. At 1/8th scale, the wingspan is 63¾ in. and a .61 motor and four-function radio are required. Wings fold fully rigged for transport, just like the real thing.

GLOSSARY OF
R/C MODELLING TERMS

A

ABS	A type of plastic popularly used for vacuum forming.
ACTUATOR	Device for moving a control surface or throttle by electro/mechanical means.
AERIAL	A metal rod (usually collapsible) which radiates the transmitted signal, or a trailing or rigid wire on a receiver, which collects the signal.
AILERON	Control surfaces on the wing(s) of an aircraft to control it in the roll plane.
AIRBRAKE	A device which slows the aircraft down so that it's angle of descent is steepened.
AEROFOIL	Aeroplane wing, tailplane or fin.
AMPHIBIAN	An aircraft or vehicle operating from land or water.
AMPLIFIER	An electronic circuit designed to pass more current than that which controls it – i.e. a high output for a low input.
ANALOGUE	A control system which depends on a variation of proportions of the signal
ANEMOMETER	Wind speed meter.
ANHEDRAL ANGLE	The opposite of dihedral angle.
ANTENNA	See Aerial.
ASPECT RATIO	Ratio of chord and wingspan or width/length.

B

B.A.	British Association – a thread form on nuts and bolts.
BALLAST	Weight added to balance a model or to increase it's wing loading.
BALLOONING	Rising flight path of a model when landing with too much up elevator, or a single-channel model turning into wind.
B.A.R.C.S.	British Association of Radio Control Soarers.
BATTERY	Electrical power source.
BATTERY BOX	Box with contacts to carry batteries, generally used for pen cells.
BEAM MOUNT	A horizontal plate or beams or bearers designed to hold an engine with lugs each side of the crankcase.
BLIND NUTS	Nuts with spiked lugs which lock into the wood so that the screw or bolt may be tightened without the nut rotating.
BLISTER	Any streamlined protrusion on an aircraft.
B.M.P.R.A.	British Miniature Pylon Racing Association.
BOOM	A thin, rod like, rear fuselage supporting the tail.
B.S.F.	British Standard Fine – a thread form for nuts and bolts.
BUBBLE CANOPY	A cockpit canopy standing proud of the fuselage.

243

RADIO CONTROL GUIDE

C

CANARD	A "tail-first" aircraft, i.e. main plane at rear and stabilizer (tailplane) at front.
CAPACITIES (engine)	The swept volume of an engine's cylinder, expressed in cubic inches or cubic centimetres.
CAPACITOR	A radio component which holds current.
C.G. (centre of gravity)	Balance point of a model.
CHANNEL	See explanation in Chapter 1. (Footnote.)
CHARGE	To renew electrical energy in a battery cell.
CHARGER	Equipment for charging batteries.
CHORD	The distance from leading to trailing edge of a wing or tail.
CLEVIS	A connecting link between the end of a pushrod and a servo or control horn.
CLOSED LOOP	Also known as "pull-pull", this is a means of operating a control surface with flexible wire "pushrods". See Chapter 9.
CLUNK TANK	A fuel tank in which a weighted flexible tube picks up the fuel irrespective of the angle of the tank.
CODER	An electronic or mechanical device for automatically timed transmitter pulses.
CON ROD (connecting rod)	A rod which translates the reciprocal motion of a piston to the rotary motion of the crankshaft in an engine.
CONTACT POINTS	Platinum pieces which form electrical contacts on a relay or switch.
CONTROL HORN	A lever fixed to the control surface which connects with the pushrod or control cable.
COWLING	A streamlined covering for an aero engine.
CRYSTAL	A natural mineral ground to resonate at a fixed frequency. (Used to control the oscillation frequency of a radio signal in a transmitter, or oscillator stage in a receiver.)

D

DATUM	A line or point from which measurements are taken.
dB (decibels)	Strength of an output or sound measurement.
DEAC	A commercial rechargeable battery, much used in radio control outfits.
DEAD STICK	An expression used to describe a power model gliding after the motor has stopped.
DECALAGE	Difference in angle of incidence between the upper and lower wings of a biplane.
DECODER	Electronic circuit to identify a control signal.
DIFFERENTIAL (ailerons)	Mechanical linkage to give greater deflection on the up-going aileron.
DIGITAL	An electronic pulse counting and positioning system of proportional control.
DIHEDRAL	Upward angle of wings or tailplane to give inherent stability. Sometimes stated in degrees, but often quoted as a measurement at the tip, from the horizontal.
DIPOLE	A single rod element aerial.
DOWEL	A piece of wood, metal, etc., which may be of round, square or oblong section, and used to join two items (normally wing halves) together, or for rubber band attachment points, etc.
DOWN THRUST	Angle of the engine to prevent excess climb.
DRAG	A resistive force produced by (and on) an object passing through the air. There are several types of drag, but to go into these is beyond the scope of this book.
DUCTED FAN	A short bladed fan, used instead of an airscrew, operating in a close fitting tube or duct, to generate thrust, and totally enclosed at its periphery. Used to simulate jet aircraft.

RADIO CONTROL GUIDE

E

ELECTRICAL NOISE Unwanted signals produced by metal to metal loose joints.
ELEVATOR Hinged part of tailplane effecting longitudinal control.
ELEVON Control surface on a flying wing or delta model that serves as elevator and ailerons.
ENGINE CONTROL Speed control of the engine by various means.
EPOXY A chemical setting resin adhesive also used in glass fibre construction.
ESCAPEMENT Electro-mechanical device, generally powered by a rubber motor, to actuate the controls on a single-channel model.

F

F.A.I. Federation Aeronautique International — the International body controlling aviation.
FAIL-SAFE A safety system to set the controls in a safe stable condition and close the throttle in the event of a system failure, or signal failing.
FAIRING A "streamlined joint".
FIBREGLASS A resin and glass form of construction.
FIELD STRENGTH The measurement of the power of a transmitter as radiated.
FILTER (fuel) A porous pad inserted in the fuel line to prevent dirt reaching the engine.
FILTER (electronic) A circuit which rejects all but a frequency to which it has been tuned to pass.
FIN Vertical stabilizer.
FIN STRAKE An extended leading edge of the fin along the fuselage.
FIXED-WING As opposed to "rotary wing" (i.e. helicopters).
FLAP A trailing edge control surface to increase lift or drag.
FLAPERONS Ailerons which (by composite controls or "mixers") can act, simultaneously, as flaps.
FLEX Flexible insulated multi-strand wire.
FLUTTER When a flying surface sets up acute vibration and twisting. Often caused by excessive airspeed.
FLUX Chemical used to facilitate clean joints for soldering. Often incorporated in the solder.
FLYING WING A model with no tailplane and/or no fuselage.
FREQUENCY Generally refers to the frequency of a radio signal expressed in megacycles per second (Mcs. now written MHz.).
FRISE AILERON Special design to compensate for drag on the downgoing aileron.
FULL HOUSE A model with all control surfaces and engine independently controlled.
FUNCTION See explanation in Chapter 1.
FUSELAGE "Body" of the aircraft.

G

GALLOPING GHOST A pulse proportional system using only one motor in the actuator, works on single channel to operate elevator and rudder.
GEAR Collective term for radio control equipment.
GIMBAL Universal pivot system to allow movement in all directions.
GLITCH Momentary condition caused by interference or electronic failure. Gives unwanted control movement in model.
GRADIENT (wind) Differing wind speeds at various heights, important in slope soaring.
GROMMET A rubber or plastic bush to protect wire exits in a case, also used to absorb vibration in mounting equipment.

RADIO CONTROL GUIDE

H

HARNESS	Wiring between parts of a radio system.
HIGH LIFT	A wing section capable of carrying heavy loads at low speeds.

I

I.C. (or i.c.)	Abbreviation – see integrated circuit.
INCIDENCE	The angle at which a flying surface (wing or tail) is "rigged" relative to the datum line of the model.
INSTALLATION	Collective term for the radio control equipment fitted in the model.
INTEGRATED CIRCUIT	A sophisticated method of manufacture which avoids the use of individual components in the circuit.
INTERACTION	Unwanted movement of other controls in the model when one is operated.
INTERFERENCE	Reaction of the equipment in the model to other transmissions.
INTERMEDIATE MODEL	A model with a few independent controls, such as rudder, elevator and engine.
INVERTED	Flying upside down.

J

JUMPER	A short wire connecting sections of a circuit.

K

KNOCK-OFF	A system of mounting a wing or tailplane so that, in the event of a crash or heavy landing, they will knock-off of the fuselage without causing damage.
KWIK LINK	A trade name now in general use for an adjustable clevis.

L

LAMINATION	Layers of material joined together. Plywood is a good example of lamination.
L.E. (Leading Edge)	Front edge of a flying surface.
LINEAR	In a constant progression, as in a control surface movement, or output arms of some types of servo.
LINKAGE	Generally a mechanical coupling between the servo or actuator, and the control surface, or engine throttle.
LONGERON	The main longitudinal members of a fuselage.
LONGITUDINAL DIHEDRAL	The difference in angle between wing and tailplane.

M

mA (milliamps)	A measurement of current.
MECHANICAL LINK	The mechanical coupling between two or more moving parts.
METER	A sensitive device for measuring current, etc.
MHz	MegaHertz per second – the frequency of the basic signal.
M.F.F.A.	Model Flying Fields Association.
MICROSWITCH	A sensitive mechanical switch which is operated by a very small movement.
MID-AIR	Mid-air collision between two models.
MIXER	Electronic or mechanical device which permits a composite movement – see "Flaperons".
MIXTURE	The fuel and air in various proportions fed into the engine.
MODE	The method of operating the transmitter control sticks.
MOMENT ARM	Broadly, the "length of fuselage between the wing and tail" – usually measured in wing chords.

RADIO CONTROL GUIDE

MONITOR
A radio receiver for checking (by audio or visual means) and determining if the air is clear or which frequencies are in use.

MOTOR PLATE
A composition, wood, or metal plate carrying the engine which is in turn bolted to the model.

M.P.B.A.
Model Power Boat Association.

MULTIMETER
A meter with various ranges of measurement for milliamps, amps, volts and ohms, etc.

MULTI-MODEL
A model with more than one independent control operated by more than one channel of information, or having more than one independent function. Often used as a description of an aerobatic model.

MUSH
Sinking flight in a partly stalled condition.

N

NEEDLE VALVE
Fuel mixture adjustment on a model engine.

NEGATIVE (electrical)
The case side pole of a battery shown by a black — sign.

NEGATIVE (rigging)
As in a flying surface having its leading edge lower than the trailing edge relative to the datum.

NICAD
Nickel cadmium accumulator (battery).

NITRATE
A fuel additive for diesels (also Nitrite) and a type of dope.

NITROMETHANE
Fuel additive for glow-plug engines.

O

OVER-CONTROL
Application of too much control movement which causes the model to deflect past its intended path.

OVER-RIDE
A slip device in a linkage to allow a large servo movement to operate a small control movement.

P

P.C. (printed circuit)
A glass fibre or plastic laminate board on which has been bonded a layer of copper, which is then etched to leave a pattern of conductors into which the components are soldered.

POSITIVE
The centre pole of a battery expressed as a + sign (red).

POT (potentiometer)
A variable resistance with connections at both ends and movable centre.

PROGRESSIVE CONTROL
A control which is not self-centring.

PROPORTIONAL CONTROL
A system in which the control surfaces move in a degree of deflection proportionate to that of the control stick on the transmitter.

P.T.F.E.
A plastic having low friction — used for bearings and control linkages.

PULSE
A short signal or passage of current.

PULSER
An electronic circuit which generates pulses which, for control purposes, are variable.

PULSE PROPORTIONAL
A control system in which the symmetry and rate of pulsing is varied.

PUSHROD
Linkage between servo and control surface.

P.V.A.
A type of adhesive (polyvinyl alcohol) water based.

R

RADIAL MOUNT
Method of fixing the engine to the model where lugs on the rear of the engine are fixed to the front bulkhead of the model. There are available radial adaptors for bearer mounted engines.

RADIO LINK
The transmitter and receiver combination without reference to the control system as a whole.

RADIO CONTROL GUIDE

RADIO RELEASE	Radio operated tow hook release for tow launched gliders, so that moment of release may be decided by the pilot and not the person towing the model.
RANGE	The maximum distance over which a radio link will operate.
R/C (radio control)	Control of a device by means of a radio signal.
RECEIVER	An electronic device for receiving radio signals.
REED	An electro/mechanical device for de-coding control signals, used in early multi-control systems.
REFLEX	Reversal of camber on a flying surface as on flying wing or delta aircraft.
RELAY	An electro/mechanical switch comprising an electro magnet and an armature carrying contacts.
RELAYLESS	Type of receiver which has a transistorised switching circuit output instead of a relay.
R.O.G.	Rise off ground.
ROOT	The part of a flying surface that abuts the fuselage.
ROTARY WING	Used to denote helicopters, etc., as against "fixed wing" aircraft.
RUDDER	Movable vertical control surface producing yaw.
Rx	Abbreviation – see receiver.

S

SCISSORS SPRING	A type of spring used mainly on control sticks to return them to the neutral position.
SEPARATION	The point at which the airflow breaks away from the contours of the aerofoil. Also the MHz difference between radio spots.
SERVO	Electro/mechanical device for moving the control surfaces.
SERVO TRAY	A plate or moulding on which several servos may be mounted for ease of installation.
SIDE THRUST	Angling of an engine to one side to counteract torque and thus provide a straight flight path.
SIDEWINDER	An engine mounted on its side.
SILENCER	An expansion box which, fitted to the exhaust of an engine, reduces the noise.
SINGLE CHANNEL (S/C)	A control system operated by only one type of command.
SKID	A long rail beneath the nose of a glider instead of (or as well as) a wheel, to protect model in landing -- like a sledge runner.
S.M.A.E.	Society of Model Aeronautical Engineers.
SNAKE	Trade name now in general usage for a flexible pushrod and sleeve type of control linkage, generally made from P.T.F.E. or nylon.
SOLDER	Low melting point metal alloy used for making electrical and mechanical connections.
SOLENOID	An electro/mechanical device which converts electrical energy into mechanical movement.
SPINDLE MOULDED	A wooden part machined to shape on a machine with a high speed rotary cutter.
SPLIT	A frequency approximately mid-way between the internationally agreed six 27 MHz spots.
SPOILERS	Devices made to protrude from surface of a wing to "spoil" the lift effect when required for landing, etc. Mainly used on gliders.
SPOT	A pre-determined position in the frequency spectrum.
SPRAY BAR	Pierced tube through which fuel is introduced into an engine.
STALL	Loss of lift due to loss of flying speed. The stopping of an electric motor under load.
STANDING WAVE	Upward movement of air currents.
STRIP AILERONS	Full span control surfaces on the wings.

RADIO CONTROL GUIDE

STYROFOAM	Expanded polystyrene used in wing construction.
SUPERREGEN (superregenerative)	A simple and more widely responsive receiver which can only be operated one at a time.
SUPERHET (superheterodyne)	A receiver circuit with a crystal controlled oscillator to give it sensitivity over a narrow wave band, thus several outfits on different frequencies within the model band may be operated together.
SWAMP	Excess power from a transmitter at close range causes unwanted response in the receiver.

T

TAP	A battery connection to provide an intermediate voltage, similarly on transformers and coil. A tool to cut female thread
T.E. (trailing edge)	Rear edge of a flying surface.
THERMAL	Rising bubble of warm air.
TOGGLE SWITCH	A manually operated lever switch.
TONGUE AND BOX	A method of wing or tail attachment that, while strong in the up and down plane, allows the flying surface to knock-off easily and without damage in the event of a rough landing or crash.
TORQUE	Reaction in a rolling plane caused by engine power reacting against its propeller drag.
TOW HOOK	Hook fixed on underside of glider fuselage for attaching the tow line.
TRANSFORMER	Comprises separate wire windings on a metal core, to reduce or increase an alternating electrical current passed through it.
TRANSISTOR	An electronic component capable of switching current.
TRANSMITTER	An electronic device for producing radio waves.
TRIM	Setting of the control surfaces and rigging to provide straight and level flight.
T-TAIL	Tailplane on top of the fin.
TAILPLANE	Horizontal stabilising surface.
TRIKE U/C	Three-wheel undercarriage.
TURBULATOR	Protuberance on leading edge of wing to produce turbulent flow.
Tx	Abbreviation — see Transmitter.

U

U/C	Undercarriage.
U.H.F.	Ultra high frequency.
UNDERCAMBER	Concave undersurface of some wing sections.
UNDER-ELEVATED	Trimming of a model such that it will not climb, or even needs constant effort to maintain height.
UNDERFIN	Part of the fin below the fuselage.

V

VACUUM FORMING	A method of moulding items from sheet plastic.
"V" DIHEDRAL	Spanwise angle of wings or tail forming a shallow "V".
VENTURI	A tube reducing at its centre to speed up the airflow at that point. Used in the carburettors of engines.
V.H.F.	Very high frequency.
VOLTMETER	Sensitive device for measuring voltage.
VOLTS	A measurement of electricity.
VORTICES	Spiralling airflow caused by unequal pressure.
V-TAIL	A tailplane with dihedral. By using this the vertical surfaces (fixed rudder) may be dispensed with.

RADIO CONTROL GUIDE

W

WARPED — Twisted.

WARREN GIRDER — Or "Warren Truss" — a triangulation method of framework construction.

WASH-IN — More incidence at the tip than at the root of a wing or tailplane.

WASH-OUT — Less incidence at the tip than at the root of a wing or tailplane.

WATT — Measurement of an electrical load.

WINCH — A geared towline spool for launching gliders.

WING LOADING — Measured in ounces, etc., per square foot, etc., the weight of the model divided into the wing area.

WIRING HARNESS — Electrical connections in the form of flex between the parts of a radio installation.

X

XTAL — Abbreviation — see Crystal.

Y

YAW — Side to side "waggling" movement produced, or corrected by, the rudder.

Z

ZERO-ZERO — Rigging of a model (generally aerobatic) in which the wing and tailplane are either parallel to the datum, or both at the same small angle of attack.